MARIA

Gestalt at Work

Gestalt
at Work

INTEGRATING LIFE,
THEORY & PRACTICE

The collected works of
Seán Gaffney
> VOLUME I

Edited by
Anne Maclean

THE GESTALT INSTITUTE PRESS
433 Metairie Road, #113,
Metairie,
LA 70005, USA
http://www.gestaltinstitutepress.com

1.800.GESTALT – or – 504.828.2267
ateachw@aol.com

Library of Congress Catalog Card Number: Applied For
ISBN: 978-1-889968-04-9

This book was printed in the United States of America

Cover and Book Design: Lesley Maclean (New Zealand)

To order additional copies of this book, call 1.800.786.1065 inside
the USA or 504.828.2267 from outside.

Dedication

To my colleague, friend,
First Reader and now Editor

Anne Maclean
(a.k.a Annie Mac)

With affection
and gratitude

Gaffy

Contents

Foreword

It is not often that such a diverse collection of Gestalt writings emerges from one person, and so it is with great pleasure I introduce the first of two volumes, *Gestalt at Work: Integrating Life, Theory & Practice*. Glancing at the contents I am struck by the breadth of the work and the writing that Seán Gaffney has undertaken over seven years. These thirteen pieces include articles, chapters for books, papers and poetry; in all a considerable contribution to gestalt literature. Within each section articles are presented in order of publication, providing insight into the development of his thought and practice.

His roles are many—gestalt psychotherapist, supervisor, trainer, organisational development trainer, group facilitator and teacher—and while teacher is implicit in these roles, one of the exciting aspects is how he also teaches through his writing. Not every teacher has the capacity to support their work through professional writing.

Seán Gaffney is an inveterate traveller and takes his work into the world—Ireland, Sweden, Norway, Finland, Estonia, Latvia, Poland, Denmark, Hungary, Italy, England, Scotland, Russian Federation, Australia, USA, Singapore, Portugal, the Netherlands, Israel, Canada, Greece, Spain, Mexico, New Zealand and South Africa. He has worked for universities, gestalt training centres, organizations and businesses, local groups and individuals and presented at professional conferences. Of particular interest in this collection, is the exploration of gestalt groups and group work in Volume 1, and cross-cultural considerations in Volume 2. Some of his work with groups shows the richness of the field through a case study, through the different physical locations of his work, the different requirements of the participants or their employers and rounds off with an article for practitioners who are at the beginning of their facilitative work with groups. In his explorations across multi-cultures he highlights differences and similarities, customs and environments, subtleties and the impact of language. Such writing makes a valuable contribution to a world needing more inter-cultural understanding. In both books he offers gestalt as the ground of his work and sheds light and relevance on gestalt theory and methodology.

One of the delightful aspects of this book is to view the collection as a series of figures arising out of the ground of practice and experience, where the concepts of gestalt are demonstrated with ideas being revealed as they develop. Then, those ideas are put to practical use within therapy, supervision and training, bringing still new ways and more ideas—enhancing the liveliness of his teaching and then further writing.

So, the descriptions of his work show possibilities with which to explore and extend the reader's knowledge and practice in all sorts of settings. The teacher is revealed both as an individual on his journey and, a therapist in action—demonstrating the importance of exploring and understanding gestalt psychotherapy in greater depth.

Seán invited other practitioners to respond to his writings and their responses are published along with what he had originally written. Such comments bring further consciousness to the articles and take the writing to a deeper level, expanding the possibilities for learning and practice. In some cases, Seán offers a written conversation between the author and other participants—a lively process—as seen in *Gestalt at Work: A Gestalt Organisation and Systems Dynamic Case Study* and *Gestalt with Groups: A Developmental Perspective*. Not all of us would put our work under this more public spotlight.

His own journey reveals life and death, his sorrows and joys and speaks briefly yet heart-warmingly of the fine-tuning that has happened and continues to happen to make him more of whom he most truly is. Some of you who know him personally, will know his sense of humour, his staunch Irishness, and his willingness to stand up and be counted when he has something to say or write. In his accounts of personal history and within his work, the spirit and heart of this man is revealed. His willingness to let his experiences speak invites each of us to read and acknowledge the pain and suffering of being human, as well as the deep joys and satisfaction of being alive and able to work and to write, and of our need for company on this journey.

I invite you to see what themes and threads you discover, what mystery you may encounter as you read, what excites you as you consider this collection.

Anne Maclean
Christchurch
New Zealand
2009

Gestalt at Work

I.

On Being Absurd:

Søren Kierkegaard 1813-1855

ABSTRACT: This paper raises some aspects of Kierkegaard's life and work, and posits a possible relevance for the Gestalt practitioner. This includes Kierkegaard's position as a source not only for the existentialism of Sartre, but also for the thinking and living of Laura Perls and Paul Goodman. In addition, the author's personal and professional responses to the influence of Kierkegaard are a central theme throughout the article.

KEY WORDS: Kierkegaard, existentialism, Gestalt, faith, angst, existing individual.

Introduction

This is a brief, idiosyncratic and unashamedly partisan introduction to the life and work of Søren Kierkegaard. He was a Danish Christian and thorn in the flesh of established Danish Christianity, a lifelong member of the Danish bourgeoisie and one of its most vibrant critics, as well as an 'existing individual' who chose to speak authentically in the voices of what became a chorus of pseudonyms. He was as much an often lonely raconteur as he was a loquacious hermit. He was an existentialist, psychologist, preacher, social critic, tragic lover, figure of ridicule—and at all times a person who met, and attempted to influence, his environment as a fully responsible, existing individual; also at all times aware of and responsive to his environment's influence on him, and his need to respond.

This article began as a last-minute two-page list of headings in capital letters for a presentation at the Gestalt International Study Center's 'European Roots of Gestalt Therapy Conference' held at EPG (Ecole Parisienne de Gestalt) in Paris, March 2003. The presentation was very extemporaneous and included my spontaneous imitation of Kierkegaard's hunch-backed, short-trousered, slightly manic conversational style, as reported by his contemporaries. This was my preferred mode for the Conference, and I felt it was particularly appropriate to a presentation of (and on) Kierkegaard who, despite the calculated complexities and dilemmas of his written work, enjoyed nothing more than a stroll around Copenhagen, in animated and deep discussion with whoever he met who chose to walk and talk with him—until the period of his being satirised and ridiculed.

Following the presentation, I was asked if I would consider producing a written version. By this stage, I was hooked—I wanted to share Kierkegaard with, at least, the Gestalt world, where I felt he was generally little known, or was stood in the shadow of one of his followers, Jean-Paul Sartre, or was even ignored altogether (though not by his fellow Danes in the Scandinavian Gestalt community).

Being 'hooked' on Kierkegaard is no laughing matter. I was both supported and frustrated by the fact that I can read him—with minor linguistic difficulties—in his original Danish, and have no problems reading him in close-to-the-original Swedish translations or translated into English. So I have had access to three Kierkegaards—including, that is, three times his various pseudonyms!

I worked at expanding and deepening the draft, at the same time holding to the general freewheeling style that, I began to sense, was most appropriate. Kierkegaard did not write 'for' an audience, he wrote 'to' his reader, infuriatingly faithful to the Socratic tradition of eliciting what the reader already knew but didn't yet know that they knew. So I will switch from the marginally more formal text of this piece to my parenthetical ruminations on my process as I revisit, revise, and renew the second version of my original skeleton draft.

One of the last texts of Kierkegaard was entitled *Concluding Unscientific Postscript to 'Philosophical Fragments'* (Hong & Hong, 1992)—'Philosophical Fragments' being the title of an earlier text of his

(Kierkegaard, 1985). The title itself contains much of what Kierkegaard represents: paradox to the point of contradiction (*Concluding* and *Postscript*); the relentlessly subjective perspective of an 'existing being' (*Unscientific*); and the irony and playfulness of the reference to his earlier work.

It would therefore be much in the spirit of Kierkegaard if I were to subtitle this work: 'A *Fragmented* Introductory Unscientific Prologue to Existentialism—and Gestalt?' Fragmented inasmuch as it is composed of bits and pieces of his full and rich life; the juxtaposition of *Introductory* and *Prologue* inasmuch as it is both an introduction to and presentation of his influence as 'the Father of *Existentialism*'—and referring also to his position (in my personal opinion!) as an early *Gestaltist*, in his living and his thinking. And Kierkegaard truly lived his thinking, and made meaning of his living. This article is clearly 'Unscientific' in the sense that I am no expert on Kierkegaard. I have read rather than studied some of his works, and a number of books and articles about him. My view here is highly subjective and selective (Kierkegaardian?).

Mmm... Am I guilty here—to coin a phrase—of praising with faint damns? A decisive turning point in the evolution of this article was my participation in the EAGT Writers' Conference, Thessaloniki, Greece, 2004, where I submitted my second draft as a conference paper. The Writers' Conference process is illuminating, incisive, gentle, collegial, supportive, and wonderfully creative. In responding to the reactions, comments, questions and suggestions of my conference colleagues, I became amazed at how well I 'knew' Kierkegaard, not just 'about' him. I experienced an increasing awareness of a deeper personal resonance to him. My colleagues' encouragement to explore more fully and describe this resonance and its impact on me as a person and, in consequence, as a Gestalt practitioner, restructured the ground of my draft, and new figures emerged.

One of these figures—which actually first emerged spontaneously at the Thessaloniki Conference—was that my well-thumbed and well-read paperback edition of extracts from Kierkegaard's 'Journals' was bought in London in 1963. So when I took the first exhilarating steps in my formal Gestalt training some twenty years later, my special interest in Kierkegaard as part of the ground for the figure of Gestalt therapy was, I now under-

stand, rooted in my previous—and curiously forgotten—acquaintance with him. I was meeting an old friend whom I had ignored for many years, and for whose renewed friendship I was now more ready.

Kierkegaard's Early Life

He was born the last of seven children. Five of these had died, the oldest of them at the age of thirty-two. His father saw this and much else in life as a curse that God had put on him for having, as a teenager, blasphemed and raged against God. As a result, Kierkegaard grew up convinced that he would also be dead by the age of thirty-two.

There is a strong Biblical theme emerging here—the curse of the father descending on the son—a theme which would later become central to his thinking, in his own particular variation. And there is also the theme of Death, as a constant companion of the 'existing individual'. As a boy, he was close to his father. One of their interactions was that young Søren would sit in an adjacent room while his father was entertaining the local dignitaries. When they had left, his father would invite Søren to sit in the Bishop's chair and be the Bishop, expressing the Bishop's opinions and attitudes. Then the local politician, then the soldier, and so on. Some early 'empty chair' work? This experience and his learning from it would return in another form in his writing (see below).

He studied theology in Copenhagen, and then took his Master's degree in Berlin, where he became immersed in and enthusiastic about Hegel. His thesis was on Socrates and his use of irony and paradox—another theme that would become figural in his thinking and writing. On his return to Copenhagen and the easy life of an intellectual living well off his father's inheritance, he became thoroughly disenchanted with Hegel and all attempts to provide a systematic philosophy of life. He also turned against the Protestant Church in Denmark, and its imposition of a system on its members. As a result, he never formally assumed the position of pastor, to which he had been educated. (His elder brother, Peter, did). Characteristically, he turned his back on the established Church, criticising it mercilessly and publicly, while always retaining a strong personal belief in God. Søren Kierkegaard, the individual with his lived existence, was emerging.

Kierkegaard, Existentialism, Gestalt

I want here to place Kierkegaard in relation to Existentialism—and maybe, therefore also Gestalt. His ground was his own Christianity, Socrates and paradox, his rejection of Hegel and the Church as systematic burdens imposed on free people who therefore then became anonymous. He lived as an 'existing individual', and forcefully propagated both the concept and the lived experience of 'existence' in a way that was directly to influence, for example, Brentano, Husserl, Heidegger, Sartre, and Jaspers. With this influence, he became the ground for European existentialism. The Kierkegaard-Heidegger link leads directly into existential analysis (van Deurzen, 2002; Spinelli, 1997; Cohn, 1997), our therapeutic sibling if not twin. (Indeed, a younger sibling who took the name, 'existential therapy', we had almost chosen for ourselves (Wysong and Rosenfeld, 1982)). The Kierkegaard – (Brentano) – Husserl – Heidegger – Sartre chain leads into the existentialist roots of Gestalt therapy.

We know that Laura Perls knew her Kierkegaard (Wysong and Rosenfeld, 1982)—indeed, German was the first foreign language into which Kierkegaard's work was translated in the late 19th century. This is how she responded to a question about her earlier interest in 'existential philosophy':

> *Oh, certainly. It was in my academic education. I worked for many years with Paul Tillich. As a student I read Kierkegaard and Heidegger; also the phenomenologists: Husserl and Scheler.* (ibid., p. 15)

Paul Goodman also knew his Kierkegaard (Stoehr, 1994). Stoehr specifically mentions Goodman's preference for Kierkegaard's 'religious existentialism' as opposed to the 'nihilism' of Sartre. Indeed, in *Growing Up Absurd* (Goodman, 1956), we find the following:

> *It then becomes necessary to stop short and make a choice: Either/Or. Either one drifts with [society's] absurd system of ideas, believing that this is the human community. Or one dissents totally from their system of ideas and stands as a lonely human being. (But*

*luckily one notices that others are in the same crisis and making
the same choice)* (p. 134).

Not only does Goodman use the title of one of Kierkegaard's books
in this passage—*Either/Or* (Kierkegaard, 1987)—but he also echoes
Kierkegaard's choice of dissent and loneliness. There is much in Goodman's book which echoes Kierkegaard's comment in his *Journals* (Hong
and Hong, 1975): 'Man has made a discovery ... the way to make life
easy is to make it meaningless' (Vol. 3, p. 346).

In addition, the passage quoted above from Goodman comes from
the chapter on 'Faith', another major theme in Kierkegaard's work,
which will be considered below. So Kierkegaard was in the ground of
influential voices in the founding of our first Gestalt therapy institute
as well as in the early explications of our theoretical stance. And he is
still around: two major recent works by Gestaltists contain sections on
his influence—*A Well-Lived Life* by Sylvia Fleming Crocker (1999) and
Beyond Individualism by Gordon Wheeler (2000), (even if the latter
author, in my opinion, misses the point of Kierkegaard's 'individualism'
and thus paints him critically with the same sweeping brush he uses
on Sartre). In unabashed support of Kierkegaard versus Sartre, I quote
the following (Kierkegaard, 1958):

*Deep within every man there lies the dread of being alone in the
world, forgotten by God, overlooked among the tremendous house-
hold of millions upon millions. That fear is kept away by looking
upon all of those about us to whom we are bound as friends and
family; but the dread is nevertheless there and one hardly dares to
think of what would happen to us if all the rest were taken away*
(p. 129).

Engaging with Kierkegaard

Kierkegaard was a prolific writer. His *Journals* cover volumes; his
scurrilous and constant attacks on the established Church appeared
in countless pamphlets in his own name; also in his own name, he
published a series of religious texts. Then there is his major contribution
to philosophy and psychology—in a series of books written under a

number of pseudonyms with Kierkegaard either as their 'editor' and/ or 'publisher'.

These range from the bishop, the politician and the soldier at his father's dinner table, to a whole group of 'authors' (including the wonderfully paradoxical voice of 'John the Silent' in full flow! Not to forget 'Johan the Climax' being followed by 'Anti-Climax'!). These 'authors' wrote their own works, or appeared in group debates in the work of other pseudonymous authors. They could hold opposing opinions; they could happily contradict each other; they could tease out the last drop of possible nourishment in an idea. Simultaneously, Kierkegaard would comment on their work in his Journals!

Or, as Hong and Hong (2000) put it:

> *The difficulties for a reader of Kierkegaard's writings are due in part to the multiplicity of pseudonymous writers who present their own views in a complex dialogue. Avoiding a conclusive system, Kierkegaard lets each pseudonymous writer have his voice.* (p. IX)

Kierkegaard himself puts it more typically in his *Journals* (Kierkegaard, 1958):

> *My role is the joint role of being the secretary and, quite ironically, the dialectically reduplicated author of the author or the authors.*

Or, in the words of the tragicomic (and slightly absurd!) hero of *Therapy* by David Lodge (1996), who embarks on his own, special Kierkegaardian journey when all else fails:

> *Reading Kierkegaard is like flying through heavy cloud. Every now and again there's a break and you get a brief, brilliantly lit view of the ground, and then you're back in the swirling grey mist again, with not a fucking clue where you are* (p. 109).

Airing contradictory views is where Socrates re-emerges: for Kierkegaard, each individual has the freedom and choice to decide for themselves. These writings are dialogues with the reader, teasing, playful, serious, paradoxical, and contradictory—the final word is always left to the reader, the other existing individual. As I said, Kierkegaard did not write *for* his readers—he wrote *to* them.

The philosopher, Gordon Marino (2001), captures this directness well:

> *In contrast to my original academic sensibilities, Kierkegaard convinced me that serious and, for that matter, scholarly writing need not be synonymous with being objective and impersonal... For Kierkegaard, a serious author is a concerned person who strives to speak to his reader in a meaningful way about meaningful issues* (p. 13).

Kierkegaard's *Journals* (1958) again, on his writing: 'The task must be made difficult, for only the difficult inspires the noble-hearted' (Vol 3, p. 331).

In his thinking and practice here, Kierkegaard, with his 'task... made difficult' is maybe not too far from the following:

> *Thus the reader is apparently confronted with an impossible task: to understand the book he must have the 'Gestaltist' mentality, and to acquire it he must understand the book* (Perls, Hefferline and Goodman, 1951/1994, Vol. 1, p. XXIV).

He conversed with his readers in his books, as he did on the streets of Copenhagen and the pathways of the Danish countryside with friends or anyone he chanced to meet, bending his hunchbacked form down and looking up to catch their eyes, all the while gesticulating animatedly. He was an existing individual reaching out to others in their existence. His individualism was not exclusive of and separated from that of other individuals—though it was certainly exclusive of and separated from any systematic elite or mass view that enslaved the individual in its demands for conformity and unthinking, unfeeling obedience. Hardly surprising then, that he had an appeal to Paul Goodman and Laura Perls, two very 'existing individuals' engaged in supporting the development and emergence of other, equally free, existing individuals, from their contemporary environment of mass conformity.

Angest (Angst)

Kierkegaard, the existing individual whose existence was primary, in a world where death was an ever-present possibility, carried another major theme—*angest* (perhaps better known in its German form of *angst*). I am choosing not to attempt a translation here—none of them work for me. However, if you have ever felt your mortality deep in your bones and your gut so that your heart misses a beat; or if you have ever agonised over the meaning or meaninglessness of your lived existence; or if you have ever found yourself in a place where nothing made sense and you still had to make a choice and be responsible for it...well, I hope you get my meaning. Kierkegaard called *angest* 'the giddiness of freedom'. What a beautiful phrase!

If you have been in your *angest*, then what it 'means' in English is not particularly important. You have been there, done that and you have the T-shirt with *angest* woven into every fibre. *Angest* is a natural ground for the existing individual, the source of the search for meaning, the making of meaning, the creative embracing of life.

At this point in my Paris presentation, I pressed the 'play' button of a music-centre, and the room was filled with the snarling, taunting voice and music of Bob Dylan. 'God said to Abraham, kill me a son'....Dear Reader, if you happen to have 'Highway 61' nearby, please play it—loud and unclear! Get into the mood, feel the agelessness of the theme of Abraham and Isaac...then Kierkegaard...then Dylan...And now me writing to you...and you responding...as existing individuals, becoming and being in our choices, with all the responsibility of choice and the angest both of that responsibility as well as the existential uncertainty of our choices and their consequences. We each have our 'Highway 61' where the 'killin's to be done', the choices made, where we change and are changed.

The Leap of Faith

This raises the next great theme for Kierkegaard—'the leap of faith', taken without rational support or logical analysis, simply taken as the only choice that is figural, fully trusting our need for and ability to take it. This emerged in his various pseudonyms' treatment of Abraham and Isaac—how could a father be willing to sacrifice his son because God told him to? This is also another variation on the father-son theme so central to Kierkegaard's upbringing and life. What finally emerges is that Abraham trusted *himself*, in his love for his son, in his obedience to his God, in his choice of aware action as a living force of a complex field. Taking his son up the mountain to sacrifice him did not in any way 'make sense'. Laying his son on the rock did not 'make sense'. Raising the knife to kill him did not 'make sense'. Yet Abraham took 'the leap'—of faith in himself, in his God. Abraham trusted his gut, rather than his head; his love, rather than any moral or ethical precepts.

To paraphrase Kierkegaard: taking the leap is to risk losing my footing; not taking it is to risk losing myself. (This paraphrase—commonly given in both Danish and Swedish references as a direct quote—is in fact a composite of numerous passages dealing with this central theme of his, most explicitly in *The Sickness Unto Death* (Hong & Hong, XIX, pp. 34-35). At the same time, it so succinctly and elegantly expresses his thinking that it has come to be taken as an actual quotation.) Even if, in the paraphrase, we only replace the word 'leap' with the word 'experiment', this is a phrase any Gestaltist would be pleased to have uttered.

And of course, there IS a Gestaltist who has written something similar, if not in fact the same—Paul Goodman. In Perls *et al.* (1951/1994) he writes about 'faith':

> …*faith is knowing, beyond awareness, that if one takes a step there will be ground underfoot; one gives oneself unhesitatingly to the act, one has faith that the background will produce the means.* (1994, p. 123)

Later in the same book, he writes:

> *But where the self has power to draw on, it has precisely no sense of security. It has perhaps a sense of readiness: the acceptance of excitement, a certain foolish optimism about the alterability of reality, and a habitual memory that the organism regulates itself*

and does not in the end wear out or explode. (This readiness is perhaps what the theologians call faith)... A sense of adequacy and power grows as the particular problem is met and generates its own structure, and new possibilities are found in it, and things surprisingly fall into place (p. 193).

This thought returns in almost identical form some five years later in *Growing Up Absurd* (Goodman, 1956). In the chapter on Faith, Goodman writes:

Children, if we observe them, seem normally to be abounding in simple faith. They rush headlong and there is ground underfoot (pp. 139-140).

Has Goodman paraphrased here one of his favourite philosophers? Is this the voice of Kierkegaard echoing to us through Goodman – and even in our central text—a hundred years after his death? Partisan as I am, I am inclined to think so!

I am also inclined to ponder to what extent Kierkegaard's thinking and Goodman's 'versions' are in full agreement, and to what extent there are subtle and important nuances of difference in their perspectives. As I read the relevant quotations in their original textual contexts, and then place them in relation to each other, I find myself wondering if Goodman has not simply produced an 'American' version. Just as Hollywood does US re-makes of foreign films adapted fully to a US context, just as European existentialism became 'peak experiences', 'self-realisation' and maybe even the whole self-help industry, just as some contemporary Gestalt practitioners in the US are becoming 'hopelessly optimistic' (Melnick and Backman, 2002)... did Goodman also move from Kierkegaard's existential uncertainty to his own pragmatic American, optimism that there would be 'ground underfoot'??? Returning to my earlier linking of 'the leap' with the experiment in Gestalt, I find that Kierkegaard's uncertainty around losing his footing or his self is far more relevant to the experiment in Gestalt practice, the focus of which is awareness rather than a pre-defined outcome or even an unsurprising expectation that everything will be okay...

Indeed, here is a striking metaphorical variation from Kierkegaard which may support a distinction between the Kierkegaard and Goodman perspectives:

> *When a spider plunges from a fixed point to its consequences, it always sees before it an empty space where it can never set foot, no matter how it wriggles* (Hong & Hong, 1978/2000, KW III, p. 24).

These reflections prompt me to imagine that Gestalt will begin to bloom in its fullness when it completes its journey from Europe to the USA, to Latin America then back to Europe and then further around the world. As this occurs, the dynamic interplay of figure/ground will allow nuanced and/or new figures to emerge. The co-creative impact of an ever-broadening range of socio-cultural environments will increase our range of perspectives. Then we, as practitioners, can follow our selves as we are attracted by the pragmatic or the irrational, the certain or uncertain, the joyfully humanistic or the black-clad existentialistic, the meditative or the energetic—the perspectives of Kierkegaard, or Goodman, Sartre, Buber, or whoever. We can gestalt Gestalt from our shared commonality and our unique, subjective experience and perspectives.

My very sincere wish is that Søren Kierkegaard will then be given his rightful place as a past and present 'root' of Gestalt therapy. (I am here thinking of Serge Ginger's wonderful image (2003) of the tree growing its roots as it develops… The roots are never static, fixed… they reach out for nourishment, spread, grow, multiply.) So maybe Kierkegaard may be seen as an old root, now revitalised and offering more nourishment?

On Faith, Resignation, and Loving

Just as it is, Kierkegaard's 'leap of faith' is a strong summary of something at the heart of both existentialism—and Gestalt. Abraham took 'the leap' at the contact boundaries of Abraham/God and Abraham/Isaac as well as Abraham Ego/Abraham Self—and his son lived and Abraham was a new self. The dilemma facing Abraham—obeying his God by killing the son, that very same son whom God had blessed him with in old age—was resolved by an act containing two simultaneous movements:

the movement of 'infinite resignation' and the movement of 'faith'.

'Infinite resignation' means abandoning who I am/was at the same time as the movement 'of faith', I embrace who I am becoming. In Gestalt terms, I see this as an example of a gestalt destruction/formation/destruction cycle, where the past ground recedes, taking with it our favourite and habitual figures, as the emerging figure becomes the self-of-the-moment. This in turn fades as the self continues its movements of resignation and movements of faith. Kierkegaard himself took 'the leap' in breaking off his engagement to the young Regine Olsen. He had first met her when he was twenty-one years old and she was fourteen, her father a family friend of the Kierkegaards. He fell in love with her, and waited until she was seventeen, when he asked first her father and then her for her hand in marriage. Both agreed. A year later, in a dramatic fashion, he suddenly and very unexpectedly called off the engagement. He leaped into his lived existence, his writing, his passion in reaching out to other individuals, his acceptance of himself in the big world of ideas and writing and influence. He never stopped loving her (nor she him), and she was his sole beneficiary on his death. Their paths crossed now and then in Copenhagen, their exchanges minimal, their regrets palpable, until she married and moved abroad. He managed to reach the conclusion that he would anyway have been a bad husband, too engaged with other things. And maybe he just did not want to become a father ....

The philosopher Gordon Marino offers an interesting and very personal perspective (2001). He was in the middle of both his graduate studies and a painful divorce. He was skipping classes, hanging out in a coffee-shop *cum* bookstore, feeling sorry for himself with a touch of being a martyr of love. One day, he bought Kierkegaard's *Works of Love* and finished it within twenty-four hours. It changed his life: he discovered

> ... *the distinction ... between self-love and other love that had never visited me before ... Kierkegaard seemed to whisper ... 'If you love her so much, then you ought to be able to put her happiness before your own. And if she is better off without you, which even you have to admit is a strong possibility, then you ought to be able to part with her'* (p. 13).

Kierkegaard's place in the intertwined perspectives of religion, philosophy and psychology can be summed up in two quotes. The first is from Ernest Becker:

[Kierkegaard] gave us some of the best empirical analyses of the human condition ever fashioned by man's mind. But ironically, it was not until the epoch of the scientific atheist Freud that we could see the scientific stature of the theologian Kierkegaard's work… The noted psychologist Mowrer summed it up perfectly… 'Freud had to live and write before the work of Kierkegaard could be correctly understood and appreciated' (Becker, 1973, pp. 67-68).

Kierkegaard's position as existentialist and Gestaltist is neatly covered in the concluding words of H. P. Blackham in his chapter on Kierkegaard:

His own example is a caution against the pitfalls which beset the point of absolute choice; but first of all it is (and remains) a summons to make an absolute choice. Because he elaborated painfully in flesh and blood his formidable epigram over Christians and human beings, 'calculated to make people aware', he is the boldest and the greatest of existential thinkers (Blackham, 1961, p. 22).

I would like to close with some phrases from Kierkegaard—the first two as examples of his style at its most whimsical, yet with depths of meaning:

My life achievement amounts to nothing at all, a mood, a single colour. My achievement resembles the painting by an artist who was supposed to paint the Israelites' crossing of the Red Sea and to that end painted the entire wall red and explained that the Israelites had walked across and that the Egyptians were drowned (Oden, 2004, p. 281).

Long live the stagecoach horn! It is the instrument for me for many reasons, and chiefly because one can never be certain of wheedling the same notes from this horn. A coach horn has infinite possibilities, and the person who puts it to his mouth and puts his wisdom into it can never be guilty of repetition, and he who instead of giving an answer gives his friend a coach horn to use as he pleases, says nothing but explains everything. Praised be the coach horn! It is my symbol (Oden, 2004, p. 51).

The next two from Kierkegaard as an early Gestaltist (?):

If one is truly to succeed in leading a person to a specific place, one must first and foremost take care to find him where HE is and begin there (Kierkegaard, 1859/2000, p. 460).

This is a fine summary of the application of the 'paradoxical theory of change' (Beisser, 1970) much loved by contemporary Gestalt practitioners. It is followed soon after by this:

Even though a person refuses to go along to the place to which one is endeavouring to lead him, there is still one thing that can be done for him: compel him to be aware (Kierkegaard, 1859/2000, p. 464).

Indeed, for many Gestaltists, awareness *is* the place to which we are supporting our clients' journey—and beginning where *they* are matches how we work.

On first reading the above quotation, I reacted to Kierkegaard's use of the word 'compel'. I let it roll around in my reflections, where it soon became 'compelling'… that is, strong, engaging, energising. I thought of my own Gestalt therapist of fourteen years…yes, 'compel him [me]) to be aware'. She had a warm, supportive, fully present silence with me as I wrestled with my demons until I sat before her, aware, vulnerable, supported in my work by her compelling silence, and then sharing my—our —change in a warm relational silence as the work was integrated.

A final quotation, and a particular favourite amongst, I admit, many particular favourites:

Something wonderful has happened to me. I was caught up into the seventh heaven. There sat all the gods in assembly. By special grace I was granted the privilege of making a wish. 'Wilt thou', said Mercury, 'have youth or beauty or power or a long life or the most beautiful maiden or any other of the glories we have in the chest? Choose, but only one thing.' For a moment I was at a loss. Then I addressed myself to the gods as follows: 'Most honourable contemporaries, I choose this one thing, that I may always have the laugh on my side.' Not one of the gods said a word; on the contrary, they all began to laugh. From that I concluded that my wish was granted, and found that the gods knew how to express themselves with taste; for it would hardly have been suitable for them to have answered gravely: 'Thy wish is granted' (Poole and Stangerup, 1989, p. 241).

Some Professional Conclusions

As a Gestalt practitioner, I am aware of the extent to which Kierkegaard informs my practice. The driving force of choice, grounded in personal integrity, as a force of a dynamic field in sharp contrast to the felt or rationalised need for certainty about outcomes of any choice, is equally evident in my clients, whether therapeutic or organisational.

It is sometimes as if choices 'should/must' be made with predictable outcomes as the ground for the figural choice. Kierkegaard's concept of the 'leap of faith' (rather than Goodman's) seems to me to capture our existential dilemma: to choose, grounded in the felt need to choose, rather than in the certainty of a safe outcome from the 'right' choice – this latter being more a rational decision than an existential choice of an energised figure, however irrational. This Kierkegaardian approach allows the figural choice to emerge from the dynamic and developing ground of the now, and includes the existential responsibility for the choice itself as well as a shared responsibility for its future consequences. This approach also leaves room for our *angest* to become a creative force of the field in the moment.

Since my own thinking is increasingly coloured by the 'existential dilemma' of the continuum 'individual – group – organisation – collective' (Gaffney, 2006), I am also taken by Kierkegaard's attempt to resolve the tension of the field between himself as an existing individual and the many mass systems he perceived as his environment—the established church, the bourgeoisie of Copenhagen, the followers of Hegelian philosophy, and the editor and journalists of *Corsair* (a Copenhagen magazine) who hounded, satirised and mercilessly ridiculed him with articles, caricatures and scurrilous reviews. He had tested all of these boundaries, sometimes pushing and poking at them, and eventually, towards the later years of his rather short life, they had begun to push and poke back. However, the meeting at the boundary which might have become possible in this process was never realised. The various environments resorted to the moralising and criticising that so easily comes to those who support their own righteousness, while Kierkegaard, hurt and misunderstood, retreated into his *Journals*.

Many—if not most—of my clients battle with this tension: how to be fully themselves in the context of their lives, their relationships, and their work. I know that I certainly do, and have done for some time. I am also aware of my need to be aware of my projective tendencies, and regularly to test my assumptions with my clients in this area. At the same time, I can feel how Kierkegaard has touched upon a core existential issue here in his focus on choice, on being a 'self' WITH others or losing 'self' in others.

Most of all, Kierkegaard has touched me, the 'existing individual', up to 150 years after his death ... or, rather, 150 years after his life. Since, in Gestalt terms, use of self is a core concept, methodology and competence, then my contact with Kierkegaard has changed me. I am now another self than the one who started this article as a presentation in Paris in March 2003, who discovered his many links to Kierkegaard over time (42 years!), and who can now read Kierkegaard in peace—again!—without having to take notes for this article!

References

Becker, E. (1973). *The Denial of Death*. New York: Free Press Paperbacks.

Beisser, A. R. (1970). The Paradoxical Theory of Change. In Fagen and Shepherd (Eds.), *Gestalt Therapy Now*. Harmondsworth: Penguin Books.

Blackham, H. P. (1961). *Six Existentialist Thinkers*. London: Routledge & Kegan Paul.

Cohn, Hans W. (1997). *Existential Thought and Therapeutic Practice*. London: Sage Publications.

Fleming Crocker, S. (1999). *A Well-Lived Life—Essays in Gestalt Therapy*. Cleveland, USA: GIC Press.

Gaffney, S. (2006). Gestalt with Groups—A Cross-cultural Perspective. *Gestalt Review, 10*(2). Cape Cod: GISC Press.

Ginger, S. (2003). Workshop Presentation and Documentation. GISC ROOTS Conference, Paris.

Goodman, P. (1960). *Growing Up Absurd*. New York: Vintage Books.

Lodge, D. (1996). *Therapy*. Harmondsworth: Penguin Books.

Melnick, J. and Backman, S. (2000). *A Hopelessly Optimistic Perspective on Small Systems*. Workshop, AAGT Conference.

Perls, F., Hefferline, R., & Goodman, P. (1951/1994). *Gestalt Therapy: Excitement and Growth in the Human Personality*. New York: Julian Press.

Spinelli, E. (1997). *Tales of Un-knowing—Therapeutic Encounters from an Existential Perspective*. London: Gerald Duckworth & Co. Ltd.

Stoehr, T. (1994). *Here Now Next—Paul Goodman and the Origins of Gestalt Therapy*. San Francisco: Jossey-Bass Publishers.

Bibliography

Because of the variety of sources used in this article, taken both directly from translations of Kierkegaard's work as well as from collections, selections, biographies, etc., I am including here ALL the sources which contain material that I have used in the preparation of this article.

Auden, W. H. (1999). *The Living Thoughts of Kierkegaard*. New York: NYRB.

Bukdahl, J. (2001). *Kierkegaard and the Common Man*. Grand Rapids, Michigan: William B. Eerdman.

Chamberlain, J. & Rée, J. (2001). *The Kierkegaard Reader*. Oxford: Blackwell.

Garff, J. (2000). *Søren Aabye Kierkegaard—En Biografi*. Copenhagen: G.E.C. Gads Forlag.

Hannay, A. (2001). *Kierkegaard—A Biography*. Cambridge: Cambridge University Press.

Hannay, A. & Marino, G. D. (1998). *The Cambridge Companion to Kierkegaard*. Cambridge: Cambridge University Press.

Hong, H. V. & Hong, E. H. (2000). *The Essential Kierkegaard*, New Jersey: Princeton University Press.

Hong, H. V. & Hong, E. H. (1978/2000). *Kierkegaard's Writings*, Vol. I – XXVI. New Jersey: Princeton University Press.

Jegstrup, E. (Ed.), (2004). *The New Kierkegaard*. Bloomington: Indiana University Press.

Kierkegaard, S. (1958). *The Journals of Kierkegaard, 1834-1854* (A. Dru, Trans., Ed.). London: Fontana Books.

Kierkegaard, S. (1985). *Fear and Trembling*, (A. Hannay, Trans.). Harmondsworth: Penguin Books.

Kierkegaard, S. (1987). *Either/Or*, (Hong & Hong, Trans.). Princeton, Princeton University Press.

Kierkegaard, S. (1988). *Stages on Life's Way*, (Hong & Hong, Trans.). Princeton, Princeton University Press.

Koskinen, L. (1994). *Søren Kierkegaard och Existentialism*. Nora, Sweden: Nya Doxa.

Marino, G. (2001). *Kierkegaard in the Present Age*. Marquette: Marquette University Press.

Oden, T. C. (2004). *The Humor of Kierkegaard—An Anthology*. Princeton: Princeton University Press.

Poole, R. & Stangerup, H. (1989). *A Kierkegaard Reader—Texts and Narratives*. London: Fourth Estate.

Weston, M. (1994). *Kierkegaard and Modern Continental Philosophy*. London: Routledge.

van Deurzen, E. (2002). *Existential Counselling and Psychotherapy in Practice*. London: Sage Publications.

Wheeler, G. (2000). *Beyond Individualism—Toward A New Understanding of Self, Relationship and Experience*. Cambridge, MA: GIC Press.

Wysong, J. & Rosenfeld, E. (1982). *An Oral History of Gestalt Therapy*. New York: The Gestalt Journal.

ᘓ

This article was published as 'On being absurd: Søren Kierkegaard 1813–1855' in the *British Gestalt Journal* (2006), Vol. 15(1), pp. 7–15, England, and is reproduced here by kind permission of the editor, Christine Stevens.

2.

On Finding My Way

A month before my eighteenth birthday, I entered Mount Saint Joseph Cistercian monastery, Roscrea, Ireland, as a novice monk (= future priest). My path there had been uncharacteristically crooked. All of my dear mother's middle-class snobbery had (damn—HAS) been passed on to me, so I always go for the top wherever I am...

Here, however, I had succeeded in getting names and addresses mixed up. Mount Melleray is/was the name of the main Cistercian monastery in Ireland, the oldest, the mother-house, so clearly 'the original and best'. Mount Melleray is in County Cork. I had sent my letter of interest in exploring a possible monastic vocation to Mount Melleray (right name), Roscrea (wrong place), County Tipperary (and wrong again!)... and it had been delivered to the Novice Master at Mount Saint Joseph, Roscrea. Father Ambrose, as he was named, had replied warmly and invited me to Roscrea for an interview. So a year before my entrance, I had made my way to the second best of the two Cistercian monasteries then in Ireland, hoping to make the best of a bad mistake.

And so I found myself accepted and entering... exchanging my clothes for medieval long-johns, white woollen socks, and a plain white soutane-like habit. All my hair was shaved off.

Thus began a core experience in my life, a defining experience, a resounding 'failure' which transformed and is still transforming my life. In fact, defining my life. And you, dear reader, are participating in this as you read...

I immersed myself fully in monastic life. Father Ambrose later told me that I had taken to it like a duck to water, and he had envied me the ease with which I embraced what had been for him a distressful period of doubt and discomfort. Apparently, my confessor, Father Thomas, had also indicated that all was well with me.

And then I ran straight into a wall, stopped dead in my tracks. I was moved to the Infirmary for a period of rest, with relaxed rules. The Assistant Novice Master, Father Canice, visited me and told me of his decision to leave the Cistercian Order and join the Capuchin Friars, a reformed branch of the Franciscans. Interestingly, the Capuchins had been my first choice when I first began considering the priesthood, an interest which had shifted towards the full monastic life of enclosed silence as it was practiced then by the Order of Cistercians of the Strict Observance, their full title. After Father Canice's visit, I felt strengthened in my choice and my resolve.

Then came the first of many visits and conversations with Father Ambrose. He had reached a decision about me which he had thought deeply and prayed about as well as talking it through with Father Canice, my confessor Father Thomas, The Prior, Father Lawrence and The Abbot, Dom Camillus. His decision was that I should leave. His feeling was that I was wasted in a monastery. He saw me as a preacher, a teacher, someone who communicated his world to others. An enclosed monastic life of prayer and silence was stifling who I was, not developing me. God, he said, would not call me to a life which lessened who I was.

I argued, fought with every fibre and nerve in me, held out, held on, pushed, asked to talk with the others involved and named…and always came back to hearing the calm statement that I was a preacher, a teacher of others, a communicator whose vocation was not yet clear—except that it was not as a Cistercian monk. Finally, I left the monastery, filled with my sense of failure. I had failed to become a monk. I had even failed to complete my novitiate period of two full years.

All the fanfare of my leaving family and friends was now replaced by the embarrassed silence of a low-key return. Over a period of two years, I made efforts to re-join, always with the same consequence: this was not my vocation, I needed to let go and find it, maybe still the priesthood though not necessarily so. Just let go, follow your path as it comes, pray, trust, be open…

My final attempt was at the new foundation by the Cistexrcians of Roscrea, at Mount Bolton, Athy, County Carlow, where Father Ambrose was now Dom Ambrose, Abbot of the new community. He actually greeted me on my first visit there with a huge smile, a warm welcome, and a loud, laughing "NO!". So I finally gave up.

Having had a number of temporary jobs—night worker at the Irish Post, goods clerk with the Irish Railways, builders' labourer—I now moved to England to become a Student Psychiatric Nurse. By the end of my first year there, I had been chosen to join a specialist programme for a combination Registered Psychiatric and General Nurse qualification. I was well on my way into a career in nursing, with a choice of future paths.

Then a female patient claimed that she had been raped by a male nurse. Her only description was "an Irish junior"—our uniforms defined us as Staff, Senior (qualified) or Junior (student). So the Hospital Board, faced with a police inquiry and a major scandal if the supposed incident were investigated—whatever the outcome—decided in its infinite British wisdom to fire ALL Irish student nurses, more than half of the student body at the time. Thus ended my career in nursing...though my training stayed with me!

I moved to London, and straight into the 1960s. If it could be done, I did it. If it could be tested, I tested it. I needed jobs to pay my rent and buy my food and the like. Careers were something the others had, not us, certainly not me. Free and in free-fall, I had a ball...endlessly!

Then my alcoholic father was imprisoned for bad debts, and I hastily returned to Dublin. Amongst my many short-term jobs was a period as Front of House manager for a travelling repertory company. It was during this period that I met my Swedish future wife.

So I returned to England, she and I moved in together and eventually married. I needed a job...and got one with an Italian domestic appliance company. Within a year, I had moved up 'in the ranks' into middle management—and a position as trainer for new staff. Later, I moved company, and found myself as Senior Sales Trainer and Customer Relations Trainer. And so began a period as Management Trainer, first in England, then Ireland, then Sweden.

We had moved to Sweden in 1975. My early jobs were partly as an independent Management Trainer in English for multinational Swedish companies, and also as an adult education teacher. I took a post graduate qualification in the Teaching of English as a Foreign Language (TOEFL) and eventually got a position as an English

Teacher at the Stockholm School of Economics (SSE). Within a few years, I was head of the Languages and Communication Department at the School as well as a lecturer at the Institute of International Business at SSE in Cross-cultural Management. This was soon followed by a senior Lecturer position at the SDA Business School of Universitá Bocconi, Milan, Italy as well as The Riga School of Economics, Latvia.

While all of these things were happening I started on and completed my Diploma in Gestalt Therapy, my Diploma in Gestalt Organizational and Systems Dynamics and started my Ph.D in Gestalt with Groups.

And then I found myself in Ireland in the late summer of 2000 as faculty for one of the Gestalt programmes with which I work. I had hired a car and was driving to the far south-west from Dublin Airport. The road passes by Roscrea. I found myself stopping there to get a mobile-phone battery charger ... and looking at the road-sign to Mount Saint Joseph Monastery. And deciding that I was too busy and did not have the time. So I drove on.

Our usual end of session faculty meetings were over quickly. Colleagues were leaving for the States. I found myself with a day to spare in terms of my planned travel back to Sweden, where I still live.

So I started out on my journey back to Dublin Airport. After a few hours, I was approaching Roscrea again, this time from the opposite direction. I knew that I could have driven directly to the Guest House at the monastery, yet chose not to. I tried a couple of roadside hotels around Roscrea, without any luck—there was a big local sports event on and everywhere was full. I drove on, intending now to go straight back to Dublin. A good hour past Roscrea I saw a sign for a hotel, and drove in. They had a vacancy.

The next morning, I returned to Roscrea and to Mount Saint Joseph. As I arrived, I realized that it was exactly 40 years that week since my formal induction as a novice. I cried. I entered the church. I watched as 12 monks and one white-clad novice filed in for midday prayers. Those 40 years earlier, there had been 120 monks and seven novices. I recognized most of the monks. Their singing was as ragged as I remembered it from my time there, though now weaker. There I sat and listened, tears streaming down my face—as they are now, with the memory of that moment, and a CD of the Monks of Roscrea playing which I got last Christmas from one of my sisters. I sat still in my place long after the monks had left.

I had not recognized any of my novice friends, and certainly not Father Ambrose. What had happened to them? Like me, out in the world outside our chosen place? And Ambrose dead and buried by now?

I got up to leave, reluctant to take what would probably be my final step out of that world of such deep importance to who I am. Slowly, I began leaving. In the vestibule to the church, there were the usual pamphlets and prayer-sheets. And—could it be true? A photograph of Father Ambrose on a sheet announcing his retirement as Abbot of Mount Bolton—the previous week! Alive and well, and living in Mount Bolton!

Have you ever driven in a car and felt you were flying? Have time and space ever disappeared into abstractions with which you have no time, or space? Has a two-hour journey taken what seems to be five minutes? Has a two-hour journey seemed like a life-time?

I arrived. Well, that is—my body arrived. More than that I cannot say. There was a stillness and restfulness about the place—and then I remembered: yes, our siesta time, from lunch onwards for about 90 minutes.

A relic of our continental roots. So nothing happening here. I went into the church, which was just beginning to be built at my last visit there—the "NO!" visit. Again, I cried, as I am crying now. So much of who I was, became and am, is here. Was here at the time I am describing, and is here now as I re-visit it. And not even physically "here" in Mount Bolton, or 'here' in Stockholm. No—here in Mount Saint Joseph and my fellow novices, postulants, monks and brothers from that time and place in a world which transcends time and place. Here in a timeless, placeless here and now.

I walked out into the garden. A figure approached me slowly, using two walking-sticks. I knew him well. Brother Alberic, I thought. We had played with a rugby ball in the corridors of the Guest House before my entry, and later on my return visits when even he shook his head at me to say 'no'. He looked at me, and greeted me by my monastic name. I did the same with him. He embraced me, and asked 'Does

Ambrose know that you are here?' I replied that he did not. Brother Alberic transferred a stick to another hand, took my hand in his and said 'Brother, you are the last of his novices he knows anything about... he is still in touch with all the rest of you... he will be delighted to meet you.'

And so I met Father Ambrose again, after some 35 years. We sat and chatted as if time had both stood still and yet also gone by. I asked him if he remembered his words to me about teaching, preaching and communicating. 'Oh yes' he said, 'I do. I have always worried about whether you would remember them'. So I told him what I now do. We talked about psychotherapy and the confessional, and agreed that the difference is that confession offers that which psychotherapy cannot offer a Catholic, namely forgiveness. We also spoke of a dilemma he had: he had been chosen as the Cistercian Orders' international advisor on novices. 'How could they', he said, 'of my fifteen novices only two made it through to profession as monks, and only one as a priest'. I responded: 'Ambrose, that's why. You know who is who. You have helped us who are not ready to find our path in life. You have always supported us to find our vocation.'

I spent three hours with Ambrose that afternoon. There is no meeting in my life so far that can match those three hours or their epilogue. None.

Ambrose excused himself to attend Vespers in the church. We agreed to meet and part afterwards. I sat in the church for vespers. Afterwards, I came out and found Ambrose and a vaguely recognisable figure, supported by crutches, waiting by my car. Ambrose said: 'You may remember Father Raymond' and gestured towards the figure by my car. Yes—yes, of course I did! Father Raymond!

Father Raymond reached out his hand to shake mine and then said: 'Brother, Father Thomas was your confessor. As you know, Thomas was not always in the best of health. So I took over at times as confessor for the novices. I will always remember when you needed a confessor, and were directed to me. I still remember the look of shock on your face at meeting me and not Thomas. I have always felt that I failed you in some way, and want to tell you how sorry I am. Thomas was a great confessor. I was never as good as he was.' After some 40 years, I found myself absolving Father Raymond.

Forgiveness is not to be underestimated.

For the record, I teach in four universities internationally, I teach in eight Gestalt institutes internationally, I supervise Gestalt therapists, I supervise Gestalt OSD consultants, I write on Gestalt in each of the English language journals, I write on MBA teaching, on international consultancy. I communicate my world to others.

And right now, dear reader, I am writing to you on the spirituality of life-coaching by the greatest expert I have ever met—Father Ambrose O.C.S.O—who was in turn supervised by ... well, come on: what/who is your name for Father Ambrose's supervisor?

Whose ultimate client I am ... gratefully, and humbly.

უ

This article was published in *InnerSense* (2007), Vol. 1(1), pp. 42-47, and is reproduced here by kind permission of the editor, Brian O'Neill.

3.

In His Own Voice:

INTERVIEW WITH BELINDA HARRIS

The context for this interview was the AAGT Conference, 23-27 July 2008, in Manchester, England, where Seán co-led with Charlie Bowman the welcome and opening plenary session.

BELINDA: *I'll start with a personal question, Seán. What brought you to Gestalt therapy? Why Gestalt for you, at whatever point in your life it was?*

SEÁN: There are probably two answers, or one answer embedded in the other. Mm. In fact, I first clearly understood and publicly acknowledged their connection only a few days ago, at Charlie Bowman's pre-conference workshop on the history of Gestalt therapy, which included our own histories as practitioners. So my answer begins in my earlier life, when before my eighteenth birthday I entered a Cistercian monastery and felt completely at home. I really, really felt it. But before my two-year novice period was up, my novice master, Father Ambrose, called me and said, 'I've been thinking a lot about you, brother, and you don't belong here. You're a teacher, a communicator. If you really want to be a priest be a preacher but the contemplative life is just a waste of your talents.'

Do you remember how you felt when he said that to you?

Devastated. Utterly, totally devastated.

I think one of the devastations was the sense that I had somehow failed. I'd failed something and here I was, now twenty, and a failure;

I'd gone to do something, strong and powerful in my commitment —and I blew it. I made several attempts to get back in and he always met me with a big smile and 'No, you just wait', he'd say, 'just wait'. Then he became Abbott of another monastery so I went there. I always remember meeting him and he just stood there and laughed and said 'Seán, the answer's still "No"'.

I then had a very bohemian life, including London in the sixties. Anything you could do I did it, and if it could be done to excess, I did it to excess. After a few years of going back and forth between Ireland and England, I found myself in London about to get married and needing a job, got a job and within about three months I was asked to train new staff. Then I got another job as a kitchen salesman and within about a year I was asked again, would I take care of the training of new staff. I suddenly found myself a trainer. I began to understand something but very slowly, it hadn't really gone home yet. Then I moved to Sweden and became both a management trainer and a language teacher.

Sweden?

My ex-wife is Swedish. We had lived in England, then in Ireland, and then in 1975 moved to Sweden. I ended up lecturing at the Stockholm School of Economics and then became Head of the Language and Business Communication Department. Then I was clearly teaching, and teaching teachers and training and doing all of the things that Father Ambrose had predicted would be better for me. I wrote in one of the Australian journals (Gaffney, 2007) that I met him again in the year 2000. He was quite an old man. Almost by accident I happened to meet him and I told him what I had been doing. I told him 'I'm a teacher, a therapist, I train therapists, I write'. He stood there and he just said 'Aah'. I said, 'You were right'. He said, 'I know. I was always worried whether you'd ever understand it too.' There's a sense in which that devastating event when I was twenty… somehow the shift from a devastating failure to the joy and the pleasure and the success and the competence as a communicator and teacher and author and, I suppose, 'preacher'.

Anyway, to get back to answering your question about what brought me to Gestalt therapy—the second and more formal, rational answer would be: in 1986 my youngest son died of leukemia. He went very, very quickly, exactly two months and one week from diagnosis to death. This totally threw me.

One of the many consequences of this was that my wife completely crumbled and eventually was diagnosed with paranoid schizophrenia, and because of the complications of the medical system in Sweden there was no way in which she could be prescribed treatment, or helped unless she agreed to it—or I threw her out, if I literally put her outside the door and phoned the authorities and said there's a person with grave diffculties, somebody homeless outside my door, then they would come. I actually had this debate with various authorities. At the same time she was and is the mother of our oldest son. So there was a period when I was living in an apartment with my wife who was becoming my ex-wife, because in the middle of all this she divorced me, and my son who had lost his little brother. The circumstances were extremely demanding.

One of the consequences of where my wife was, was that she reversed day and night totally. So she was up all night and slept all day so everything was chaotic, there were always separate lives being lived completely out of sync in this small apartment. Eventually, after much manoeuvering and in cooperation with her former employer— the hospital where she worked part-time and where our son had died—eventually, they managed to create a situation where they could proactively take care of an employee and they arranged for a period in a kind of residential treatment centre. That created a situation where there was a little bit of space, so I had a grieving process going on for myself, and supporting my son, my ex-wife who now was clearly in the middle of a very severe grieving process, and yet all of these things had been arrested in some way…

Arrested?

Held up, slowed, hindered. Suddenly now there was space, so this was all floating around in me. In my job as head of department I was asked to go to an exhibition of new pedagogical ideas, training and development and things like that. I arrived on the last afternoon and as I was charging around collecting brochures to prove I'd been there more than anything else, somebody jumped out in front of me and said 'Are you in crisis? Would you like to change your life?' I said 'yes and yes' and she handed me a brochure for a Gestalt residential. I already had some experience of therapy, first with my wife and both sons in family therapy, then my wife dropped out and I continued with the two boys until my son's sudden illness and death. Then they took me and my son separately, and then I dropped out as the conditions at home became overwhelming... anyway, I came home and registered and found myself in a 3 x 4-day Gestalt therapy group. I went almost immediately from that into Gestalt therapy training. I knew I'd come home. This is where I wanted to be.

The reason for naming and connecting these two crucial and formal starts of my life in Gestalt is now clear to me: I had not quite finished my training when I began co-leading Gestalt therapy residentials with other people and came very quickly into being a trainer on the training I'd already done. This happened again when I did the Cleveland international organisation programme, I went from student to faculty.

So... mm... this is still new for me, still emerging as a clear pattern, and in this week, in this interview. Maybe I can project here onto Father Ambrose that when he spoke of me as a teacher, communicator, preacher, he was thinking of me doing so from my religious conviction...as a natural expression of who I am, or was then.

Coming into Gestalt therapy how and when I did probably saved my life. I mean I was so deep in my grief and my guilt and my shame and my inadequacy that I could just as easily have 'taken to drink' as we say in Ireland, or wallowed in self-pity and become a perpetual victim, or God knows what. I came into Gestalt as a client in crisis, became a therapist and trainer, brought my learning into my university teaching and management training, became... whole, I suppose, integrated. I see that as a connection from the monastery to teaching to Gestalt therapy.

I am now, as a therapist, trainer, teacher, consultant, working from who I am, from my philosophical convictions. Who I am and what I believe in is fully in my work. I have understood that learning is change, and change is learning, and I'm learning and changing all the time—and passing on my learning to others. So it wasn't just a coincidence that I happened to go to that exhibition or that I happened to go on the residential.

From the start of my training in the eighties Gestalt has been more and more a philosophy of life for me. It's a way of working. It's in my university teaching. It just flowed naturally into that. It's become a way of being for me connected to a specific event in the eighties and a specific event in the early sixties. Both of them quite devastating.

In different ways…and both of them quite formative…

Extremely. My dead son is involved here somewhere in another, more directly influential way. One of the things I did as a consequence of that period around his death and his mother's obvious painful grieving was to decide 'I'm going to become a better person. I probably wasn't the best father in the world; I probably favoured his big brother more. I clearly wasn't a good support to my wife. I've got to be a better person. I need to do something to be a better person.' When I graduated from the Gestalt Academy of Scandinavia and the group of us were sitting there I said, 'Thanks to my son, I promised myself to be a better person, and thanks to these four or five years I believe I've become one.'

That's a very powerful set of connections, isn't it? Really, really powerful. I've got to ask you this because I've never experienced you as a trainer but is there a bit of Father Ambrose in you in the way you work?

Yes, two things are very clear to me from Father Ambrose. One is that I would never hesitate to tell someone 'I don't think Gestalt is for you. I don't think it's the right place for you', so that's connected to him. The other thing that's connected to him is that during the three-hour conversation I had with him in 2000 he said, 'You know, they've asked me to be the trainer of the new novice masters in the Cistercian order all round the world. I can't understand why. I had fifteen novices and only two of them actually became monks and one of those has since left.' I said, 'Ambrose, that's why, that's exactly why'.

There's something of a connection there in that what seems like failure at the time is actually a huge success.

Yes, that's it. I said something to Ambrose like, 'You had clearly the ability to ask yourself 'Is this the right place for this person or not?' Not, is this person good enough or is this person right for this place, but is this place, is this life right for this person? If you thought it wasn't, you never hesitated to say so.' 'Oh,' he said, 'I never looked at it that way.' He was a little bit absorbed in the thought that he had failed.

In the same way that you had been...

Exactly, so we had a funny sort of conversation around it that, as a Cistercian novice master, he could regard me as one his ultimate successes.

I feel really touched by that story.

So am I.

And it's very hard to know what to ask you next that won't somehow take away or trivialise what feels like a very precious set of disclosures. And yet, now I've got you, I don't want to lose you!

OK, I'm here!

One of the things that struck me when I first met you at the opening plenary of the conference is your Irishness, and how Irishness feels like another precious part of you. I'm aware that you live in Sweden and also work in Ireland. Can you say a little about your relationship to Ireland and what it means to you?

My relationship to Ireland is ... well, if I'm asked to say or write something about myself in fifty words, I usually start by saying 'Irish by birth, culture and conviction'. Growing up I had a very strong sense of Irishness, largely because I learned the language when I went to school at the age of five or six and I was extremely proud of my growing fluency, that I could happily converse in Gaelic and access its wonderful literature.

With the kind of Irish Christian Brother education I later got, if they weren't paedophiles they were sadists, but whatever else they may have been they were passionate Irish nationalists. That grabbed me, that sense of fervent pride in a collective identity, that there was a sense of belonging. I also grew up in Dublin; my teen years were the mid '50s onwards, when the activist ideals of revolutionary Ireland were still quite potent.

There was always the possibility of becoming associated with the IRA at the time, as did many of my school friends. In my own case, my maternal grandfather had been very involved as an Irish Republican activist in the pre-1916 times but then chose to go the political route and to see whether we could get independence by political means. He had such a powerful influence on me that I felt this tug between wanting to do something active, wanting to maintain this identity I felt so attached to, that I really felt I belonged to, and yet some kind of respect and great love for my maternal grandfather, the feeling that he wouldn't do something that wasn't good. So maybe if he'd seen another way, then maybe there was something in it. So I always felt caught in that tug. In a sense, I think, this is pure interpretation on my part, but I think I put my political nationalist fervour into Irish literature, music and art, and this whole expression of Irishness, and that has stayed with me.

As I grew older and became aware of what Irishness means...I mean I moved to London at a time when, if you were looking for a place to stay, windows would have a sign 'No Blacks, No Irish'. If it only said 'No Blacks', the landlord was probably Irish, so there was this identity thing. It was very, very powerful being called Paddy by anybody and everybody, simply because of the way I spoke, and it brought with it this awful sense of being personally anonymous. At the same time I could feel 'Well, fuck you, call me Paddy 'cos I am Irish...I can buy that', a feeling of belonging to something bigger. As I moved up through life and began teaching—one of the things I lecture in is cross-cultural management—it became clear that it is impossible to separate me from that environment. If I am to honour who I am, I need to include that. There isn't a Seán that is distinct from my Irishness.

And you knew that early on in your career?

I knew that probably . . . I'd put this somewhere around the mid-sixties and early seventies because at that time I was involved in the revival of traditional Irish music in Dublin and hung out in all the music pubs and knew all the guys and got into that whole world of revival of Irish language and culture through music and through words, two things we're kind of good at. There it really came home to me that whilst I wasn't brought up in a family environment that had any particular interest in Irish music and certainly not in the Irish language, my contact with the music and language had really resonated in me. The more I found myself acknowledging that the more whole I felt. If you get me, you get my Irishness. . .

Sounds like a really strong core in you from your adolescence, into your time in London.

Yeah, and just getting stronger. I don't think it's possible to separate these things, and maybe that's a part of my being Irish! And I really can't and won't stop myself here from connecting with my particular pleasure at the most recent 'Irish' issue of the BGJ—Bronagh, Des, Sarah of the 'Galway Fallons', and myself . . . 'the colony strikes back'!

That's a palpable pride in identity! You said earlier that in London you had a real sense of belonging, this 'call me Paddy if you want' suggests 'this is where I fit'. It sounds really exciting, there's an energy in it.

There was, there was.

And then I'm imagining you going to Sweden and I'm wondering what happened to your sense of belonging?

Well, I think that's an excellent question. Firstly, I learned the language comparatively quickly. I thought as soon as I can pass the university entrance exam for non-Swedes, I'll be fine. So I went to lessons, six hours a day, five days a week, until such time as I passed that exam and then stopped taking lessons and just soaked up the language. It took about four months, and this then gave me the opportunity to feel more grounded in myself.

So you're a fast learner.

Well, in a sense I had learned a second language when I was five or six so the ability was there somewhere. The bad thing was that when I added a third language, my Gaelic began to disappear. It's very hard to get it back because I'm not in that environment. Then I had established a way to enter Swedish society to the extent I needed to. I had a sense of maintaining my Irishness because both of my children had very Gaelic names. I didn't want them to lose a connection because they were clearly named as Irish children, so that aspect of passing on something of my identity remained fairly strong. My wife at the time was fed up with Ireland and everything Irish (including me), which of course encouraged me to be a little more Irish in reaction. I became more fascinated by the fact that the differences due to cultural upbringing are so much a part of the person. I told my wife, 'You know there were a lot of things that used to drive me crazy and I thought it was you. Now I realise that a lot of Swedes are driving me crazy in exactly the same way. What really pushes my buttons is your Swedishness meeting my Irishness.' So I became interested in it there. I realised there are some things I cannot change, there's no way, so I might as well celebrate it. I can't hide it, so that's what I've done.

A thread running through everything you've said is hanging on to what's important to you.

OK, yeah.

So if I think of a week in Seán Gaffney's life outside this conference, what's the most important part of the week for you?

Well, the week in Seán Gaffney's life would have to depend on where I was. I spend sixty to seventy percent of my working life outside Sweden. A week in my life could be lecturing in Milan, could be a supervision group in Belfast, could be a training group in Denmark, could be a training week for the international OSD programme anywhere in the world, or a week in Cape Cod with consultants. One of the joys in my life is that I don't have a typical week.

So, what sustains you when you're in these different places?

What sustains me is that I don't have a typical week. What sustains me is that I would find it physically impossible to become bored, being focused, stimulated and connected, wherever I am.

So the stimulation sustains you?

Yes, always meeting something new, intellectually, socially, meeting different people, new challenges … a phrase that comes to mind right now is 'always being alive'. In some ways I don't have the time to die because I spend so much of my time always being alive.

I feel really impacted by that as well. [tearful]

Well, as we're talking, that's what comes up, Belinda. That feels really important to me too.

Yes, I'm really taking that in.

OK. So I hope to die in the middle of doing something I enjoy, an opening experiential plenary at a conference, for example.

Oh no, the closing plenary, please! [both laughing]

What a way to go! That sense, that's what really keeps me going. It means that in between all of that I have very intense periods of wanting to be totally alone.

I wanted to ask you about that.

I have a house in the Swedish countryside and I can spend six weeks of the summer there on my own. Visits by arrangement…

So that's a space for you to recharge?

Mmm, just a space to be utterly alone, and there are certain important spaces like that. Like the anniversary of my son's death, for example. I will not do anything for a few days before or after—that space is sacred because I know it's going to hit me and I want to be available when it does. It has every year for twenty-something years.

Twenty-two.

Twenty-two. Yes. Next month, in fact. So, being alone, that movement, to actually go somewhere and say, 'Listen, I'm not talking to anybody, not going to meet anybody'. I have a few of my favourite movies on DVD. I might watch them three times a week because I enjoy them. Time on my own is important to me.

Someone who knows me very well and who's at this conference said the other day, 'You know, you're the only person I know who has the ability to go suddenly absent without leave in mid-sentence, if you need to', and it does happen. I can suddenly feel 'I've had it'. If I get that feeling I can close down and disappear ... I'm reminded here of a Van Morrison song with a chorus that starts 'Well, I think I'm going AWOL, disconnect my telephone' ... or another favourite by Nanci Griffths with the astounding opening line 'I'm going to take an early plane to anywhere but here'. So maybe a mixture of feeling overwhelmed ... or underwhelmed ... or just needing a retreat ... maybe that piece of the monastery that is still alive and well in who I am ... so yes, I like to go AWOL.

And I really appreciate that you haven't done that in this interview. And I just want to say this, I'm really aware that when you talked about dying my immediate thought was 'God, what a loss that would be to the profession'. I don't feel I know you. I know a really precious part of you now but even though I've only known you for a couple of days from a distance I have a really strong sense of what a huge loss that would be and what you probably mean to other people out there.

The funny thing is that when you say that I think, 'What the hell is she talking about?'.

I believe you, and I understand that. But it's true. Thank you for your time.

You're more than welcome.

References

Gaffney, S. (2007). On Finding My Way. *Inner Sense—A Journal of Australian Spirituality*. Wollongong, Australia: Ravenwood Press.

ૐ

This article was published as 'In his own voice' in the *British Gestalt Journal* (2008), Vol. 17(1), pp. 51-56, England, and is reproduced here by kind permission of the editor, Christine Stevens.

4.

A Journey Through Mourning

In memory of my son, Dara Gaffney
May 9, 1972 – August 9, 1986

Allow me to begin with some extracts from the interview by Belinda Harris, published in the British Gestalt Journal (Gaffney, 2008), which started me off on the reflections described in this article:

BELINDA: *I'll start with a personal question, Seán. What brought you to gestalt therapy? Why gestalt for you, at whatever point in your life it was?*

SEÁN: *There are probably two answers, or one answer embedded in the other. Mm. In fact, I first clearly understood and publicly acknowledged their connection only a few days ago, at Charlie Bowman's pre-conference workshop on the history of gestalt therapy, which included our own histories as practitioners. So my answer begins in my earlier life, when before my 18th birthday I entered a Cistercian monastery and felt completely at home. I really, really felt it. But before my two year novice period was up my novice master, Father Ambrose, called me and said 'I've been thinking a lot about you, brother, and you don't belong here. You're a teacher, a communicator. If you really want to be a priest be a preacher but the contemplative life is just a waste of your talents.'*

I have described this experience in the first issue of Inner Sense (Gaffney 2009). It has become more and more formative for me as I look back on my life, and now more clearly connected to the topic of this article: a journey through mourning and the meaning of a life…

SEÁN: *Anyway, to get back to answering your question about what brought me to Gestalt therapy: the second and more formal, rational answer would be: in 1986 my youngest son died of leukaemia. He went very, very quickly, exactly two months and one week from diagnosis to death...*

And later in the interview:

My dead son is involved here somewhere in another, more directly influential way. One of the things I did as a consequence of that period around his death and his mother's obvious painful grieving was to decide 'I'm going to become a better person. I probably wasn't the best father in the world; I probably favoured his big brother more. I clearly wasn't a good support to my wife. I've got to be a better person. I need to do something to be a better person'. When I graduated from the Gestalt Academy of Scandinavia and the group of us were sitting there I said, 'Thanks to my son, I promised myself to be a better person, and thanks to these four or five years I believe I'm becoming one.'

So let me now, after a brief detour into the safer territory of quoted references, go straight to the point: shortly after the fourteenth birthday of my youngest of two sons, he became ill, with very diffuse symptoms. I took him to our local clinic, where the diagnosis was an infection of some sort, with prescribed antibiotics and a week's rest. He appreciated the week off school, though did not seem to be getting over his symptoms of tiredness, mild though diffuse pain, and a general listlessness. Despite his prescribed freedom with no school and no homework, he showed little interest in TV or videos.

On June 1, 1986, he had severe pain, mainly in his stomach. His mother—a social worker student and a part-time assistant nurse—took him to the emergency ward at our local hospital, where she herself worked. I was away, teaching. My wife phoned me that evening to say that Dara had been immediately transferred to the cancer ward of the Children's Hospital, which, she knew, was the leukaemia ward.

I returned immediately and went to visit him. He was clearly unwell and in pain. My wife was very concerned, using her experience in the hospital and conversations with the nursing staff. I was...well, optimistic is the wrong word. Maybe reassured that he was in a good hospital and with my belief that treatment worked.

Two days later, my wife and I had a meeting with his doctor, a soft-spoken and gentle man originally from northern Africa. He declared the diagnosis—acute myelocetic leukaemia—and spoke of the chemotherapy treatment that would start immediately and continue for about two or up to three months. If the cancer was arrested then, it would be time to maybe start looking at such interventions as a bone marrow transplant and he would need to start taking samples to establish who would be a suitable donor, probably our oldest son. He was clear about the statistics: 60% chance of improvement, 40% chance of moving into a terminal condition. For this particular form of leukaemia, the average for Sweden (population 8.5 million) was four cases per year.

My son was in the leukaemia ward on the eighth floor of the children's hospital. The ninth floor had been adapted for parents and relatives to spend nights there in order to be near their children. My wife and I took a room there so that one of us at least would always be around, day and night, using a shift system on weekdays, and staying there for most of the weekend. My wife and I re-arranged our work schedules so that we could attend to both our sons.

Reflecting back to this period, I am now more aware than I was then, of the differences in how my wife and I heard and interpreted the information we regularly received. For her, the doctor was preparing us for the worst. For me, he was keeping us informed of progress without making any promises. She became more and more withdrawn, at times impossible to reach in any way that I knew how. We became more distanced from each other, sometimes only meeting briefly as we took over from each other at the hospital. The few hours we might be at home with our other son, we did the practical things together that had to be done and otherwise kept our exchanges to a social minimum.

As we moved through July, it was becoming increasingly difficult to distinguish between the impact of his leukaemia and the impact of the chemotherapy on Dara's condition. His immune system was degraded by the treatment and he was susceptible to heavy colds, sudden fevers, exhaustion, complete loss of appetite, and days which he slept through from one to the next.

By the end of July, a mere two months after admission to the hospital, his condition was worsening on a daily basis. All talk of a bone marrow transplant was now out of the question. The personnel moved an extra bed into Dara's room so that my wife and I could choose to sleep there with him in his room. I slept there the three last nights of his short life. My wife was working nights during this time, dropped in to see him during the night, and slept at home during the daytime.

When I awoke on the morning August 9, 1986, Dara was asleep, breathing shallowly and his whole body burning hot with fever. There was an intern on duty that morning and I asked him to check on my son and tell me what was happening. He asked me where my wife was. I told him that she was at home, sleeping.

"I think you better call her, and get her here" he said. I did, and she came. We were at our son's bedside when he died, early that afternoon.

Our eldest boy, Naoise, was on his way back from Ireland that same day. Because of very strained relations between my wife and my family in Dublin, none of us had been back to Ireland since coming to Sweden, 11 years earlier. Naoise was a dedicated scout and troop leader, and, the previous year, his troop had planned a study visit to Ireland in the first week of August, ending this very day. I had earlier phoned a close friend of mine and told him of the situation. With an amazing effort and great ingenuity, he had traced Naoise to the harbour where he was waiting to board the ferry. With the help of the ferry personnel and scout leaders, Naoise was put in a taxi and was on his way to Dublin Airport with a flight booked by my friend back to Stockholm where he would be met and brought straight to the hospital.

His brother died while all this was happening. The ward staff arranged for Dara's body to be brought to the hospital chapel so that Naoise could say his farewell when he arrived later that evening.

(Months later, Naoise told me that he had spoken with Dara about the trip to Ireland and his own willingness to stay in Sweden. I was amazed and moved to hear that Dara had spoken of possibly dying, and that he did not want to deprive his brother of a trip that was so important to him. If he went, and Dara died, then Naoise would anyway have been back to Ireland and met their cousins, whom Dara did not remember—he was two years old when we moved to Sweden. If he didn't go, and Dara died, then this would always be between them…)

As is common in Sweden and a shock to me, the funeral was to be some 10 days later. My wife reminded me of a christening we had attended at the Catholic church in central Stockholm, where we had both been impressed by the priest, a German Jesuit whose name I got from the father of the christened child—Pater Peter Hornung. I phoned the church and found myself speaking with Pater Hornung for almost an hour. I could feel and sense his care, gentleness and warmth.

A few days later, my wife and I met Pater Hornung. 'My name is Peter Hornung', he said, 'that's "honung" with an "r".' 'Honung' is Swedish for honey…(right now, in mid-sentence, I think of Karen Horney, the psychoanalyst, also 'honey' with an 'r'). We spent almost an afternoon with him in what was a gentle combination of counselling, pastoral care, and the practicalities of our son's funeral. Amongst these was the hard practicality of our family not being parishioners, and our son not formally baptised. This meant that we could not have a full church funeral. What Pater Hornung proposed was that we have a private funeral in the chapel at the Catholic section of our local cemetery—located directly in view of the balconies on the eighth and ninth floors of the children's hospital—and a memorial mass, which he would celebrate, the Saturday after the funeral, in the church.

My wife attended the funeral, and not the mass. Pater Hornung had suggested that we bring some of Dara's favourite music with us. I remembered him telling me once, with a young teenager's earnestness, that Annie Lennox of Eurythmics was the best singer in the world. I prepared a tape with her singing 'I walk into an empty room/And suddenly my heart goes boom—There must be an angel/Playing with my heart'. Annie Lennox was for my son; today, I can realise that the song was for me. Since then, I still can't hear it without opening up to my memories, or closing down in a non-supportive environment, knowing that I can raise the song again later and be open to its influence.

I still and often remember that mass. I had put an announcement in the Deaths column of the main newspapers and was amazed to find the church absolutely full. Almost all of the Swedes, including classmates, teachers, neighbours, family friends had a flower with them to place on the non-existent coffin, having confused the memorial mass with a funeral. Pater Hornung noticed this and immediately said that he would stop at an appropriate moment during the mass to allow these flowers to be placed on the altar, which he did. When it was time for his sermon, he stood silently on the side of the altar, looked up and around and said words I have never forgotten. I am convinced as I write that what follows is more verbatim than it is a paraphrase:

'At a time like this, when we remember a fourteen year old boy, some may wonder about the meaning of life. What is the meaning of Dara's life? I can tell you his meaning for me, who never met him and who buried his dead body. YOU are the meaning of his life to me. Here I am, a German Jesuit, a missionary and a parish priest, speaking to a church full of … non-practicing Catholics, since I recognise nobody; Lutherans in name though maybe not in practice; agnostics, atheists, humanists … and more besides. This is a dream come true for me—thanks to Dara, whose life made this possible. The meaning of Dara's life is not what he achieved or failed at in his fourteen years. The meaning of his life is in the influence of his life and death on us he leaves behind, and on how open we are to allowing that meaning be a part of our lives as we go on living. If we forget him, then his life and death become meaningless to us.'

There was a long silence as he finished and returned to complete the mass.

⌘

Allow me here to return to the BGJ interview, where I summarise the immediate and subsequent events:

In 1986 my youngest son died of leukemia. He went very, very quickly, exactly two months and one week from diagnosis to death. This totally threw me. One of the many consequences of this was that my wife completely crumbled and eventually was diagnosed with paranoid schizophrenia, and because of the complications of the medical system in Sweden there was no way in which she could be prescribed treatment, or helped unless she agreed to it—or I threw her out, if I literally put her outside the door and phoned the authorities and said there's a person with grave difficul-

ties, somebody homeless outside my door, then they would come. I actually had this debate with various authorities. At the same time she was and is the mother of our oldest son. So there was a period when I was living in an apartment with my wife who was becoming my ex-wife, because in the middle of all this she divorced me, and my son who had lost his little brother. The circumstances were extremely demanding. One of the consequences of my wife's condition was that she reversed day and night totally. So she was up all night and slept all day so everything was chaotic, there were always separate lives being lived completely out of sync in this small apartment. Eventually after much maneuvering and in cooperation with her former employer— the hospital where she worked part-time and where our son had died... eventually, they managed to create a situation where they could pro-actively take care of an employee and arranged for a period in a kind of residential treatment centre. That created a situation where there was a little bit of space, so I had a grieving process going on for myself, and supporting my son, my ex-wife who now was clearly in the middle of a very severe grieving process...

ꝭ

I had started writing poetry in my very early teens, in both English and Gaelic, and have continued ever since, though nowadays in English and Swedish. I have only ever published three—two in English and one in Swedish. One of the two in English accompanied the BGJ interview. It was my celebration of Dara's 21st anniversary. I say 'celebration' in the sense that every recognition of his influence on my life is indeed a celebration of the meaning of his life. So—yes, a celebration, no matter how much sorrow or regret or shame each poem expresses, or humour or joy. These poems, over a period now of 22 years, have become my 'Journey Through Mourning', with all its ambiguity...

Over the years, these poems have simply emerged, sometimes complete, sometimes in parts over a day or days or even weeks. I became used to being open for a line to emerge, and, when it sounded, tasted, felt 'right', I would see what followed. I have committed few of them to paper until they were finished in my body.

My intention here is to select from them as I, for the first time publicly, explore my mourning and its meaning with the poems as my guide. The only changes I have made for publication are concerned with clarity, never content. This selection is intended to capture the main themes which have emerged over the past 22 years, and will include my first and my most recent poem.

The first one came within days of Dara's death. Someone had asked me, in Swedish, how I was. Directly translated, this particular phrase would be "How is it?" This became the opening line of my first, unexpected poem:

I.
there is nothing it is like.

it is. it

is the gaps we leave still in our conversations.

is your place at the table empty but
still set sometimes and unset again.

is the rocking chair you'd sit in, observing
sat in by someone the day of your funeral
shock of him sitting on top of you there.

the gaps we leave still in our conversations
the place beside me at the table empty
rocking chair you'd sit in, observing
shock of you not sitting there to observe us.

there is nothing it is like.

it is all of these and more of them and none of them.

it is.

This first poem was a flower that bloomed in the wasteland of my life at that time. It opened and its seeds blew within me. Soon poems began forming spontaneously in me, and I processed them until each was finished, ended, temporarily complete. I say "temporarily", since some poems and lines re-emerged in later pieces. One theme which has never left me came in the second poem, which, in itself, was an echo of the first one:

2.
you will always be not here.

your birthdays will be would have beens,

at would have been twenty one you will be
unimaginable.

at would have been eighteen you will be
unimaginable.

at would have been fifteen you will be
fourteen still
fourteen years and three months to the day
killed by leukaemia.

you are not.
there is no you.

you are a he that was
and not a you even.

you are a he that was.
you were and are my son and I miss you not here now, not

ever.

again.

here.

My anger was a theme that emerged early and changed form over time: as I select poems now, I find I am re-visiting the times and places of their creation, and the emotions I was experiencing then— and now again, though softer.

4.
leukaemia is a cruel and brutal killer

gnawed and gnashed in you
sucked sickly at the marrow in your bones

polluted you

even the treatment
polluted you

pushed the hair out from under your burning skin
pushed your food back out through your sore filled mouth
gushed shit out of your seeping anus
sickness and treatment
polluting you

killing you

cruelly
brutally
killing you
and all our matter of fact trivialities
our let's be practical delusions
our crying won't help him helplessness our
may the end come quickly never confusion

cruelly
brutally
killing you

This poem re-appeared soon after as a variation on the same theme explicitly repeated. I remember how the ending differed with a new theme emerging, though I had no real idea of this at the time:

9.
. . . .

even the treatment
polluted him
sickness and treatment
polluting him

killing him
cruelly
brutally
killing him

this repetition a release and a reminder:

I'll exorcise his dying not
your life your life
lives on in me

Another theme was around our family:

7.
we are a square
collapsed to a triangle

one corner gone and
half our space our
distances distorted

On the night of the funeral, my wife moved out of our bedroom into Dara's room and bed. The following day, she nailed up double blankets over the window and kept the room in total darkness. Two weeks later, she was sent home from her work. I had no idea of the details at the time, and only caught glimpses of them later. One thing I learned later was that she was regarded as being on sick leave. This led to a period at home of extreme stress and unpredictability. It is only since becoming a gestalt therapist myself that I was able to see perspectives that were beyond me at the time. Amongst the stresses were occasional brief and sharp outbursts by my wife, accusing my family of things which were partly recognisable, and partly imaginary. These outbursts were also directed at me, including my inadequacies as a father to Dara: how I never loved him as much as Naoise, how I didn't take his illness seriously, how my grieving for him was inadequate and typical of the selfish person I was.

In the midst of all this, my wife sought a divorce and only needed my signature for it to become a formality, three months later. In the circumstances, I admit, with some shame, that I was relieved at the time. Her divorcing me would be one problem less to deal with. My focus was fully on both of my sons, one dead, his big brother living in a home that was fast becoming a hell. I am remembering the insoluble dilemmas I was facing: grieving for Dara, with all the shame and guilt I felt; supporting my living son, not only in his own loss of his little brother, for whom he had always been a big brother—with all that entails - but also protecting my son from an insufferable situation at home. And protecting myself from the increasingly disjointed accusations of my wife, now my ex-wife but still living in the family home ... though the family was truly collapsed in on itself.

Earlier, on my wife's initiative—she was studying to be a social worker—we had all four started in family therapy (psychodynamic) some six months previously. My wife had dropped out, following an argument with the two therapists. I and the two boys continued. Then Dara was invited to join a group of his own age. Then Naoise was invited to move to the Youth Department, which he did, and I stayed in therapy on my own. After Dara's death and the subsequent events at home, I too dropped out and Naoise continued. So I had a sense that he had a place to get support. My self-support was in dealing with the situation at home, getting back to work as a lecturer—and managing my constant grief. Divorce seemed like a way out. What I had not understood was that my wife—soon formally my ex-wife—had no intention of moving from our apartment. So for a further six months the three of us lived this strange, disjointed, disconnected life in the same space and times...

Throughout this confusing time, poems continued to emerge. My guilt and shame were themes which bloomed and spread their seeds:

8.
cold fact of your absence crying through my mind

tears of my thoughts freeze and craze in me
my dry eyes pain with the hurt behind them

my memory cringes with images of your suffering

something inside me shrivels at
thoughts of my thoughtlessness:

the hug I needed the hug I gave you your skin
screaming at the contact:

daddy, daddy please

daddy!

daddy!

more confusion than anger
an appeal more than anger
an appeal not to hurt you

I think of you begging me your father not to hurt you

images of your suffering

images of my clumsiness
Dara, Dara please

Dara!

Dara!

teach me your meaning

During this first of my twenty two years of mourning, there were moments when my sorrow met joyful memories and these themes intertwined, weaving strangely integrated patterns of polarities:

10.'
sometimes I see you.

my lips form your words in my head:

I-HAVE-NO-HOMEWORK-OKAY?
I-HAVE-NO-HOMEWORK.
YOU relax at the weekend
YOU go to the bloody bookshops
spend all day just looking at books

SO: I. HAVE. NO. HOMEWORK.
OKAY? OKAY?

so can I go out now to my friends
smirking and smiling your triumph at me…

or:

mew – mew – mew – mew – SEEK
mimicking my stammer and my clumsy Swedish
mew – mew – mewssssSEEK
say it again daddy say it again

mewmewmew
it's so funny daddy: say it again!

or:

Daddy Daddy please

Daddy!

Daddy!

18.
I'm learning to laugh again
good-hearted chuckles bubbling up from in me

Sometimes when I meet you where we've been before
I hear you clearly begging me:

Tell it again daddy please
daddy daddy tell it again
it's so funny
daddy daddy please come on daddy

You could hear the same joke twenty times and laugh
each time equally heartily
your eyebrows up under your quiff
mouth opening to welcome the punchline
helplessly creasing yourself giggling and laughing

Sometimes I meet you where we'll never be
hear you sometimes where you can't be now
know it's anyway you I'm seeing
know it must be you I'm hearing –

hear you giggling watch your mouth opening
a t.v programme maybe or your granddad's latest bargain

or something I hear of I know you'd laugh at
or something I think of I know you'd laugh at

share it with you say to someone who knew you
Dara would have laughed at that

Dara would laugh at that I say
learning again to laugh at it with you

19.
hairs in the bathtub
mine or your brother's

hairs in the bathtub remind me

moulting, your insides mangy with poisons
hair everywhere strands and clumps of it

so we shaved your head
crossed a border into no-man's-land
burned your bridges though we didn't say so

you wanted a wig but you never wore it

out for those royal tours in your wheelchair
you lifting your hat to old ladies passing
laughed baldly when we'd passed them said
stop stop quick wait here's another one ready?

bald bony dying still you

A theme which re-emerged and has followed me is the confusion of Dara's birthday. This more than anything is an annual reminder of his death, of the end of his life, the end of our physical time together.

14.
today you are would-have-been fifteen

at five i think it was twenty five
five twenty five p.m Irish time
fifteen years ago today you were born

today you are nine months dead
at 14.50 Swedish time
nine months ago today you died

the nurses didn't let me see you born

the nurses let me see you dying
the nurses let me see you die
today at 14.50 you are nine months dead
at 17.25 then would have been fifteen

i'll first relive your dying then
your birth first sounds of you

A number of other themes had emerged during this first year after Dara's death, all somehow flattened by his absence as evoked by his would-have-been-fifteen-day and now the powerful finality of his first anniversary:

25.
this night last year the last night of your life

this night last year the first night of this year

i didn't know then you were dying then

you'd asked to have the extra bed back in
this week last year the last week of your life

my turn to sleep there in your room that night
this night last year the first night of this year

i didn't know then you were dying then

i knew that you were dying but not then i mean
this night last year the last night of your life

i didn't know then you were dying then

this night last year the first night of this year

this night last year the last night of your life

There was a dreadful finality about Dara's first anniversary. A Christmas come and gone without his subtle signals and delight. A birthday come and gone and still the same age as on the day of his death. An anniversary confirming the obvious—Dara was dead and always would be, for the rest of my life. And somehow, dead but not gone and not forgotten. I understood that the meaning of his short life for me would be in how I remembered him and gave his life meaning for me through how his influence lived on in me.

For most of this first year, I felt as if I were living in a number of parallel worlds. I was absorbed by my grieving, grabbing private moments to ponder my sorrow, my guilt, my shame, my memories of Dara and his life with me, and mine with him, and mostly expressed in the poems which just kept coming. My home life was in chaos. Naoise needed more support than I could give him, and I was truly grateful that he was still in therapy. My work as a lecturer had lost much of its excitement for me—it had become a job, a way of paying the bills. My one good friend, Terry, from Wales, whose family and ours had socialised a lot together, became the channel for my feelings, and I could just let go of whatever was going on for me in his attentive company.

And then, of course, another year without Dara had started:

Sixt....

a month to go today until your
would-have-been-sixteen day

(this month I know is April and my watch says ninth)

four months to go today until your
second anniversary

(the month will then be August and my watch says ninth)

is sixteen worse than fifteen—if so why?
and first one worse than second—if so why?
surely your absence cannot match your presence
surely your life is worth more than your death:

I'll write this for you now not then:
you were you are—not would-have-been

Early in the Autumn term of 1987, I found myself at a Training and Development Exhibition as part of my work. A woman stepped out from a stand as I rushed past and asked: 'Are you in crisis?' 'Do you want to change?' 'Yes and yes', I replied. She handed me a leaflet for a 3 × 4-day Gestalt residential. By the end of this residential, I felt that I had come home in some way. I applied to the Gestalt Academy of Scandinavia for their 4–year Diploma Programme in Gestalt Therapy. I started in August, 1988, two years after Dara's death. I had understood that even if I never became a 'better' person, I could at least open myself to change.

Some pieces from this period:

MAY 19, 1990

at would-have-been-eighteen today
you are not with me now

you were and are and always will be
fourteen years and three months to the day

ALL SOULS' DAY, 1991

I light a candle for each of you:
My granddad, my father and my son.

You, granddad, thought I could be your son
Heard in my voice your dead son's echo…

You, my father, just never knew how to be one
Hoped you could be one if I became your son.

And you, my son, hoped I would be your father.
And now I'm learning how to be your son.

I stand here last of our four generations
Alive in the lives of you, my special dead.

MAY 9, 1991

Dear Dara,
okay, okay: I'm still not really good:
but you will agree I'm changing.
so: thanks for being you,
thanks for your patience.
love,
Daddy

I completed my training in May, 1992. I can see now, as I write this sentence, that I started the month of his death, and finished the month of his birth. Between his dying and his birth…That summer, I attended a 4-day residential Psychosynthesis retreat, where the following poem emerged:

SILJAN-SONG

On a hill above Lake Siljan I give myself an hour
And watch the trees around me being trees;
And watch the grass around me being grass;
And see each bush, plant, weed and flower.

On a hill above Lake Siljan I give myself the time
To see ants, busy, on a mottled stone;
To hear each birdsong, separate, distinct;
To sit here, waiting for a rhyme.

On a hill above Lake Siljan, I'm happy to just be,
Accepting all the ups and downs I've had,
Accepting all the paths that lie ahead:
On a hill above Lake Siljan, I'm learning to be me.

On the first anniversary of Dara's death, I established a ritual which became obsessive. First, a visit to the florists at the cemetery entrance close to the Catholic graveyard, where I bought two potted white wild daisy plants, and two protected candles. I would then go the chapel where we held the funeral service, and plant the daisies and light a candle at the small mound opposite the chapel with a crucifix. After some time there, I would walk to the hill on which the Memorial Garden was, where Dara's ashes had been strewn. Here I would again plant daisies and light a candle and reflect. I did this for fourteen years.

And then came Dara's fourteenth anniversary. I can remember sobbing and shaking with tears as I sat by the chapel and realized he was now dead as long as he had been alive. Still sobbing, I walked to the Memorial Garden. I sobbed and moaned with grief. Suddenly, I was stilled, then exhilarated: I did not need any empty rituals to commemorate him. My life was my commemoration. My work at opening to change. My work at being a good father to his brother, Naoise. All that I did to give meaning to his life through the influence of his life and death on me, and, through me, on others: my therapy clients, my training groups, my supervisees, my university students—all had Dara to thank for any value they found in working with me. I walked laughing down the hill, and have not been back there since.

Since then, my only 'ritual' is to keep the days around his anniversary completely free, and also to celebrate his birthday. I never know how I will be impacted, simply that I will be, in one way or another.

And the poems still came, old themes returning, new ones poking up like wild flowers, all becoming perfect parts of a colourful bouquet of celebration. This process over the 22 years since his death can be captured in the two most recent anniversary poems:

I.

you are twenty one years dead today.

twenty.

one.

years.

dead.

today and then i saw you die and see you die again.

i stood and stand now by your bedside.

my finger touched and touches now the heat of your hand.

i did not touch you more than that, it caused you pain.

your startled wide-eyed stare.

your startled wide-eyed stare a shift and you were gone.

i dared to touch your burning hand.

you neither moved nor sounded.

you are twenty one years dead today.

and now again I dare to touch your burning hand.

i take your hand to guide us through this day.

2.
my guilt my shame my sorrow and

the black hole of your absence:

forever fourteen.

your brother now a man of thirty seven.
forever fourteen.

and me with two weeks now to sixty five.

and you are still

forever fourteen

still

the black hole of your absence all these years.

This was as cathartic an experience as was that of his fourteenth anniversary, though fundamentally different. In the first, I went from helpless grief, shame and guilt into the joy of discovering that Dara was in me and with me, not in a chapel or a Memorial Garden. On his twenty first anniversary, his death and total physical absence from my life hit me deeply.

He was not with me in my life now as a 35 year-old man. He had been missing physically from my life for 21 years, though always a presence as a permanent 14 year-old, fixed and frozen in time. The Autumn which followed was a strange period, of mild depression, loneliness, and reflection.

The summer of 2008 became special for me. The interview with Belinda Harris came as a total surprise in terms of its theme —a personal portrait—and the pathways on which Belinda and I wandered. I had never before been so public about Dara's death and its influence on my becoming a Gestalt therapist. I spent the week following the interview in Belfast with three good friends, among them Brian O'Neill, originally from Belfast. I met members of his family there as well as four delightful young children on the street where we were staying, and who were convinced that I was Santa Claus on a trial trip to the Falls Road area, checking it out for Christmas … they sang "Jingle Bells" for me. Seventeen times in a raucous row and I enjoyed every minute of it. These children then came to talk with me every time I stepped out onto the street for a cigarillo. I became aware of how much I enjoyed their presence and how open I was to their endless questions. Not at all the self-importantly impatient and busy person I could often be with Dara during his lifetime.

I returned to Sweden, where I live, and then went down to my isolated house in the country as the anniversary approached. A poem emerged in the usual way: an opening line that clicked into place and the rest simply followed. I had it clean and clear in my head before I wrote it down. Here it is:

AUGUST 9, 2008

1.

awaiting you to rise in me again
ready as always to meet you when you come

meet you sometimes where we've been before and
places where you've never been I think you'd like
I meet you and I feel you smile and nod

and always and forever fourteen

I celebrate your birthday every year
your deathday too
always and forever fourteen

2.

something is changing for us now

I started fixing place and day
never to forget you:

the chapel where your funeral was with
annie lennox singing of an angel

the hillock where your ashes
whitened the wild grass then
washed by rain absorbed by the wet earth

and always august ninth

and then that day when you were
fourteen years dead

fourteen years living and now
fourteen years dead

sharp painful flamed epiphany
cauterized my wounds

I came there dulled with grieving and regret
and left in joy

those places unimportant just the day
I haven't been there since

3.
so you are in me with me now
not out there somewhere like a ghost

not appariton and not
séance calling of the dead

for you are in me with me now
anywhere and always

4.
this day a meditation now on
life and death

on life my life and yours and on
our short lives together

and you are in me with me now
alive in my aliveness

on death, your death and mine
and you are in me with me now
and will be in my dying

5.
I took my time in getting here
and glad I did

we've been here for awhile I feel
just took me time to know it

where you are in me with me now
everywhere and always

ॐ

Writing this paper meant revisiting my large collection of what I call 'Dara poems' for the first time in many years and reflecting on the patterns of my mourning. I also took out the last photographs we had taken of him, not knowing then that they would be the last, and reflected on how his life and death had so thoroughly informed my life. I have worked hard at being a good father to Naoise, better than I had been to Dara and better than my own father had been to me.

I came into Gestalt therapy training as part of my openness to change. This involved an obligatory two years of regular therapy, which became fourteen in all. I had stayed in therapy with my female therapist until I felt I had worked with all of the issues I needed awareness about in order to change into always being in becoming me.

Death was a major and recurring theme of my therapy. Dara's death, of course, and my journey through mourning him. And other deaths: all my life I had lived in the shadow of my dead uncle, who had died at the age of fifteen before I was born—and whose name was Seán. I was christened Seán Joseph, always assuming that my second name was after my maternal grandfather. In the late 1990s, my one surviving maternal aunt decided to order a new gravestone for her family grave and to include Dara's name. She also left two spaces blank—one for her and one for me. While checking out of the records, she discovered a grave she knew nothing about—her maternal grandparents—and went to pay her first visit there. She was amazed to see that a four-day old baby was buried there who could not possibly have been her grandparents'. After some further investigation and a conversation with her 95 year-old cousin, she discovered that her mother had given birth to a baby who died in hospital and was secretly buried. It was a boy, and his name was Joseph. So I have been carrying the dead with me all my life. And then my son ...

And then another, and wonderful person: in 1988, on a Psychosynthesis residential week in England, I met and fell in love with a younger, beautiful and gentle person, Cathy. I had said something about the congruent wildness of her hair. 'It's a wig', she replied and went on to tell me that she had had an operation for a brain tumour and had just completed her course of chemotherapy, so she was actually quite bald. I told her about Dara ... and felt a strong urge not to desert her in her illness, to let my love lead me. Less than a year later she moved to Sweden and we lived together until her death in 1993. I took the last six months of her short life off work and was her primary carer up to and including her death. Again, I found myself with a spare bed alongside someone I loved, and this time someone who knew I loved her ... and I could hold her hand as she died.

So yes: death and mourning were major themes of my therapy and my Gestalt journey.

No wonder then that I could so easily and honestly respond in the interview:

BELINDA: *So the stimulation sustains you?*

SEÁN: *Yes, always meeting something new, intellectually, socially, meeting different people, new challenges ... a phrase that comes to mind right now is 'always being alive'. In some ways I don't have the time to die because I spend so much of my time always being alive.*

Writing this, I am aware more clearly of how inter-connected and integrated the 21 years of my life in Gestalt are with my 22 years of mourning my son and finding meaning. And this is what Gestalt has given me: the opportunity to stay with my grief while recognising my joy, a support for allowing change to happen, a way of being in the world which is also a way of working in and with the world. It means allowing myself to be as gregarious socially as I am, and also still, quiet and reflective in my work as a Gestalt therapist, trainer, supervisor and group facilitator. And no matter how apparently polarised my behaviours may be, I am always me in and through them.

And, right now as I bend over the keyboard, a very special memory: I was working in Belfast in the late 1990s with a supervision group. One of the participants had mentioned her son—Naoise. Another had just become a father to his second son—Dara. So I told them that I felt moved to be reminded of my two sons in the presence of this group.

Previously, when I was asked in purely social settings whether I had any children, I would usually say 'Yes, a son.' I became accustomed in Gestalt settings to say 'Yes, two sons, one living, one dead.'

In writing this article, I can feel myself saying 'I have two sons, each living though in different ways.' And without each and both of them, I would not be who I am today.

So my thanks to my uncles Seán and Joseph, both dead before I was born, and in whose shadow I was raised; to my son Dara who has given so much meaning to my life in his death; to Cathy, who gave life to the word 'relationship' in the short time we had together; and to Naoise, my son, companion and best friend in this journey through mourning.

჻

This article was published in *InnerSense* (2009), Vol. 2(1), pp. 9–29, Australia, and is reproduced here by kind permission of the editor, Brian O'Neill.

Gestalt at Work:

A Gestalt Organisation and Systems Dynamics Case Study

Prologue

Edwin C. Nevis, PhD

The following case study by Sean Gaffney represents an important milestone for *Gestalt Review* and is the first of many case studies we hope to publish. It is an attempt to provide a detailed, step-by-step story of an intervention, and to look at it in terms of Gestalt theory and methodology. As use of self is a cornerstone of this approach, Gaffney provides us with numerous examples of his statements and of his inner experience as he does the work. We are gifted with a paper that struggles to combine the best aspects of the third-person perspective of the detached theorist-researcher and the first-person perspective of the engaged practitioner/co-creationist.

We are presented with the story of an engagement against a backdrop of theory, and a running account of the feelings and thoughts of the interventionist who drives the engagement. Though this might seem an obvious way to write a case study, most are written either in the first person or the third person (I suppose that we might consider transcripts of dialog, such as in therapy sessions, to be examples of a second-person perspective.) To combine both is a daunting proposition, but it seems to be the only way to integrate the use of theory in action and the use of self—one's thoughts, sensations, feelings, images, and so on—to guide and understand one's work. Gaffney's paper points the way for others to follow.

By presenting the ongoing story of this case in great detail, Gaffney allows us to see the chaotic nature of system intervention, and to appreciate the need to be highly flexible.[1] As Organizational Development (OD) has become more of a rational exercise in planning and implementing change, it is humbling to see how events have a force beyond anything we can anticipate. Once again, we see the value of the Gestalt practitioner's stance of openness and 'going with what is,' and of the concept of 'the system is doing the best it can, given the field conditions,' which is an extension of the Gestalt concept of *Pragnanz*, And Gaffney does not give us a rosy picture of the hero-intervener riding off into the sunset in full glory. He allows us to see his confusion, his hurt, and the times when his interventions may have been less than elegant.

A third reason this is an important case study is that the organization being studied is an entity created to deal with one of the most overwhelming problems of our modern times. We get a glimpse of the way people in the system try to cope with things, and we see how different and how similar this is to what occurs in a business/work setting. As not-for-profits, NGOs, and governments now are becoming our clients more and more, it is important that we share with each other our experiences in working with them.

COMMENTARIES BY NIEBUHR AND WYLEY [2]

Just as Gaffney's paper is a milestone, so are the commentaries that follow it. They are written by a physician (Niebuhr) and a community/economic development specialist (Wyley), not by traditional organizational consultants. Both authors are involved with complex, interdependent systems whose work transcends the normal boundaries of a single organizational entity. They are pioneers in applying the Gestalt approach in these arenas, as are the other Gestalt-trained people

---

[1] Richard Wallen, my co-founding father of Gestalt OD, used to say: "If you want to do this work, you need to be as flexible as a wet noodle."

[2] Both Niebuhr and Wyley were students of mine and of Gaffney, Hanafin, Rainey, and Stratford in the Gestalt Institute of Cleveland International Organization & System Development Program. Niebuhr also completed the Intimate Systems Program of the Gestalt International Study Center. Both continue to be active in further Gestalt study at these institutes.

who Wyley mentions in her paper. They introduce us to a world that seems far removed from that of individual Gestalt therapy, yet they make it clear that by applying Gestalt concepts and methodology, they can have more impact in what they do in the general realm of social action.

Wyley and Niebuhr do not share as much of their personal experience in doing the work as does Gaffney, but they are resolute in trying to use Gestalt concepts to understand what is happening. Though they do a good job of this, my sense is that their contribution may be greater in showing Gestalt practitioners the limits of our theory for understanding complex social phenomena, and raising the need for us to become more conversant with other theories.

Finally, these commentaries are important because they show us that expert consultants who normally focus on content are choosing the Gestalt approach as their process theory of choice. Would that more workers in the area of HIV/AIDS and other intransigent social problems could say the same. Perhaps bringing this about is our next frontier.

⤳

ABSTRACT: This article will combine a case study approach with reflections on the application of theory in an organizational consultancy from a Gestalt perspective. As the work developed, my reflections on Gestalt theory increasingly informed the work and also my understanding of the theory.

Introduction

The application of the psychology, philosophy, and methodology of Gestalt therapy to an organizational setting has a history as old (or as new) as Gestalt. Elliot Shapiro, one of the original members of the group that became the New York Institute, was an influential educator and educational administrator whose work, during and after his NYI days, makes him the first Gestalt Organizational Development (OD) practitioner. In *An Oral History of Gestalt Therapy* (Wysong

& Rosenfeld, 1982) and in Hentoff (1966), we have the story of a man who practiced rather than preached; that is, who worked with, rather than wrote about organizational change through his impact on individuals, groups, systems, and communities. His work deserves a focused Gestalt perspective.

His is an example of one approach to the application of Gestalt theory in organizations—to simply do it. Others both do it and write about it, thus spreading knowledge and developing theory. Roughly speaking, there are three traditions already established here: applied theory, with generic exemplifications; 'how to' literature; and case studies, with their focus more on the work than the theory.

The applied theory approach is well-exemplified by Alevras and Wepman (1980) and Nevis (1987). If Shapiro is the grandfather of Gestalt OD, then Nevis is the founding father through his work, his writing, his teaching, and his example. Together with colleagues at the Gestalt Institute of Cleveland and, more recently, The Gestalt International Study Center, Nevis has developed and supported a growing body of applied theory.

Clark and Fraser (1987) and Herman and Korenich (1977) have written for the manager and trainer, with a practical, hands-on approach in which theory is presented through exercises, with a view to application in a work setting.

Case studies are represented by Ennis and Mitchell (1970) and, more recently, Farrands (2001). Here, the practice of Gestalt OD is the primary focus, supported where necessary by reference to theory. This approach brings us into the work and into the processes of the consultant, and shows us the unfolding story of the consultancy. There is liveliness and unpredictability as we follow the consultant into, through, and out of the client organization. As fellow Gestaltists, we can join vicariously with the practitioner; as non-Gestaltists, we can get a feel for what Gestalt OD is all about.

These and other writings in the field provide a broad and deep overview of the subject.

In this article I combine case study and applied theory perspectives. As the work developed, my reflections on theory increasingly informed the work and my understanding of the theory; my reflections and my practice became increasingly interwoven. In addition, an opportunity arose to present theory formally, both as background to the OD process, and as an intervention in itself. As a result, this article is a case study in applied Gestalt theory that I trust will support fellow Gestalt practitioners in appreciating the rich applicability of our core theory to organizational and systems settings.

The names of people and places have been changed, even though the work was in the public domain. This has been done to preserve the integrity of the people concerned, as well as to recognize the sensitivity of the client's work with people diagnosed as being HIV-positive and as having AIDS.

For the overall frame for the article, I use the Gestalt Cycle of Experience/Energy/Contact as applied to Gestalt consultancy; that is: Scanning, Awareness with Figure, Energy Mobilization, Action, Contact/Change, Meaning-Making, Withdrawal. This version and others are commonly used at The Gestalt Institute of Cleveland as a pedagogical tool.

Scanning

I was contacted by Anna, who worked for Aidsphone, a volunteer organization that provided a confidential phone line, information packages, and presentations, and various support activities. The support activities typically consisted of counseling, alternative treatments (aromatherapy and yoga, for example), a support group for those with HIV, and home care through a 'Buddy system' for those who were terminally ill with AIDS. The organization had gone from the phone service to personal support for the terminally ill and, increasingly, to support for their HIV-positive clients.

The various medical treatments that had become available had led to an increase in the time involved in providing in-house support services and, by accumulation, in the numbers of people potentially requiring such services. The organization needed consultancy support to adapt to the changed context of its work. Anna explained that there was a new focus on 'empowering the service users' as part of the organization. I arranged a meeting during my next visit to the area.

My first meeting was with the Director, Birgitta; Carl, who trained the Aidsphone volunteers and Buddies as well as held information meetings at schools, the workplace, and community organizations and Anna, the counselor.

The meeting was held in the organization's premises, known as 'The Centre,' a neutral and somewhat anonymous name, consistent with the context. Birgitta, Carl, and Anna interchangeably gave me the history of Aidsphone and The Centre. It had been in existence some 15 years, beginning as a confidential phone service for information, advice, and support, and run on a voluntary basis. It had become well established, and was now fully operational as a volunteer organization with a management committee, director, staff, volunteers, and premises. The organization was funded by several sources, both state and private. Carl had been involved from the beginning.

I gave a presentation of my personal and professional background, my connections to the region and my work there, and my approach as a Gestalt OD consultant. This included a brief review of Schein's (1999) categories of consulting—expert, doctor/patient and process—and my focus on process. In other words, I would work from the perspective that my presence in the organization would have some impact; I would actively be using my own experience of working within Aidsphone/The Centre as material for reflection and feedback; and I would be guided by my curiosity. In this way, they might possibly see the central issues from new perspectives, and that this could optimize their choices in terms of possible actions.

Theory in Action: Overview

My description of how I intended to work contained compressed and generalized versions of the following: Use of Self, Awareness, Contact Modalities, Lewin's Field Theory, interventions at the contact boundary, and the Cycle of Experience as frame and methodology. A brief introduction to each of these follows.

USE OF SELF

This is, for me, the essence of Gestalt, whether in my work as therapist or consultant. Gestalt is an integrated philosophy, psychology, methodology, and creative adjustment at the organism/environment contact boundary. It is integrated inasmuch as it flows organically from the self involved—in this case me—and no other. Gestalt Organizational Systems Dynamics (OSD), as I see it, is not a transferable checklist of techniques; it is a lived process for change. Any other Gestalt colleague could have done a great job with this client and the work would have been totally different from mine. This is, I believe, our inner strength as Gestalt practitioners, and our dilemma in explaining our work to the environment. It is never, in my experience, a dilemma with the clients we have honestly and openly met as our environmental other.

Awareness

Awareness is complex and difficult to define as a construct, and it is just this complexity and difficulty which keeps us Gestalt practitioners on our toes! Awareness and Use of Self are inextricably linked—my task is to be open to, and aware of, emerging figures from the ground of my organism/environment contact. My task and my methodology is to be open and to welcome these figures nonjudgmentally. This nonjudgmental welcome includes initially allowing all my judgmental opinions to be fully figural for me and then allowing them to fade or be bracketed into ground again. I need to be fully present and to selectively share my figural awareness in support of contact with my client and opportunities for change.

Contact Modalities

Use of Self involves Awareness at the co-created contact boundary of me-as-consultant/client. This is where Self emerges—me as Self and Client as Self. With which contact modalities are we, out of habit or choice, meeting each other? As 'the other' to the client, what can I learn from this through awareness? The generally agreed upon contact modalities are: confluence, egotism, introjecting, deflecting, projecting, retroflecting. Each of these, whether practiced by me in my developing awareness, or by my client in my phenomenological experience, provides useful experiential data about our relationship.

Field Theory

I distinguish between Systems Thinking and Lewinian Field Theory (discussed later in this article). For me, our work as Gestalt OD practitioners is to be part of, experience, and differentiate from (as organism to the client as environment) the client as a dynamic field, both in itself and with us as a force within the organism/environment field.

Interventions

Our Creative Adjustment as Gestalt Practitioners at the co-created contact boundary of ourselves/client supports a creative experimentation in the moment, interventions which emerge spontaneously and are charged with their own energy. This is Use of Self as Theory in Action: a philosophical and methodological attitude grounded in learning, experience and integration.

Cycle of Experience

Originating as the Contact Cycle—forecontact, contact, full contact and postcontact—this was refined and expanded as a teaching model at the Gestalt Institute of Cleveland. Transposed to an OD context, this generally becomes: scanning, figure with awareness, energy, action, contact/change, meaning-making, withdrawal.

Scanning Continued

We then moved towards the work itself. The focus of the initial meeting was 'the service users'; that is, those people who used The Centre's in-house services. The issue was that they were seen as part of the organization, and needed to be empowered to play a more active role. This became more clearly an issue of attendance: usually, only four to five people came regularly to the Support Group at The Centre; of those, maybe three came most weeks. 'Empowering the service users' was clearly figural for the Director: This was her mandate from the Management Committee, and the primary focus of the consultancy. My response was to point out that empowering another pre-supposed having the power to do so, and could therefore be seen as confirmation of a power imbalance in the relationship. As such, it could be counterproductive, especially in a context in which no such power imbalance supposedly exists.

All four of us discussed this point, with Anna and Carl seeing how this could fit their experience. Birgitta took the point without hesitation. We continued to look for a contract formulation that would match the original mandate; be acceptable to Birgitta, Anna, and Carl with their hands-on perspective; and be acceptable to me as the task of the consultancy. This resulted in the following agreement, which I signed:

> My brief is to support the organization in finding ways to influence the perceived/virtual/real balance of power, so that service users have the opportunity for a greater degree of proactive participation in the management of their situation; and to engage all parts of the whole organization – management committee, director and staff, volunteers, and service users—in this process.

Theory in Action #1

This was my first intervention. The work began at the moment of my entry into the client system, and the contracting phase is often where the first interventions occur. This first one created a change in the contract and therefore also a reframing of the presented problem.

The timeframe was a maximum of 10 days, in one- or two-day blocks, over a period of eight months. There would be a review after six consultancy days. We agreed on the daily fee so that David, the accountant, could be directed to apply for funding.

I would hold a series of individual and group meetings, during which I would gather information, form impressions, follow my curiosity, feed back my impressions, and monitor the impact of the work. The contract was renegotiable by both parties at any time. Anna was to be my contact.

Awareness with Figure

My next visit was for one day. I met with the Director and staff members individually, as well as with the service user group. I presented myself, the focus of the consultancy, and its method, at the beginning of each meeting. The focus was generally understood, though not always with any energy. My sense was that I was welcomed by almost everybody, but there was a certain amount of skepticism in the air, most clearly directed at me and my way of working. Generally, people showed a willingness and openness in my meetings, which slowly began to suggest a need to offload, to be heard, to influence, to make a contribution.

I also quickly encountered a major aspect of Aidsphone/The Centre—an obsession with secrecy that seemed to have no boundaries. For example, all staff apart from Anna could never greet service users by name because staff were not supposed to know them, and their visits were highly confidential. Anna would only use names with the group in the meeting room. During my meetings, it would occasionally happen that a person would hesitate and check whether a name could be used or not. The staff practiced a degree of political correctness with respect to confidentiality that made communication among them about their work often complicated and even near-impossible.

The Director and staff were all clearly concerned with the issue of 'the service users'; that is, those people who directly used The Centre and any or all of its services: counseling, alternative treatments, social gatherings, or Support Group meetings—or more specifically, the service non-users. Most of the staff's attention was being given to those who could potentially use the services, and chose not to. These people were sometimes known; they had at some time or another used The Centre. Others belonged to the statistics of HIV in the Region: more people could use The Centre than ever did. All of the staff were concerned with these non-users, though only Anna had any direct responsibility for that area of operations. I was curious about this, and also moved by the obvious concern that was being expressed.

I met five service users, four men and one woman. I could sense frustration, anger, resignation, willingness, criticism, warmth, irony, loneliness—everything all at once. The anger, criticism, and irony were directed at the staff and at me. My exact fee was brought up, and how such a sum could be much better spent. The salaries of the Director and staff also came under fire, as well as the luxury of a 9 to 5 job with HIV/AIDS: 'Some people have to put up with it all the time.' The prevention posters were mentioned: 'A bit too late for some of us.' The willingness and warmth were there too: I was protected and defended as well as criticized. The central point with which I was left was that each person present wanted and needed to be seen as a person, each with his/her own context and difficulties, not as a member of a non-existent homogeneous group. I was deeply affected by this meeting. There was so much life and energy, illness, and medication; and so many test results, diagnoses, and prognoses. I had met five people who lived in a somehow separate world in which generalizations no longer applied, and in which each person had to rediscover how to live an everyday life.

My reflections at the end of that first day were a curious mixture of the crystal clear and the murkily confused. I felt strongly that the service users did not in any self-defined way belong to the organization, and were not in fact even a self-defined group. As such, it would be difficult for the organization to succeed in any effort that presupposed either one, or—as was the case—both of these as facts. The management committee, Director and staff seemed clearly convinced of these presuppositions, to the extent that they were almost principles that underlaid their work. Clearly there either was a connection I could not make, or a deep gap into which I was gazing from the edge. I was aware of being impressed by the staff's obvious concern for the users, and also aware of the affect on me of my meeting with the Support Group. I could feel my emotional involvement, my protectiveness, and also my vulnerability.

I then did what I usually do: I allowed my impressions, reflections and the experience of the first visit to merge into my ground, and waited for whatever energized figures would emerge.

On my next visit, I met four members of the management committee, including the chairperson, Francesca, and continued with the Director and staff meetings. As we all introduced ourselves, Francesca casually mentioned that we had met earlier. We had, at the service user meeting the previous visit. Gregory, who had also been there, introduced himself as if for the first time. I was meeting the political correctness/confidentiality/secrecy communication mode of The Centre. I went along with it then, realizing that I would soon have to decide how best to function in my work and deal with this aspect of the consultancy. I wanted to respect the required confidentiality, and yet not become enmeshed in the secrecy. I was confused by this and other issues during this meeting. There seemed to be two main foci for the committee that were mutually exclusive. One was to engage in hands-on direction of the work of The Centre, detailing mandates for the director. The other was to engage in strategic planning, using the director as a resource and guide in identifying the current and future needs of the organization. I felt at times as if I were attending two meetings simultaneously.

I raised this last point (Use of Self), comparing it with the position of the director and staff: if the management committee is ambivalent about its function, then this ambivalence is likely to impact on the work of the Centre. Since the Committee met every second month at most, there could be long periods of uncertainty in the organization. There was general agreement about this. The point was that not everyone felt enough was being done with the service user issue, and as a result, they tended to want to become more involved. We had a good, open discussion.

My last meeting on this visit was with three volunteers, including Gregory! Again, he and I met as if it were for the first time. I was reluctantly complicit with this. I knew I would have to deal with this confidentiality/secrecy issue soon, before it began to cloud my experience and my judgment. At the same time, confidentiality was the foundation of the volunteers' work, as I had had it described to me. They worked alone in the phone room on a shift system. They met when their shifts overlapped. They also had old connections with each other, having trained together on Carl's courses for volunteers. The training involves explicit exchanges in realistic simulations between the trainees, thus creating a closeness and honesty among the volunteers. Their work is one-to-one phone dialogues on anything and everything to do with HIV/AIDS.

I soon realized that the volunteers were ideally placed to observe the whole system of Aidsphone/The Centre, and all its subsystems. They also connected all the functions of Aidsphone/The Centre: They dispensed information and advised on further actions, in addition to supporting people with HIV/AIDS who used the phone as a service rather than visit The Centre. They agreed that some people started with Aidsphone, then progressed to using The Centre. This meant that the volunteers could agree on their having a vested interest in The Centre as an organization worth recommending to potential active users. As long as there seemed to be any doubt on this point, they would have to consider how that would impact their work. And there were some doubts: they raised some non-specific criticisms about The Centre, generally along lines similar to those raised in the Support Group. My sense was that more could be done, but so far, no one was being specific about what that should be. I also had a sense that they were echoing the staff's wishes and drive to give more support without a clear sense of what to do and how to do it.

I had by now met the chairperson and management committee, director and all staff, the HIV Positive Support Group, and the volunteers—all the subsystems of Aidsphone/The Centre. I was now feeling the frustration of these people who were dedicated to caring for others and feeling inadequate. This was how I was feeling: wanting to support everyone I had met, and recognizing that the levels of dedication I was meeting were beyond me, that I could at best make only a very minor contribution, and that I would come and go and they would still be there, day after day, dealing with people in deep existential dilemmas.

My reflections after this day were deep, personal, and serious. The word 'dilemma' was alive with experience and meaning. I needed to meet this dilemma in myself as I continued the work. I also needed to raise awareness that this was the nature of the work of Aidsphone/The Centre: to work within an insoluble dilemma. Nothing anyone could do would ever be 'enough' for people with a life-threatening illness, surrounded as they were by dead and dying friends, partners, and even strangers since HIV/AIDS statistics are broadcast in the media. I needed to be able to come closer, and remain marginal; to understand, yet comment freely; to respect the norms, yet be willing to challenge them.

Theory in Action #2

I was beginning to sense and experience the strong force towards Confluence of the Client Field. The service users were expected to become confluent with each other and then also with 'the organization.' I was also being drawn into such a confluence at the same time as I was resisting this attraction with as much awareness as I could muster. In some sense, I needed to hold the marginal, Egotistical position, at the same time as I needed to be willing to immerse myself, with aware confluence, as part of the dynamic field of the client system. The work was dynamically alive!

Further Scanning

Anna had been in touch with me and said that the staff at both the clinic and the social workers' office at the local hospital had heard through the grapevine about the consultancy, and would be interested in meeting me. I agreed to see them. This would give me some sense of the wider context in which the organization functioned, as well as a better understanding of the formal, statutory support services available to those who also used The Centre.

Both the clinic staff and the social workers spoke of the great importance HIV patients attached to confidentiality. They tended to want to spread their visits out in such a way that there were never too many HIV patients in the waiting room at the same time. This clearly paralleled the situation at The Centre. Many patients found themselves unemployed and homeless after being diagnosed, with families or partners who no longer wanted them; or feeling the pressure to move from where they were known to more anonymous housing. The secrecy issue was again a stumbling-block here; the slightest suspicion that any information had been 'leaked' was enough to cause a patient to break contact. Again, the confidentiality/secrecy threshold was difficult to pinpoint, since everything had somehow become subsumed in secrecy for the HIV patient. Both the clinic and the social workers praised Aidsphone/The Centre, and recommended its services to their clients.

These meetings had taken the whole afternoon. I left the hospital at dusk, a light drizzle falling steadily. I walked around the city in the rain and growing darkness long into the evening. I was feeling depressed, lonely, alone, inadequate. I reflected on the social environment of this Region, where sexuality was kept down; where sexually transmitted diseases were stigmas, even 'Acts of God'; where homosexuality was dismissed as unnatural. Secrets and lies were natural in such an environment. All of these things I had understood earlier and could rationalize. Now, as I walked, I could experience the oppression, the grim reality of the clinic staff and the social workers—most of all, the hopelessness of being a victim with no way out, no safety, no trust. I felt how I was carrying all the unexpressed and inexpressible existential anxieties of the users, the staff, the volunteers, the director, the management committee—and, of course, myself. I had now been close enough to the deepest issues for all of my own experience of terminal illnesses and deaths to visit me, of helplessly watching loved ones waste away and die, of wanting to do more, and nothing ever being enough.

[As I write this, I am reminded of how this day affected me. I can feel heaviness. I feel drawn back to the consultancy, the people I met. I am aware of being in two places: at my house by a lake in Sweden, a brilliantly sunny day, a fish caught late last night soon to be prepared for dinner; and also, in a darkening city in the rain, exposed and vulnerable.]

Theory in Action #3

AWARENESS WITH FIGURE—ENERGY MOBILIZATION

By now, a number of themes were emerging for me as I met and re-met the client system. These figures were clear and energized enough for me to select them as the issues around which I would attempt to raise awareness at a forthcoming general meeting with the director and staff. I was moving from Awareness to Energy to Action.

Action and Contact/Change

I opened the meeting with Birgitta, Anna, Carl, David, Erik, and Harriet, a part-time assistant to Birgitta in her role as chair of an umbrella organization for HIV/AIDS services. After a brief review of the method, sequence, and progress of the consultancy, I introduced the five main areas on which I had decided to focus, the first three concerned with my impressions, and the next two more content-based:

- Confidentiality/Secrecy
- Shame/Blame
- Focus on Failure
- The Organization
- The Service Users

My intention was to spend the most time on the last two items, since these, in effect, would become part of my re-negotiation of the original contract or at least, a reframing of it. Having reflected openly on my experience of the first three issues, I then talked about an organization having two forms: what it could/should/might be, and what it actually is in practice. An organization defines itself, and is defined by others, and the more congruent these definitions are, the less room there is for ambiguity. Ambiguous organizations are difficult to relate to and work in.

My experience of Aidsphone/The Centre was that the service users did not in any way identify as part of the organization. The organization served them; they used the organization's services. They neither were, nor wanted to be, part of the formal organization. Some made individual choices to join the organization: Francesca as chairperson, Gregory as committee member and volunteer. As a result of their choices, they were formally members of an organization called Aidsphone/The Centre. As such, they were truly empowered service users: self-empowered.

I explained that one of my initial confusions was based on the implicit assumption within the organization that 'service users' was actually a recognizable and homogeneous group, and that this assumed group was seen as part of the organization. I could find no evidence of there being such a group—especially when the service *non*-users somehow were being added to it. During my meeting with the 'Support Group,' I met a number of strong individuals with distinct needs who needed the freedom to come and go as they needed, or wished. In fact, the only possible 'group' would be the particular collection of individuals who chose to attend the Support Group on any given alternate Wednesday. This 'group' might even include a number of people who generally attended and were recognizable to each other as 'members of the Support Group.'

Yet, it was precisely this group that was being used as evidence for the failure of The Centre to engage users: 'The group was so small'; 'Only a few come regularly'; 'They don't take many initiatives'. I asked the staff to consider that the more these people were used as proof of failure, the more likely they were to satisfy that particular self-fulfilling prophecy. I asked them to see the users as individuals, making individual choices in difficult existential contexts: sometimes needing support, sometimes happy to see that they could do without it.

I then moved on to consider the term 'service user.' I found it unclear in the full context of the work of Aidsphone/The Centre. So I asked a few rhetorical questions: What are people called who use the phone line? Who comes to information meetings? Who requests information presentations at schools, workplaces, communities? Who attends such meetings? The response was clear: service users! So then I asked if they had any statistics on how many phone calls the volunteers had handled, how many information meetings were held, average attendance, and so on. Soon, we discovered that Aidsphone/The Centre had some 4,000-5,000 service users per year, all of whom were being offered the best services that the organization could provide in the context of time, funding, staffing, and available resources.

I suggested the new term 'Centre user' for anyone in the now small, bounded subsystem of the larger whole. I suggested, with humor, that 'non-user' be non-used.

We then had a long and animated discussion about the ramifications of the last two points: the organization as it was, and a fresh and congratulatory perspective on 'service users.' This was an exciting and encouraging session: the room filled with energy and proposals and ideas.

My reflections that evening were around the animated and confirming response to the five figures I had chosen to present. My sense was that I had 'spoken the unspoken,' and maybe even the 'unspeakable'; that is, made public what was known and/or thought individually, though never shared or acknowledged collectively. I had in fact possibly made a first intervention in the areas of 'Shaming/Blaming' and

'Confidentiality/Secrecy'; and perhaps even the 'Focus on Failure'. The same applied to my presentation of 'The Organization' and 'The Service Users': despite the previous assumptions (or politically correct wishful thinking?) in these areas, there were no protests at my reflections. This led me to wonder where, in fact, the earlier assumptions about service users being part of the organization had come from, who was representing them, and how strong were these ideas as part of the field?

Theory in Action #4

I also gave some thought to the distinctions between 'the system' and 'the organization.' The system—as an arbitrarily bounded integrated unit—would clearly include all parts of Aidsphone/The Centre: the service users (as reframed), the Centre users (as reframed), and the clinic and social worker units at the local hospital. Aidsphone/The Centre was a definably bounded subsystem, as was the hospital, and then, the Centre users. Two formally defined, organized, and reasonably stable subsystems, and a subsystem of individual subsystems, some of which occasionally happened to share the same space at the same time, were embedded in each of the other two subsystems. The here-and-now nature of the Centre users as a subsystem contrasted clearly with the history, development, and strategic planning of the other two subsystems. Aidsphone/The Centre and the hospital existed, and would continue to exist, independently of the individuals currently working there. The Centre users only existed as long as any individual chose to be involved. Could this be some clue as to what was happening?

I was aware that I was also moving into my preferred context, Lewinian field theory. While I believe that systems thinking supports my work in terms of being able to use it as a descriptor of a given client over time, my working focus is on the field as the dynamic characteristics of the system at any given moment.

Here, Kurt Lewin's notion of 'the life-space' (in Marrow, 1969) plays a central part. As Lewin conceived it, Behavior = f (Person + Environment), a concept clearly in line with Perls, Hefferline and Goodman's (1951) 'organism/environment'. In this perspective, I as person/organism have each subsystem and any combination of all subsystems as my environment, and vice versa. Each individually, any combination, and all of the named subsystems are organism to me as environment; that is, the in-the-moment-field as I experience it, and as my environment/environments experience it as organisms to me as environment.

I really resonate to the dynamics of the co-created, distinct, and connected concept of this existential field. In this instance, I was meeting my client as the wholeness of my existential field. Since I believe in the field of the client—with an existence before, during, and after my presence as intervener—I was also open to learning something through my experience of our contact. The field of the client existed independently of me (its history and established internal relationships) as well as in response to my presence. I was aware that I was now moving into the delightful and unpredictable area of the dynamic field of forces of the work.

My feeling was that the afternoon session had freed both the staff and, indirectly, the Centre users, from entanglements they didn't need. I was aware that I had probably crossed some invisible boundaries somewhere— presenting figures that so easily engaged and energized could mean that forces were now in movement which previously may have been held in check. By whom? How? And what would happen next? I became aware that Birgitta had been a little less enthusiastic than the others. During the meeting, I interpreted this as her keeping her managerial cool, letting the staff have their day. Now, I was uncertain. What had been a day of clarity was now becoming complex.

Change: Meaning-Making

On my next visit, I met Birgitta, individual staff members, and another version of the management committee. Birgitta, the Director, was pleased with the previous staff meeting. She felt we had clarified some important issues, especially with respect to the organization, and that it had been healthy to raise the other impressions and get them out into the open. She was particularly taken with how much unnecessary secrecy she had discovered herself dealing with, and how much uncertainty the level of secrecy had caused. She felt that the staff had benefited from the meeting. At the same time, she had some concerns about staff and management issues: she felt that she was having to spend more time on staff issues. Also, she felt that her relations with the management committee were strained.

We discussed these points in detail. At one point, I could feel my concern for Birgitta, and also a sense of my possible/probable responsibility. I asked whether she had managerial supervision. She had, though not formalized and regular. I suggested that she give it a thought. I was aware of the attraction of moving into managerial supervision with Birgitta, both in the moment, and as a possible future contract.

All my warning bells and sirens went off at once. I needed to regain my focus on the work in hand and on this meeting with Birgitta as part of that ongoing process. I found myself making a generalized comment about what can happen in an organization when a perceived external difficulty is resolved—that internal issues have time and space to surface. Now that the 'service user issue' was no longer a staff focus, then maybe issues internal to the workplace were surfacing. Birgitta saw the logic in this, and the possibility that it might be just a phase. By moving to the general, and then back to the specific work at hand, I had balanced my own dilemma. The bells and sirens stopped ringing. I was unsure, however, as to what extent I had supported Birgitta in resolving anything.

The individual meetings with staff all centered on the general meeting and its consequences, both individually and collectively. Each now felt greater enthusiasm and focus in their work. They related more to each other, could see the interconnectedness of their contributions. The Centre users were no longer 'Anna's problem', for which she received her colleagues' sympathy; the Centre users were now everybody's clients inasmuch as they all used Aidsphone/The Centre services. Individuals had taken initiatives in seeking clarification regarding what was formally confidential, and what was optionally confidential. Some users were now greeted by name, others not, depending on the individual concerned. Anna now joined Carl on some of his presentations, where she could give a view from her counseling and support role. Anna and Carl now worked together for the same organization, whereas before, they had worked as if they were two separate functions of two separate organizations, Aidsphone and The Centre. David had enthusiastically launched a major funding drive: he felt much more confident about his work and its value to the full range of users. Erik was very pleased with how everything had gone: He felt much more free and personally engaged in his work. Harriet commented on the open and active atmosphere in the staff office.

All of this began to form into a simple figure for me. The staff felt self-empowered, and were behaving accordingly. I gave some thought to the proposed original contract—'to empower the service users'—and to Birgitta's even more obvious need for the support of good supervision. Self-empowered staff are great, and hell to manage if you don't expect to have to, and their empowerment happens overnight. I could sense that my work was coming to an end, and that I needed to be clearly bounded in relation to the issues that seemed to be surfacing. I reminded myself of my contract: '... to support the organization in finding ways to influence the perceived/virtual/real balance of power, so that service users have the opportunity for a greater degree of proactive participation in the management of their situation ....' I needed to keep this in focus.

That evening, I met three members of the management committee: Francesca, Gregory, and someone I had not met previously, Jannika. As Jannika had missed some previous management committee meetings, I needed to go back over the process and bring her up to date. She and I had some misunderstandings, as she was thinking in terms of a standard evaluation report that would justify previous funding and support more funding. Standard evaluations were part of the typical procedures for volunteer organizations in the Region. We finally sorted this out, and continued. I had decided to present my impression of the meeting with the director and staff, and the changes that seemed to have arisen as a result. Jannika wanted to reframe each comment I made into a conclusion, followed by a point for action. I found that I was having difficulties—frustrated at having to go over the process again, at having to explain in detail what had happened, at not being able to get to the point of this meeting. I became defensive, and a little impatient—I felt that I was having to manage the meeting. In effect, I was having to manage the management committee.

Withdrawal?

I returned a number of times to my impression that my work was basically finished. I needed a final round of meetings to close my work with all concerned parties. Then, still more questions came up. I explained that I was having difficulties going back and forth between issues, much as I understood the necessity for doing so. I expressed my uncertainty about the level of continuity in the management committee, and the effect that this was having on me: Instead of working with ongoing developments, most of the time I was back at the beginning.

I was moving from being defensive to being offensive! I backed down, and made another try at meeting the three members where they were, rather than where I wanted them to be. We reached a reasonable flow, and ended on a friendly note.

Theory in Action #5

My movement from where I wanted the client to be, to where my client actually was fits with 'The Paradoxical Theory of Change' (Beisser, 1970). Change occurs dynamically when 'what is' is acknowledged and supported, leaving the forces of the field in the moment free to self-organize.

I had a lot to reflect on: major changes with staff, probably having a positive impact on their relations with Centre users; some strain around Birgitta; and an unsatisfactory meeting with the management committee. I had moved too fast there. I had stayed with my intention, and not been sensitive to the needs of those who were there. Or maybe I was presenting to Francesca and Gregory, at Jannika's expense, punishing her for being so out of touch?

Or was this how Birgitta could find herself? Going over the same issues again and again, each time some member happened to turn up after absences? Was I acting on Birgitta's behalf?

And where was I, Seán, in all of this? I needed to experience and explore how enmeshed I seemed to be becoming, and also to find a place for myself on the margin. My empathy was clearly with the members of the support group, and also, clearly with the staff. So I could easily be enmeshed in either of these subsystems. I admired and respected the volunteers—no enmeshment there. I sympathized with Birgitta. I was ambivalent about her: I felt she needed more than I could or would give her in the context of the work—and in this, I was avoiding enmeshment. I was marginal to the management committee—and yet, my defensiveness said something about getting entangled in something there. I had a lot to work on!

At the same time, my sense was that this consultancy was at an end. I had worked the contract, and was on the cusp of the move from doing the work to the point of closure. I decided to move into closure of the contract. In a discussion with Anna, I talked about the value of meeting as many as possible of the various parties at the same time, in order to report back to all concerned. Anna saw that a good opportunity for such a gathering would be the Annual General Meeting (AGM) in early June. So I suggested that my next visit would be my final one, that it would last two days, and it would close with an oral report to the AGM.

Two weeks later, Anna called with the news that the management committee had instructed the Director not to allow me into the building again until I had produced a written report, which the management committee approved. She also scheduled a telephone time for the Director to call me.

Scanning!

Anna was apologetic, and seemed even a little resigned. Birgitta was frustrated: she had acted within her mandate in engaging me, in agreeing to the focus of the work; she had regularly reported to the committee on the progress of the consultancy, and on her and the staff's positive reactions—and yet, here we were in an embarrassing situation. She was being forced into a relationship with me that was not congruent with her own experience and choice. I was aware of how easy it would be for me to form an alliance with Birgitta, and worked hard at maintaining a relatively neutral position, promising to produce a brief report along the lines I had already indicated to the management committee.

I was amused at myself. When last in The Centre, I was concerned by my tendency towards a deeper enmeshment in the system, and now

I was being pushed out to the margin by the formally strongest force of the field. I like to see the field as the dynamic characteristics of a system at any given moment, and it now seemed as if the management committee and I were the major forces, and that the field was self-organizing around us.

Awareness? Figure? Energy?

When my amusement faded, my feelings became anger, frustration, superiority, and shame, mixed with a desire for vengeance. If they insisted on a report, then they would get one!

Initially, the events around the report—and my feelings about them—were constantly figural. How could they? How dare they? Who did they think they were, and who did they think they were dealing with? I was angry, self-righteous, morally indignant, frustrated—so near to completing the work (and good work!)—and now: 'No further meetings until the management committee has received a written report.'

Revenge: I'd show them! They'd be lucky to get two pages of mainly headings and little content. Then I'd insist that they honor or at least renegotiate the contract. I would behave formally and impersonally. They deserved no better!

And shame: Clearly, I had done something wrong, made a bad mistake, become blinded by my own self-importance, disrespected or pushed a boundary or two, let good people down. I deserved to be put in my place.

Awareness – Figure – Energy

I moved from feeling to feeling, opinion to opinion, decision to decision. I allowed myself full freedom to express everything that moved in me. I composed opening after opening for the report: angry, bitter, sarcastic, cold, disappointed, nonchalant. Slowly, a figure began emerging, or rather, my ground began structuring itself (Wheeler 1991).

I began to think about how I might condense and focus all that I had experienced into a report as an intervention. This became a clear and energized figure: I would continue my contract and my assigned task by designing a written intervention. I could sense how I was back on track, how all the emotional energy had been channeled into a focus on contact: how I could prepare a report that met the management committee—indeed, the organization—at a co-created contact boundary, where change might occur. This was my challenge, my task, and my ethical, professional responsibility to my client.

Theory in Action #6

A reflection I had at the time: I have now absolutely fully experienced the paradoxical theory of change (Beisser, 1970). I had stayed with what was—my anger, frustration, and revenge—and, rather than chase any figure that was current, I had allowed a new figure to emerge, organically and fully congruent with who I was in the field of this particular piece of work. The nature and intentionality of my contact at the boundary of me/the client had changed radically.

Action

I began planning and writing the intervention. After three weeks of focused and intensive work, I believed I had written a report that might create contact and support change. It certainly expressed my experience of the work, my feelings, thoughts, and reflections.

As an indication of the scope of this Interim Report, here is the Contents Page:

WORK-IN-PROGRESS CONSULTANCY REPORT: JULY 2000

Distribution
    Chairperson
    Members, Management Committee
    Director
    Centre Staff

Contents
1. Background
2. The Consultancy
3. Comments

4.   Issues, First Impressions, and Comments

5.   Reflections on theories in practice, with examples

6. Preliminary Conclusions

Theory in Action #7

Having written the Interim Report, I now had a clearer sense of the levels at which the dynamics of the field were being played out, self-organizing around possible sets of themes. For example, the will to do better was interacting with the uselessness of doing anything—life and death were wrestling with each other, and death was in the lead. The formal organization was defining the Centre users as a homogeneous group confluent with the other subsystems; that is, in a way that did not match the users' own individual experiences. So they reacted—individually and possibly semi-collectively with their Egotism—through withdrawal and absence, two great deflecting behaviors; with complaints (projecting); and with anything that could support their difference.

Contact – Change

In my report's 'Preliminary Conclusions,' I covered aspects of the organization as it was, rather than as hoped for, or assumed. I continued to discuss the issue of who a 'service user' actually was, as covered in the article. I concluded with the following comments:

> As I read back over these pages, I am amazed at the complexity of the Centre and its work. I am also impressed by all who work in and for the organization, at the motivation, energy and willingness to learn that they contribute, as well as their various skills and areas of competence and personal experience.
>
> There are still a number of issues that interest me and arouse my curiosity, and I would like to raise these issues in a series of questions. These questions contain a mixture of summarizing reflections, hopes, encouragement, and feedback.

1. What would happen if the organization regarded the concept 'service user' as any user of any of the varied services offered by the Centre?
2. What would happen if attention was shifted onto the people who actually come to the Centre to avail themselves of its services, giving them the services they need, and discussing with them what else they need and whether it was feasible to provide it, as well as engaging them in dialogue?
3. What would happen if the management committee worked at establishing clearer boundaries for its work?
4. What would happen if the Director and staff saw the volunteers as a bridge between the various activities, and looked at ways of using this already present resource in more ways than they are used at present?
5. What would happen if all parties within the organization worked at defining and clarifying their boundaries in relation to each other?

6. What would happen if the issue of confidentiality was defined and applied in a consistent manner throughout the organization, and if the answer to every new question that was asked was communicated to all concerned?
7. What would happen if the organization celebrated its successes, and worked at developing what it is good at?
8. What would happen if The Centre simply advertised its presence and current services among potential users?
9. What would happen if none of the in-house services were ever cancelled as long as at least one user came at least every second time?
10. What would happen if the organization did none of these?

I trust this work-in-progress report will in some way support the good work of The Centre, and I look forward to an opportunity to discuss it with any and all interested parties.

I sent off this work-in-progress, this written intervention. I was in contact with Anna, and requested that she ensure that the chairperson and Director got their copies at about the same time, and that copies were sent to management committee members at the same time as the staff received theirs.

Anna got back to me with the news that of course, volunteers and Centre users had heard of the report and wanted to read it. So Birgitta had decided to make it available to anyone who wanted it. She had also given the management committee a deadline of a month, at which time, in the event of not hearing otherwise, she would invite me back to complete the consultancy. Anna's own opinion was extremely positive: she felt the report supported her in her work, and opened up new perspectives for her. She added that others felt similarly, and that Centre users who had read it generally viewed it favorably.

After a month had gone by, Birgitta—through Anna—invited me back to finish the job. I arranged for a two-day session some six weeks later, to include individual meetings where requested, Director and staff, volunteers, Centre users and management committee.

Meaning-Making

Before arriving, I had arranged the schedule with Anna: Day 1, a.m., individual meetings; p.m., Centre users; evening, volunteers. Day 2, a.m., individual meetings; p.m., Director and staff; evening, management committee.

On arrival, I was met with the news that I would not be meeting the Director, and that my evening session with the volunteers was moved to another location. The following story emerged: A staff member—let's say, named X—had a grievance with the Director's behavior, which had not been resolved. Another staff member, Y, supported X by raising a similar grievance. Since this was also unresolved, there was general support among the staff for these two issues to become formal complaints to the management committee. This did not lead to any satisfactory resolution.

The management committee then formed a disciplinary subcommittee to deal with the issues involved. Since this announcement, the Director had not come to work during office hours, but rather at night and on weekends. The subcommittee was meeting X, Y, and Birgitta at The Centre that evening, at the same time as I would be meeting the volunteers elsewhere.

I was not too surprised, as I had seen signs of tension beginning to build around Birgitta and her relations with the committee and staff. What did surprise me, as the morning wore on and I was given more and more details, was the slightly dramatic nature of the complaints—and the air of happy and busy efficiency that was so evident. That—and the enormously positive response to the report, with expressions of gratitude and congratulations—were surprising.

Each meeting confirmed these first impressions. Staff members were in a good mood, clearly enjoying their work; they had read and discussed the interim report, and were looking forward to getting down to work.

I returned after lunch for the support group meeting—this was the Wednesday they would normally meet, from about 2:00 p.m. on. When I walked into the room, I was taken aback. It turned out that there were fifteen Centre users there. Many had copies of the report with them. The others had asked Erik to make copies for them.

My meeting with them was scheduled from 2:00 to 4:00 p.m. I am aware that I still have difficulty finding words to describe my experience during those two hours. I was interrogated, grilled, cross-examined, supported, laughed at and with, thanked, appreciated. They held a highly dynamic dialogue that was tense, earnest, critical, and appreciative, swinging from one person to another around the room.

Most could see the shame/blame patterns, and their part in co-creating them. The same was true for the focus on failure—they would not get better and, at best, simply not get worse. So yes—failure. There was curiosity about what they may have induced from the Director and staff—and they had various unprintable suggestions.

The Trauma Cycle was a focus of attention: most recognized it in their own and others' behavior, and gave various examples. It was very important to them that the Director and staff completely understood that part of the report.

There were some amusing moments with respect to scapegoating, with various suggestions as to who was who (including some of themselves individually). The concept clearly had resonated with those who had read the report, and their examples were understood by the others.

This meeting was intense, serious, funny, casual, dynamic, repetitive, warm, hot. The room bubbled with life. As the time approached 4:00 p.m., they moved on to planning a bus trip to the coast (which the Centre would pay for), and some were volunteering to return to the system whereby one of them would go out with Carl to schools and workplaces, and talk about how it was to be HIV-positive.

As 4:00 p.m. approached, I asked whether there were any further questions. I was told 'no', thanked again, and offered some handshakes—and I left what had been one the most draining, nourishing, tense, and invigorating sessions of my experience.

I went for a long walk around the city. That evening, I met the volunteers. One had been at the previous volunteers meeting, three were new, and there was Klaus, who had been at the support group earlier that day. Klaus immediately said that I could greet him as Klaus—he had given some thought to the secrecy issue, and was now going to actively work against it. So he was Klaus, HIV-positive, volunteer, Centre user. He had thoroughly enjoyed the meeting earlier, and was looking forward to hearing how the report would be received by the other volunteers.

We went through the report, page by page. Issues mentioned in the report were confirmed, expanded, nuanced. At the part where I point to the volunteers as the synthesizing and integrating subsystem, with more to contribute if given the opportunity, one of the more experienced members, who had been at all three meetings, shed a tear. They all felt that their work had been seen and appreciated, and that they now had an opening to develop their contribution to The Centre and its various activities. This was yet another powerful meeting.

That evening, I reflected on how the field was reorganizing itself, and on which need was the organizing force. Clearly, Birgitta was in focus: staff had moved towards changing the relationship between themselves and her. Since change, however constructed, was an inevitable consequence of a process consultancy, she seemed to have positioned her reaction as that of an immovable object meeting an irresistible (?) force. The management committee was now in the roles of judge and jury. The Centre users were generally on the side of the staff. The volunteers had as their main contact a respected and long-serving staff member, Carl, and their loyalties lay with him. The social context of the Region would always support personal loyalty more than data. I was reminded of my earlier gut reaction: a tendency to want to support Birgitta, as I had, at that time, wandered around the boundary of my contracted work. My dilemma at the time of staying within the boundary of my contract, or straying into supervising her—however well-intentioned—became figural. Was this in any way also the dilemma of Aidsphone/The Centre as an organization?

Theory in Action #8

A distinction I always enjoy tracking in my work is that between the explicit/planned force for change, and the organic force for change that can often emerge as the work proceeds. In this case, the former was originally 'empowering the service users,' the latter now seemed to be 'empowering the staff' and/or any other subsystem, as all others were involved in the outcome of the Director/staff change in relationship. With regard to the management committee, I was aware that being judge and jury can hardly be as 'objective' as it seems.

As a Gestalt-oriented consultant, I could sense my excitement that the field had taken over; that it was so explicitly re-organizing itself as field and, in consequence, as a system, differently than before. Lewinian field theory (Marrow, 1969) speaks of the 'need that organizes the field.' Again, what could that need be that organized the field and impacted the system as it was now being played out?

I was alive with reflections, hypotheses, opinions, projections, and theories that evening. The field was bubbling with life, dynamics, change, and direction. The system was being redefined from within. I was back on the margin, and in the middle, and anywhere the field placed me and/or where I chose to be—and all of the above! This was Gestalt work in its most dynamic form—presence itself as intervention, rather than wholly directive interventions—and that presence (mine!) changing over time and in context. I could truly sense how the work occurred through me, through us, in relation to the client, rather than because of me. And the work occurred dynamically through the client and through our relationship as it developed and changed over time.

The following day was an exceptional experience. I began the day with the remaining individual staff meetings. My greatest 'doubting Thomas' had now become a fan. His reading of the report had con-cretized many of the issues taken up during the previous staff session. Another staff member saw Gestalt as a desirable perspective: the work and the report had opened ideas and views which had hitherto been unknown.

Staff reactions were active and energized. The report had supported them and their work; the issue with the Director was, for them, self-evidently appropriate in the context of their new perspective on themselves, individually and collectively. The individual sessions were open, personal, and affirmative.

Anna had already informed me that morning that the management committee wanted to meet the staff in my presence, so I had arranged for a two-hour session with staff only, followed by a one-hour joint session, with the option for the management committee to have a separate session for themselves.

The meeting with staff was dynamic, concrete and exciting. We went through the report, section by section. They could each recognize the points that had been taken up earlier, and those that were new. Erik described his reaction to the report as parallel to his experience of Stanley Kubrick's film, '2001: A Space Odyssey': each reading revealed something new in the same way that each viewing of the film opened new insights and interpretations. We worked together through the staff's sense of excitement and focus on the report. Anna and Carl were filled with ideas and projects. David had found a new focus for his funding efforts. I could feel myself drawn into the sense of excitement and empowerment expressed by the staff.

I felt how drawn I was to following the enthusiasm expressed by the staff, and how I also held myself on the margin, looking in at them, checking my own experience, and reflecting on them-and-me. A lot had happened—and was happening—and fast.

The management committee arrived. There were five of the eight members—Francesca, Gregory, and three members I had not met before. One of the latter, Lars, I knew by reputation as Senior Lecturer in the counseling degree program at the Region's well-respected university. I knew that Gestalt did not have a good reputation in the Region; indeed, at a training session I ran with local social workers, one of them had spoken of 'Gestalt and battery', a play on the police term 'assault and battery', and a reference to the confrontational training style they had previously experienced. I felt a little unsure.

This session opened with the management committee, led by Francesca, the Chairperson, asking the staff for their impressions of the consultancy in general, and the report in particular. This started slowly, then became animated and enthusiastic: staff members' support for the process and the report were unqualified. Dialogues developed and expanded into lively discussions. At one point, it emerged that this was the first time that the staff and management committee had met. This in turn led to an open-hearted exchange of regrets that this had not happened earlier.

Lars took up the theoretical input in the report with appreciation and curiosity. While acquainted with the content, he was interested in the idea of theory as a foundation for process work, and the link from my experience to theoretical considerations. We had a brief and engaging exchange on this issue.

The atmosphere was friendly and focused. Carl and Anna talked about the changes in their routines and the areas of co-operation they were exploring. Erik enthused about the changes in attitude and behavior he had experienced. David reported how his new understanding of the organization and its work had resulted in his developing more successful funding applications than before. Francesca and Gregory expressed appreciation for the process and its impact.

I knew that sooner or later, the issues concerning Birgitta were bound to emerge. The form this took initially was the management committee's asking the staff how they were managing without the presence of the Director. The response was clear: they were managing very well. They knew what needed to be done, they were doing it, and the level of co-operation and mutual support was high.

Francesca then asked whether the committee could have a short meeting alone with me, and asked whether the staff could be available to rejoin us later. They agreed.

The committee reported that the meetings with the Disciplinary Subcommittee, X, Y, and Birgitta had not led to a resolution. Birgitta was holding to her perspective, and the whole matter would probably have to go to arbitration. This would involve a lengthy process, and her absence as Director during that time. The future was uncertain.

The question was how to manage this relative to the staff. After a brief discussion, it was agreed that the current relationship with staff was such that the most natural and productive decision was to bring them completely into the picture.

The staff returned, and our meeting ended with an open and productive exchange between the committee and staff. Reporting procedures were proposed, and a further meeting was arranged.

Withdrawal

As we closed the session—and as I formally closed my consultancy contract—I was invited for a Christmas drink with the committee. We retired to a nearby bar.

Theory in Action #9

Use of Self: yes, I was totally engaged in, with, and by this work. The client had me, and not anybody else, to work with and relate to. As a result, with as much awareness as possible, I have included my own process throughout this work. Change had occurred at the contact boundary. I was changed, both personally and professionally. The organization had clearly changed and was changing. The Centre users had grasped the opportunity for change and were now being proactive in relation to the organization.

I had been supported throughout this work by Gestalt theory, methodology, training, and integration. In the process, my understanding of Gestalt theory had deepened and become even more integrated; my competence in the application of Gestalt to organizational settings had developed; and my trust in Gestalt as a self-based contact methodology had been strengthened.

Afterword

A new Director has been appointed. The organization has changed its name, clearly indicating its HIV/AIDS focus, and all its various activities are now under that one heading. Anna is currently in her first year of a four-year masters degree program in Gestalt psychotherapy. Carl has expressed an interest in joining the next group.

Two of my supervisees in the Region recently started a counseling group at the organization for members of the support group, and applied to the management committee for funding for supervision. As a result, Francesca—still Chairperson—sent me her greetings, and my check always arrives with a personal message from David, the accountant.

And yet I still have Birgitta on my mind, and the question about which need organized this field in such a way that she ended up outside of it. Was this what she wanted, or what another or others wanted?

And what part did I play? And on whose behalf?

References

Alevras, J.S.A & Wepman, B.J. (1980). Application of Gestalt Therapy Principles to Organizational Consultation. In B. Feder & R. Ronall (eds.) *Beyond the Hot Seat: Gestalt Approaches to Group* (pp. 229-237). New York: Brunner/Mazell Inc..

Beisser, A.R. (1970). The Paradoxical Theory of Change. In J. Fagan & I.L. Shepherd (eds.) *Gestalt Therapy Now* (pp. 88-92). Palo Alto, CA: Science and Behavior Books.

Clark, N. & Fraser, T. (1987). *The Gestalt Approach: An Introduction for Managers and Trainers. Horsham,* UK: Roffey Park.

Ennis, K. & Mitchell, S. (1970). Staff Training for a Day-care Centre. In J. Fagan & I.L. Shepherd (eds.) *Gestalt Therapy Now* (pp. 339-345). Palo Alto, CA: Science and Behavior Books.

Farrands, R. (2001). Sustaining Dynamic T1ension. *British Gestalt Journal, 10*(1), 4-12.

Hentoff, N. (1966). *Our Children Are Dying (p. 72).* East Rutherford, NJ: Penguin Books USA.

Herman, S.M. & Korenich, M. (1977). *Authentic Management: A Gestalt Orientation to Organizations and Their Development.* Reading, MA: Addison-Wesley.

Marrow, A.J. (1969). *The Practical Theorist: The Life and Work of Kurt Lewin.* New York, NY: Basic Books.

Nevis, E. (1987). *Organizational Consulting: A Gestalt Approach.* Cleveland, OH: GIC Press.

Perls, F., Hefferline, R., & Goodman, P. (1951/1994). *Gestalt Therapy: Excitement and Growth in the Human Personality.* New York: Julian Press.

Schein, E. (1999). *Process Consulting,* Second Edition. Reading, MA: Addison Wesley.

Wheeler, G. (1991). *Gestalt Reconsidered: A New Approach to Contact and Resistance.* Cleveland, OH: GIC Press.

Wysong, J. & Rosenfeld, E. (1982). *An Oral History of Gestalt Therapy.* Highland, New York: Gestalt Journal Press.

Commentary 1:

CHANTELLE WYLEY, MA

ABSTRACT: The author responds to the article by relating her own awareness and figure-forming processes in grappling with HIV/AIDS in South Africa. She shares questions and issues raised in discussion with Gestalt colleagues about the potent and existential nature of HIV/AIDS, and its impact across so many levels of system. Finally, the piece suggests the potential unique effectiveness of the Gestalt approach in this context.

The opportunity to write this comes as I grapple intensely with the burdens and challenges of having placed myself (a white, educated, left-thinking, Gestalt-trained South African) as an intervener in development processes of people and communities (black, poor) facing the onslaught of HIV/AIDS. My response to Seán Gaffney's article, therefore, is related less to the (important) theory-practice relationship, or the dynamics of his organizational intervention; rather it is related more to Gestalt and HIV/AIDS—the work context of the organization in the case study (Aidsphone).

HIV/AIDS has a somewhat different face in Africa, compared to European countries. The disease infects more women than men (for example, a recent survey of 15-24 year-old South Africans reports the HIV prevalence to be 15.5 percent among women and 4.8 percent among men: Reproductive Health Research Unit, 2003). As a result, the infection rate among children is high. Women are the caretakers of the sick and the (orphaned) children, and are most affected by the epidemic. Infections in the gay community and among intravenous drug users are statistically low in the whole population.

Despite this, I connected instantly and deeply with Gaffney's figures of the complexity of working with people who confront HIV/AIDS, and of the constant presence of the shadow of death.

Intervening in HIV/AIDS

In his work with Aidsphone, Gaffney experiences (within himself and the organization) frustration and inadequacy when faced with supporting and caring in a context of acute existential dilemma. Again I found a deep connection: as an intervener in HIV/AIDS processes, no intervention is ever enough when working with individuals carrying a deadly virus that has no cure, and against a pandemic which is unrelenting and indiscriminate. Failure is constantly with us, as it is with Aidsphone.

In the midst of this complexity, and grappling with the dilemma, therapists feel immense pressure to DO something (articulated by Gaffney at the end of his 'Awareness with Figure'). On the individual level, I feel pressed to donate clothes, food, money; to somehow support stressed community-level caregivers. On an organizational/political/societal level, the media reflect the pressure to hand out condoms, distribute educational material, roll out anti-retroviral therapy, and develop a vaccine. On this level, billions are being thrown at the HIV/AIDS problem: In early 2002, the South African Department of Health implied that there was a surplus of international aid money for condoms, more than we could use.[1]

How is one to make sense of the complexity, the existential dilemma of HIV/AIDS, felt by Gaffney, myself, and many others, in the face of all the money, demands, pressures, busyness, and action?

Some Figures/Data

I began writing this article at a guest farm in the rural Eastern Cape (one of the most poverty stricken areas of South Africa). The farm has been run by the same (white) farming family since World War II, and apart from cottages for guests, it accommodates about 15 black families and seasonal workers from the nearby small town. On a quiet morning walk, I came across the graveyard for the black farmworkers. It contained 23 graves, all simple mounds, and all but one with wooden cross 'headstones'. Half of those buried were born between 1910 and 1930 and had died between 1996 and 2004, at an average age of 80

---

[1] Personal communication to the author.

years. The other half were born in the 1960s, 70s and 80s, and had died over the past eight years, in their twenties, thirties and forties. On this farm, young people are dying faster than people in their fifties and sixties. I asked a farmworker about AIDS deaths in the area. He shook his head and said 'plenty.'

I live in a suburb of Cape Town, close to the mountains and the beach, desirable property that is still mainly white- and foreigner-owned. A shack settlement ('Mandela Park') has sprung up, built by domestic workers, gardeners, and casual labor on building sites and in the fishing industry; it also houses many people involved in the informal economy (taxi drivers, hawkers, tavern/shebeen[2] operators, criminals) and refugees from nearby countries (Zimbabwe, Nigeria, and the Democratic Republic of Congo).

When we first moved here in early 2000, the doorbell rang constantly with requests for work. Over the past 2 years, the request has changed to one for food, and many applicants show visible signs of HIV (e.g., oral thrush, Karposis sarcoma[3]). Clinics in Mandela Park report infection rates of 30-40 percent in their prenatal and voluntary testing programs.[4]

Two ladies who work in my home assisting with cleaning and childcare have male partners who refuse to be tested for HIV or wear condoms. Neither of the women are successful in talking with their partners about HIV. Both have young children and were tested during pregnancy; both were negative then, but live with the constant fear of being infected. One has a brother in prison who is HIV-positive.

Mobilizing Energy

And so the pandemic comes closer, and the pressure to DO something increases. I have donated food boxes via the local church, contributed to collections at my daughter's school, fed the sufferers who ring the doorbell, talked to my domestic staff and given them literature to pass on to friends who are infected.

---

[2] An unlicensed or illegally operated drinking establishment.

[3] Commonly known as Kaposi's sarcoma in the United States.

[4] Clinic statistics from "Proposal for Funding: Extension of Hout Bay Main Road Clinic" and clinic reports, Hout Bay Health Forum.

As a trainer of people who manage development projects and programs, I have included HIV/AIDS examples in training material, and contributed to discussions about 'mainstreaming HIV/AIDS' into development planning. I have worked directly on programs and consultancies that deal with the health and HIV/AIDS sectors.

The situation seems fairly hopeless. The pandemic is huge, overwhelming; the likelihood of failure is high; the possibility of slightly relieving suffering is the only reward.

Back to Awareness

Faced with frustration, I have been casting around, reframing, redefining, shifting paradigms, looking for another way out/in.

In the biomedical sphere, I am intrigued at the South African President's dissident views disputing the relationship between the HI virus and AIDS; he suggests that poverty causes AIDS. The South African Health Minister advocates large amounts of grated garlic, beetroot, lemon juice, olive oil, the African potato, and other medicinal herbs as alternatives to anti-retroviral drugs. Both have been branded lunatic by the press, medical fraternity, and AIDS activists. They are both intelligent, seasoned politicians: Why this going outside of the mainstream bio-medical orthodoxy, in the face of such criticism? But, their views certainly point to out-of-the-box thinking (about how the AIDS disease interacts with the immune system, for example), which may be where we could be looking.

In terms of behavioral interventions, certainly the orthodox thinking and approaches related to prevention (condoms, education materials, peer education programs, voluntary counseling and testing), and the billions invested therein, are not significantly affecting infection rates (i.e., resulting in sexual behavior change), especially in Africa.[5]

Focusing on the behavioral sphere, Gestalt thinking leads us[6] to query the orthodox thinking on at least two levels:

1. The Awareness-Action interplay.
2. Whether interventions at a different system level could have greater impact.

1. Awareness to Action. Questions here could be:
    −   Have HIV/AIDS program managers leapt into action (condoms, education programs, etc.) with incomplete awareness of the complexity of sexual behavioral change, which is so linked to power, masculinity, and culture (incomplete awareness, inappropriate action)? Is there a reluctance to go into this intimate, charged, secret, emotionally potent area (hence deflection into busyness)?
    −   Why are individuals not changing their sexual practices if they are informed about how the virus spreads (high awareness, blocked at action)? Is this about 'HIV only affects others' (other races, sexes), or 'it won't happen to me' (denial and projection)?
    −   When it comes to sex, why are people moving impulsively and compulsively from sensation to energy mobilization and action/intercourse? Why are they avoiding other data or awareness-raising in the moment, and not taking responsibility for their lives, and those of others (desensitization and/ or deflection)?

2. System Level. Questions here could be:
    −   Are safe sex education and HIV prevention campaigns in the mass media and in public spaces not effective precisely because they are not going into the more hidden, private spaces (aimed at the societal level instead of individual level)?

---

[5] For example, South Africa's national HIV prevalence rate has increased steadily by just over 2% per year between 1999 (22.4%) and 2002 (26.5%) (South African Department of Health 2003). The exceptions in Africa are Uganda and Senegal. This has been attributed to strong united, outspoken government leadership, and unity within sectors of society, e.g., churches. Thailand and Brazil have also been successful in lowering infection rates.

[6] What follows came out of discussions between Ewa Eriksson (Asia and Pacific Department of the International Federation of the Red Cross, Geneva), Fran Johnston (Teleos Leadership Institute, Philadelphia) and myself, which culminated in a joint session at the meeting of the Gestalt International Study Center's International Affiliates Meeting in Stockholm in April 2004. Additional points were raised in discussion with Nathaniel Mjema (Independent Development Trust, Pretoria).

- Or, further: is it a pre-condition for change on an individual level in the interpersonal space, that there be change in the intrapersonal space?
- Or, alternatively: is it a pre-condition for the individual to abstain, be faithful and/or use condoms (A,B,C), that there be change at community level to support and legitimize this behavior change?
- Or: is mutually supportive, attuned change across a number of levels required for behavior change to manifest to the extent and in the numbers necessary to lower and stabilize infection rates?

The recent work of Edwin Nevis and others[7] on balancing intimate and strategic systems raises other questions. As interveners they suggest that we need to be familiar with both intimate and strategic behaviors, in both types of systems, and familiar with the interplay between the two; we need to keep the boundary clear, transparent and flexible. The reach of HIV/AIDS has made it the focus of international organizations, large government departments in developing countries, and the recipient of billions of dollars in aid and government funding (areas of strategy). At this level we could be in danger of losing sight of the deeply personal issues and the suffering (the area of intimacy and relationship). Can we:

- Build personal capacity to engage in the intimate sphere more strategically:[8] in the process of seeking connection/ intimacy, to be able to hold up personal goals (related to health, survival) and have one's own view on these prevail (even if this brings a break in that intimate connection, and loneliness)?
- Assist in developing strategy around HIV/AIDS by taking the issues into the intimate space, by holding relationship

---

[7] As presented by Nevis and Stuart Simon in 'Balancing Intimate and Strategic Behaviors in Families and Organizations,' a GISC seminar, Stockholm, April 2004; and as published in Sonia M. Nevis, Stephanie Backman and Edwin Nevis (2003).

[8] Thanks to Fran Johnston for suggesting thinking along these lines.

as a focus (even if this means having to suspend hierarchy, status, and persuasion, and perhaps laying the self open to being unexpectedly influenced)?

Intervention Figures

Some of these questions have been tackled in a Gestalt-informed intervention with HIV/AIDS leadership in South Africa, Swaziland, and Cambodia. The 'Leadership for Results' program was launched by the United Nations Development Program in 2002, and is designed and presented by the Teleos Leadership Institute (Philadelphia, USA),[9] with input by local facilitators. This training intervention is based on research that highlights the difficulties faced by leaders in government and non-government organizations addressing HIV/AIDS. It seeks to heighten participants' awareness of their own contact with HIV/AIDS and those infected and affected, and to explore their own behaviors related to sex and gender, while at the same time mobilizing energy and resources at many different levels (individually, in organizations, communities, institutions) to make an impact. At the same time, the intervention seeks to develop a cadre of facilitators to take the work further in the local context.

Another Gestalt-trained facilitator of development processes in South Africa has designed interactions to deepen awareness of policy makers, strategists, managers, and practitioners engaged in mainstreaming HIV/AIDS. These interventions give space to explore sexual identities, assumptions, and behaviors, deliberately engaging participants at the feeling rather than analytical-factual level.[10]

Anecdotal results from these interventions are promising, with participants reporting shifts at the intrapersonal level, in personal and sexual relationships, and in conceptualizing and managing interventions in the field. For me, meaningful contact with HIV-positive people (the infected) during the 'Leadership for Results' program brought me a different perspective on the disease.

---

[9] Faculty include Annie McKee, Fran Johnston and Eddy Mwelwa. The author worked as a local facilitator on the program.

[10] Thanks to Nathaniel Mjema for descriptions of this.

The (lack of) behavior change has been tackled by a South African social psychologist on the basis of action research/intervention over three years in a squatter camp community of black migrant mineworkers, sex workers, and youth near a mine in the Johannesburg area. Catherine Campbell (2003) makes the following points:

– Sexual behavior is not determined by conscious rational decisions of individuals based on factual information; people often knowingly engage in sexual behavior that places their health and lives at risk, and this behavior relates to complex social constructs.
– People living in marginalized, dehumanized, poverty-stricken situations have less control over their behavior than their more privileged fellows.

And, specifically—

– Migrant mine work involves dehumanized, stressful living conditions (single men's hostels; shared, cramped sleeping, cooking, and recreational space in concrete rooms) and working conditions (hot, dark, physically strenuous, and dangerous work that is kilometers underground). This deprivation results in loss of dignity and status as men. The danger of underground mining yields first-hand experience of rock falls, blasts, mutilation, and death, and a sense of fatalism. Sexual interaction ('flesh-to-flesh') with sex workers is one of the few opportunities for pleasure and expressing masculinity, releasing stress and seeking intimacy and affirmation, serving to counterbalance powerlessness and the lack of self-efficacy.
– Sex workers are aware of HIV and how it is transmitted, but their desperate economic status militates against condom use in their R20 or $4 a time encounters; insistence on a condom means that the customer would move on to the next woman, or respond with violence. The sex workers admitted that if all insisted on condoms this could change, but distrust runs high. All expressed lack of control over

their situation, dislike of the unpleasant, disease-ridden, physically dangerous work, and shame at their downgraded, undignified, stigmatized social standing.

Campbell (2003) argues that HIV/AIDS interventions need to take into account the specific contexts in which people negotiate their social and sexual lives. A pre-condition for individual behavior change is the renegotiation of social and sexual identities in relation to social power and standing.

These examples of interventions, though small given the scale of the pandemic, bring the same powerful message with respect to embracing behavioral change via exploring sexual identities, assumptions and behaviors, or sexuality, masculinity, and (gender and material-based) power. To take the message further, how necessary it is to explore and shift one's intimate boundaries/assumptions/inhibitions to be authentic and effective in working with the intimate behavior of others. The Gestalt option more clearly proffers the opportunity to approach this from an intrapersonal perspective by replacing the factual-analytical relationship with HIV/AIDS with one that is based more in feelings. Bringing this global issue into the realm of the 'I' makes taking responsibility possible, and hence action becomes possible.

Interestingly, this reverberates at a subtle level in Gaffney's experience with the organization Aidsphone. The intervention contract focused on power and participation: empowering the HIV-positive users of Aidsphone's services to participate in the organization. A split had developed between the users and the organization's management and staff. This seems to have been the result of the institutionalization of the services in the 15 years since their inception, lessening contact with those for whom the services were designed: the 'deep gap' Gaffney confronted in his 'Awareness with Figure' phase.

What kept this gap in place as an attractor of organizational energy is the Confidence/Secrecy Gaffney focuses on in the 'Action and Contact/Change' phase. Secrecy (regarding the HIV status of volunteers, identity of users of the center) blocks communication and contact between the two groups by keeping opinions (therefore participation and accountability) faceless and nameless.

Stigmas related to HIV status apply in Africa as much as in Europe, with sexual preference, habits, promiscuity, and emotions with guilt, shame, blame, anger, and reprisal keeping the behaviors that spread the disease out of the spotlight. Secrecy and confidentiality (about test results) serve one purpose at one level; namely, to protect individuals from persecution. On the other hand, disclosure about status serves a purpose at another (societal) level; namely, to enable role modeling (sportspeople, music idols leading HIV-positive healthy lifestyles), positive identification, working against feelings of isolation and shame (self-empowerment), and working against stigma and bias, which enables support and the education of others at a community level.

Gaffney's intervention illustrates this: by surfacing the confidentiality/secrecy figure, he unlocks a process of giving faces and voices to the HIV positive people, culminating in 'highly dynamic dialogue', Klaus's coming out as an 'HIV positive, volunteer, Centre user', and the HIV-positive volunteers feeling 'their work had been seen and appreciated'. Altogether this unlocked a powerful force for change/field re-organization, in both individuals and the organization.

Energy Mobilization

Gaffney illustrates a Gestalt approach to HIV/AIDS: confronting in the moment, in touch with the self, working with what comes up, remaining open to existential challenges, and challenging contact modalities. To this I would add a deeper level of self awareness-raising in the area of one's own sexual behaviors/inhibitions/assumptions to authentically work with those of others. As I conclude, I have become acutely aware of and energized about my purpose in writing this commentary.

The HI virus attacks us at the boundaries where life is created (sex for adults, and consequently, at birth for children). Put another way, we are faced with the dilemma of sex, the life-sustaining force, becoming a death force with HIV. Five million of South Africa's population of 44 million are infected or already ill (including six percent of South Africa's children and 10 percent of its youth). Thirty million are infected in Africa.[11] The scale and the significance for the globe is indisputable.

---

[11] Statistics from the South African Human Sciences Research Council, reported in the Cape Times, May 11 and 13, 2004, and the RHRU (2003).

I ask that if you, the reader, can confront HIV/AIDS by bringing it closer to your 'I,' to your intimate spaces, and through this, to your strategic interventions, then the breezes some of us feel, generated by the wings of the butterfly, will turn into strong winds.

South African HIV-positive activist Brett Anderson talks of the 'gift of AIDS', acknowledging and giving thanks for the world it has opened up to him. For us, the opportunity is to encounter our common humanity, not in terms of rosy ideals (e.g., South Africa's 'rainbow nation'), but by dealing with risk, death, poverty, sickness, orphaned children. Our work at that contact boundary could bring us the unexpected.

References

Campbell, C. (2003), *Letting Them Die: Why HIV/AIDS Intervention Programmes Fail.* London: The International African Institute; Oxford: James Currey; Bloomington and Indianapolis: Indiana University Press; Cape Town: Double Storey/Juta.

Nevis, S. M., Backmann, S. & Nevis, E.C. (2003), Connecting Strategic and Intimate Interactions: The Need for Balance. *Gestalt Review,* 7(2),134-146.

Reproductive Health Research Unit, University of the Witwatersrand (2003), *HIV and Sexual Behaviour Among Young South Africans: A National Survey of 15-24 Year Olds.* Johannesburg: RHRU; Love-life.

South African Department of Health (2003), *National HIV and Syphilis Sero-prevalence Survey of Women Attending Public Antenatal Clinics in South Africa-2002, Summary Report.* Pretoria: South Africa Department of Health.

౪

Commentary 2:

Birgit Niebuhr, PhD

Abstract: The commentary describes how, by applying three elements of Gestalt theory—levels of system, cycle of experience, and multiple realities—it was possible to raise awareness and promote action in HIV/AIDS-related workshops in Africa.

Seán Gaffney's brilliant analysis of his consultancy in a non-governmental organization working in the field of HIV/AIDS somewhere in Europe had a far-reaching effect on me, and I am grateful that he has shared his work with us in this way. I personally connected with the article in two ways: First, I was taken back to the time when the author was my teacher, at different times in various countries, introducing me to the concept of 'levels of system' with inspiring lectures, funny and yet profound.

Second, it brought me face to face with my own work which takes place almost exclusively in a complex field of horizontally and vertically interrelated systems and subsystems. Seán Gaffney's article, with a focus on field, systems/subsystems, organism/environment, and interdependence, made me recall two recent experiences in Africa where I facilitated seminars, one on HIV/AIDS at the workplace and one on adolescent sexual and reproductive health. While reading the case study, I became poignantly aware of the process in which I had been involved at that time and I felt compelled to reassess the instruments and the methodology I had used.

The two different environments I worked in—for the purpose of discussion, I will call them environments A and B—each had their own specific features.

Environment A:

HIV/AIDS' prevalence of at least 20 percent in Eastern and Southern Africa has a heavy impact on individuals and their families, and stunts local communities' socio-economic growth. The high prevalence among the economically active population in sub-Saharan Africa calls for a private sector response at the workplace. It is assumed that these 'HIV/AIDS workplace programs' will not only benefit affected individuals and their families, but companies as well, all of which are feeling the brunt of the epidemic in the form of a loss of skilled workers, absenteeism and low productivity levels and, hence, less profit. In many cases, HIV/AIDS programs in the workplace have a central role to play in raising awareness and providing social and medical support.

In thematic terms, the seminar focused on the barriers obstructing the implementation of HIV/AIDS workplace programs. In my experience, the real barriers to implementation seem to have less to do with insufficient management skills and financial resources, and much more to do with taboos, discrimination, stigmatization, and the fear surrounding HIV/AIDS and those affected by it. The challenge of the seminar, therefore, was to raise participants' awareness of these facts and to create an environment in which participants would feel encouraged to reflect on their values and explore their experiences and feelings with regard to sexuality, love, disease, and death.

Participants at the seminar were mostly representatives of private businesses from five countries in Southern Africa.

Environment B:

This West African country is land-locked and Muslim-dominated, with some of the most severe indicators for reproductive health in the region. With HIV/AIDS prevalence still around one percent, the maternal and infant mortality rate is about 50-60 times that in the West, with a high number of teenage pregnancies and unsafe, sometimes fatal abortions. The situation is characterized by a lack of accessible services offering social and medical help and is often compounded by rigorous school and family systems that disapprove of sexual activity in youth, leading to a withdrawal of support and dialogue when it is most needed.

The workshop was designed to develop a teachers' module on the topic of adolescent sexual and reproductive health which the National School of Public Health would use as part of its basic training of nurses and midwives. An initial draft of the module had already been developed and was scheduled for discussion and revision during the seminar.

The task was to reconcile the kind of teaching approach common throughout most of francophone Africa—by which I mean a top-down, learning-by-rote approach with little room for dialogue, discussion, or the exchange of ideas—with the draft module's contents, which focused on the physical aspects of sexual development and possible pathologies without giving due attention to contextual conditions or the desires, fears, and needs of young people. The challenge for the workshop was to raise awareness of the realities facing adolescents, and to point out ways of reaching and addressing this target group.

Participants were the directors and senior teachers of the two branches of the national school, one in the capital and one in a remote area close to the desert.

How could awareness be raised in these two very different, yet in some ways very similar environments?

Raising Awareness of 'Levels of System'

One approach that proved to be effective in making participants aware of themselves and their environment was to alert them to the different subgroups existing within the group (total system and subsystems). Subsystems included nationality, their company of employ, age, gender, religious orientation, tribal affiliation, preference for monogamy or polygamy, or even their upbringing in a village or town context. Participants were asked to form respective subsystems and to formulate what they would be able to contribute to the system as a whole, and what they, in turn, would need from the overall system. Another level of subsystem involved pre-existing interpersonal relationships among participants, the history and nature of which were then shared with all others present. The individual subsystem was the last one to be explored and was presented with the help of creative techniques. What did this mean in concrete terms for the participants?

In short, they experienced a process of changing subsystems, along with the inherent (conscious or not) redefinition of boundaries for each given group. Boundaries were not fixed and static, but moved and shifted, thereby stressing not only differences, but also similarities. Having shared some of their individual life histories, participants could see how their contributions and needs interconnected; thus, they were better able to relate to each other. In a way, looking at systems (a more abstract term) had created room for intimacy. This group experience also made it easier to look outside the group with greater acumen. More energy was available, so attention could turn to the issue of 'what is'.

The Cycle of Experience

From the outset, both seminars had planned to include experiential learning, such as awareness-raising exercises, body work, role play, and the exploration of feelings of fear, anger and sadness. At the same time, participants were expecting content that would provide technical support for the achievement of their specific objectives. In seminar A, for instance, this content was the straightforward presentation of cost-efficiency modules for implementing HIV/AIDS-related workplace programs; in seminar B, the content concerned concrete proposals for revising the draft module text.

After going through some of the experiential learning exercises, participants felt a need to understand where the seminars were taking them. This need was expressed in various forms, including resistance. Here, the introduction of the Cycle of Experience (slightly transformed into a 'cycle of learning') was extremely useful in helping participants understand the process and appreciate where they were at a given moment. It was important to introduce the cycle at the right time—when there was a need, an anxiety, or maybe anger. Being introduced to the cycle made participants more patient and trusting, enabling them to stay where they were and explore the different facets of the here and now—until a new figure could emerge.

From that point on, reference was made to the cycle every time we assessed where we were in the process. At the same time, by voicing what I had seen and what had moved me, I was able to integrate interventions into the feedback process.

Multiple Realities

Probably the most powerful concept for the teachers' seminar in terms of raising awareness and redefining values was that of 'multiple realities.' Acknowledging the existence and legitimacy of these different realities for each of the groups involved—teachers, nurse-students, adolescents—using different methodological approaches (role play, reflection exercises) was a precondition for defining a common reality that was binding and meaningful for all three participating groups, and it later served as a reference for the contents to be included in the module. What was this common reality? It reflected parts of each of the three realities: for the teachers, the need to teach medical and socio-medical aspects of adolescent health; for the nursing students, the need to obtain tools enabling them to counsel adolescent clients at the health center; and for adolescents themselves, the need to know what to do in order to maintain their physical and social well-being.

New Figures Emerging

The methodology supported the emergence of new figures. In seminar A, this new figure was the understanding that before and parallel to dealing with managerial and cost-related issues involved in the implementation of HIV-workplace programs, other processes had to be initiated that fostered communication about AIDS, the attendant emotions, and the development of a safe and trusting environment. In fact, the environment that had been created among participants during the seminar led one HIV-positive person to 'come out'. Furthermore, a strong wish was expressed to have a follow-up seminar after about two years to assess the changes that were expected in the individual companies/organizations in the interim.

In seminar B, the new figure was the realization among the participants that the draft module needed to be completely rewritten to make it appropriate and able to respond to the adolescents' needs. Above all, it would have to be based on the questions youths ask about sexuality and health. One particular form of acknowledgement is the fact that the participants wished to use the methods they had experienced in this seminar in their own future teaching.

Conclusion

Even though Seán Gaffney's work differs from mine in many respects, nonetheless I identified many similarities in our processes. Like him,

I found that Gestalt methodology and training provided a framework that supported my work throughout. The positive outcome of the seminars and the changes I saw made me realize just how worthwhile the Gestalt approach is in intercultural work settings—areas in which it has not been applied frequently to date.

Bibliography

DiBella, A. J. & Nevis, E. C. (1998), *How Organizations Learn: An Integrated Strategy for Building Learning Capacity*. San Francisco: Jossey-Bass Publishers.

Gannon, M. J. (2001), *Understanding Global Cultures: Metaphorical Journeys through 23 Nations* (2nd ed.). Thousand Oaks, CA: Sage Publications.

Nevis, E. C. (1987), *Organizational Consulting: A Gestalt Approach*. Cleveland: The Gestalt Institute of Cleveland Press.

Stevens, J. O. (1988), *Awareness—Exploring, Experimenting, Experiencing*. London: Eden Grove Editions.

جب

Reponse to Wyley, Niebuhr, and Nevis

I would like to begin by thanking the anonymous reviewers of an earlier draft for the fruitful challenges they set for me, and also my Action Editor, Jon Frew, whose calm patience, great skill, and warm collegial support made a final and much-revised draft possible. What began as a nudge and a gentle push from Joe Melnick finally reached a form to which others could read and respond. And so my warm thanks to Chantelle Wyley and Birgit Niebuhr for their sensitive reading of my article, and to Edwin Nevis for masterfully introducing the article and the responses.

I feel gratified and humbled by the energized responses of Wyley and Niebuhr: gratified in the sense that they could use the article as ground for their powerful and evocative figures from their own great work in areas of sub-Saharan Africa, thus spread their thinking and their Gestalt applications to a wider audience; and humbled by the extent of the social, political, economic, medical, and human catastrophes that are the contexts of their work. In the region where I worked, known cases of HIV/AIDS were counted in the hundreds. The worst-case scenarios were still only fractions of one percent of the population. The figures mentioned by Wyley and Niebuhr—and especially Wyley's constant physical closeness to HIV/AIDS—present a truly frightening perspective. I am filled with both personal and professional admiration for their work, and appreciation for the opportunity to connect with it, even at this distance. They provide eloquent voices for the people with whom they work.

Reading Wyley's comments on 'out-of-the-box thinking', I was reminded of a recent conversation with an Irish colleague who works with HIV/AIDS in Kenya. He described, with a mixture of humor and resignation, a discussion between a local social worker and a representative of a European aid agency. The agency wanted to donate a jeep to the local community. The worker explained the difficulties in maintaining such a vehicle, and the high costs of spare parts—if they were even available. He suggested instead that they donate horses and carts equal to the value of the jeep. The impact of that type of donation could be spread more evenly throughout the community, requiring little or no maintenance, and providing horse manure. The agency did not approve his request.

This highlights an aspect that both Wyley and Niebuhr raise: culturally congruent interventions stand a better chance of having an effective local impact than those that are too culturally incongruent. Throwing crates of condoms at people seems a particularly Western 'solution' in a context in which literacy levels, attitudes, levels of sexual hygiene and sex education, and family and social customs are so different. Wyley raises good questions 'on the behavioral sphere,' using both Gestalt thinking and language: she wonders about the 'Awareness-Action interplay' as well as 'interventions at a different system level.' I would like to comment from both the context of my article, and Niebuhr's response.

In teaching Gestalt, I like to talk about awareness and the 'fast figure,' as well as the 'habitual figure.' I relate these to the concept of 'ground' and the emerging, self-energized figures that can enter our awareness, given the time to do so. In other words, I spend more time at the 'Sensation' phase of the Cycle of Experience. This slowing down of the awareness process is what can allow for 'out-of-the-box' figures to emerge. This, it seems to me, is what Niebuhr describes so clearly under the heading 'New Figures Emerging.' It is also part of what happened when the 'trendy' social work theme of 'empowering' the end user was renegotiated in the case study. The ground was re-structured, and new (and unexpected!) figures could emerge.

On the subject of system levels, I was reminded of the impact of my work in shifting perceptions of the service users from a 'group' to a collection of individuals with common and shared health and existential issues. Niebuhr raised awareness with respect to dynamic and changing subsystems, and the mutual impact of subsystems and individuals on each other in a rich combination.

Wyley, Niebuhr, and I each found our way to a 'use of self' that became central to our work. I like Niebuhr's interactive use of her 'cycle of learning,' sharing 'what I had seen and what had moved me.'

Wyley's amazing final three paragraphs testify to the power, existential beauty, and sense of personal commitment that emerges when we, as Gestalt practitioners, allow ourselves to be fully present in the wholeness of who we uniquely are, being influenced by and in return more able to influence our environments, no matter how challenging.

Turning now to the generous introduction by Edwin Nevis, I need to start by unraveling some of the threads that make up the weave of my relationship to him. He has been, in turn, my teacher, colleague, and mentor, and is now my friend. He is also a legend in his own long lifetime as a Gestalt practitioner and teacher par excellence. So I feel doubly honored: that Edwin, my friend, introduced the article and responses; and also that Nevis, the Daddy of all Gestalt OSD practitioners, should so honor one of his 'sons' and two of his 'daughters.' Ah, now I feel better!

Nevis accurately recognizes 'a paper that struggles to combine' both third-person and first-person perspectives. I would simply like to add that this was also the ongoing struggle of the work itself, as is more forcefully expressed by Wyley and Niebuhr. Indeed, this seems to me to be what distinguishes the Gestalt practitioner from what he later describes as 'a rational exercise in planning and implementing change.' It includes being 'as flexible as a wet noodle' as well as 'his confusion, his hurt,' and—we should not forget—the 'less than elegant' interventions.

Nevis concludes with a challenge to the current generation of Gestalt OSD practitioners: to raise our sights beyond the level of organizations, and meet the need to work within the context of major social issues. He poses what I choose to interpret as another challenge in his comment about 'showing Gestalt practitioners the limits of our theory for understanding complex social phenomena, and raising the need for us to become more conversant with other theories'.

I find that I am increasingly working at the interface of organization and society, mainly through my work as supervisor or consultant to volunteer organizations in the field of community development in regions of the world where societies are divided by, or in open conflict about, issues such as social inequality, politics, religion, race, and sexual orientation. I would like to suggest that this type of work can be an opening for future practice-based theory-building on a Gestalt ground, as well as for the development of methodologies and best practices for the successful application and expansion of the Gestalt philosophy, theory, and approach at the level of the societies in which we, and our children, and our grandchildren live. So, Edwin, I accept both challenges, and look forward to reading evidence of the fact that others have also accepted them, in future articles in Gestalt Review.

ᘓ

This article was published by the Gestalt Review (2004), Vol. 8(3): pp. 260-262 (introduction) pp. 263-290 (article) pp. 291-304 (commentaries) pp. 305-307 (response), and is reproduced here by kind permission of the editor, Joseph Melnick.

6.

Borders and Boundaries:

CROSS-CULTURAL PERSPECTIVES FOR OD PRACTITIONERS

This chapter explores some core constructs in cross-cultural studies, both well known and lesser known, and applies them to the work of international organization development OD practitioners. The implications of national culture, individual identity, and boundaries for cross-cultural work of OD practitioners are examined. The chapter begins with a mini-case study to set the scene and exemplify the work. The mini-case is adapted from my experiences as an international OD practitioner and is intended to highlight some of the issues involved in cross-cultural OD work, as well as possible resolutions. Throughout the chapter are references, where appropriate, to other aspects of cross-cultural OD work. The chapter concludes with a brief exploration of national culture and racial identity, as well as implications for OD practitioners doing cross-cultural work.

An Introductory Mini-case

This mini-case is based on the author's experiences as an international OD practitioner. For case story purposes, the OD practitioner is named Liam Quinn.

Liam was contacted by a former client, Adam Svensson. Adam had been headhunted by a U.S. multinational and competitor to his previous company. Liam first met Adam as technical director of a major Swedish multinational corporation and worked with him as OD consultant to his division, coach to his senior managers, and trainer in cross-cultural business and management. During this time, Adam played a leading role in the acquisition and integration of an Italian company, which was a challenging and complex process, successfully completed. The U.S. company recently acquired an Italian subsidiary and pinpointed Adam for his proven experience both in the business itself and with Italian production facilities.

Adam was now located in Northern Italy as technical director at a major production facility, living nearby with his wife and daughter. He knew Liam worked regularly in Milan and arranged for him to visit his office. Liam presented himself at reception, asked for Direttore Svensson and was led by a receptionist down a long corridor to a door with a brass plate on the wall beside it. On it was his client's title and name. There was a smaller and simpler plate on the door, with an initial and a surname; he took this (rightly) to be the female secretary's name. The receptionist knocked, and the secretary came and took him into her room. She asked him to be seated and then went and knocked on an inner door, stepped into the adjoining room, and announced his arrival to Adam. Adam came immediately to the door, and soon all three were somewhat awkwardly sharing the threshold. The secretary moved back into her room, and Adam and Liam stepped into his office.

One of the first things Adam did was take him to another inner door at the far end of his room. This led into another corridor, parallel with the first one Liam was in. This corridor was the private entrance to the senior executive offices—and one of Adam's small problems. He felt uncomfortable using it and preferred to come into his office through his secretary's room, greeting her on his way. He sensed that she seemed uncomfortable with his doing this, which became one specific part of the general dilemma: the distance he was expected to keep from his staff, and especially from the factory floor. In Sweden, Adam just loved visiting the factories, whipping off his jacket, and getting into the nitty-gritty of production. Now, he felt he did not know his staff, could not distinguish between those under his management and any others. This was new to him. Liam's task was to support Adam in dealing with this dilemma. We will return to the mini-case later. First, some background to the main themes of this chapter.

Border Crossings

The notion of cultural differences has moved from exotic tales of far-flung countries and exciting travel books to an academic subject that combines aspects of anthropology, history, sociology, social psychology, and (increasingly) organization, management, and business. Indeed, Hofstede (1980) has declared that 'the business of international business is culture'. OD practitioners are more and more working at the interface of cross-cultural interactions. Those who work with multinational companies are working within the same organization, but in varying sociocultural contexts as they move from subsidiary to subsidiary. In this regard, Hofstede's work began as a study of corporate culture, only to discover that local and national culture was more a significant characteristic of local subsidiaries than corporate culture was; indeed, it thrived in creative ways despite the lip service generally being paid to the notion of a corporate culture.

Sometimes success in one context leads to work in totally different cultures, and OD practitioners find themselves challenged by the insight that what works in one's home culture does not necessarily work everywhere—or even anywhere—else. The very competence that led to the new contract may turn out to be a barrier to best OD practice in this new cultural context.

The clearest sign of a move from one sociocultural context to another is when a physical national border is crossed. In most cases, this means a change in language as well as social and business behaviors. Indeed, on arrival at an airport there are already distinctive behaviors. As an Irishman with an Irish/European Union passport and a resident of Sweden for twenty-nine years, I can compare quick and painless border-crossings into Denmark or Italy, for example, with those into the United States, Canada, Israel, Iran, and Latvia or Estonia in the immediate aftermath of the Soviet era. There is the additional experience of getting into Iran with fifteen (they counted!) stamps in my passport from Tel Aviv airport in Israel—and then into Israel with a visa to Iran in my passport. Not to mention the U.S. immigration!

Then there are the local variations in signposting at Arrivals—not to forget the taxi queue (or lack of it) as well as the negotiation options, which may or may not arise as one finally gets seated in a taxi. Then hotels do differ! For example, checking in at my regular hotel in Milan is now a long series of handshakes and mutual assurances on how delighted we all are to meet again. So it is often in these early encounters that OD practitioners can begin sensing that the environment is not what they are used to; a cultural and behavioral border has indeed been crossed. All of this can happen before starting work with the actual client!

There are important additional issues that have an impact on border crossings. First, this is a post-colonial world, with former colonies struggling still to emerge from years of submission into a new era of self-sufficiency and cultural identity. The notion that 'the West knows best' carries with it many undertones of an old and new colonialism. Those of us who are in any way representative of a form of dominance—be it racial, gender, political, historical, financial, organizational or management approach, linguistic, or other—have to be aware of and sensitive to how this may affect our cross-cultural relations. This is especially relevant as we move in areas of the world where fundamentalism of any kind has created sharply divisive attitudes based on the fuzziest of generalizations ('All Americans are evil.' 'All Muslims are aggressive.' 'All Catholics in the North of Ireland are Republican terrorists.' 'Globalization is a Western plot.') Such notions are impossible to calmly discuss or lightly dismiss.

The second issue is related to the first: anyone who opposes Western political or business ideals can now be branded a terrorist. This is enough to justify a coalition of Western powers invading another country and imposing democracy—a truly paradoxical contradiction in terms. For many people in the Middle East, this is the new face of twenty-first-century colonialism. Working recently in Tehran, I was given a clear perspective on local perceptions. I was shown a map of the region and had it pointed out to me that Iran is surrounded on each side by 'America': to the east in Afghanistan and to the west in Iraq. Then they mentioned the threat also posed by America's ally, Israel. The English-language newspapers make regular references to 'the American devil' and 'the Zionist plot'.

Whatever one thinks of the validity or realism of these perceptions, they are to be reckoned with if OD practitioners choose to work in these cultures. Preparing for a border crossing into Iran, for example, it is necessary to be mindful and respectful of the important distinction that Iranians are not Arabs, that Iran is an Islamic Republic, and that one can be arriving in the middle of Ramadan. In my own case, it could be added that I am an Irish Catholic by tradition, white, Western, comparatively well off, and living comfortably and to a high standard in Sweden. I needed to be aware and sensitive that such aspects of my background would color my perceptions of Iranian culture, and equally aware of and sensitive to how these characteristics may be perceived in the context of Iranian culture.

Generally speaking, border crossings are the focus of research in cross-cultural business. Hofstede (1991, 2001), Adler (1991), Trompenaars (1993), and Zander (1997), for example, have thoroughly researched and explored aspects of culture related to organization, management, and business, thus establishing a foundation for the work of OD practitioners. Of the authors mentioned here, Geert Hofstede of the Netherlands is recognized as having produced major work on culture and business. He began his research in the 1970s and now covers some fifty countries and regions in his work, thus covering the broadest spectrum in the field. Hofstede currently explores and compares cultures through the five dimensions described in EXHIBIT I.

EXHIBIT I. HOFSTEDE'S FIVE DIMENSIONS OF CULTURE

1. Power distance (large, small): issues and attitudes around the use and acceptability of formal power
2. Uncertainty avoidance (strong, weak): the tendency toward fixed or flexible structures
3. Individualism-collectivism: individual choice versus collective norms
4. Masculinity-femininity: assertive performance versus modest contribution
5. Long-term and short-term orientation: perseverance versus speed

Source: Hofstede (2001).

Hofstede's dimensions are useful as a guide to issues at the border of another culture and helpful in explaining the experience as one works in other cultures. For example, applying the dimensions to the mini-case that opened this chapter yields relevant and interesting information about Sweden (Adam's home culture) and Italy.

Italy is towards the large power distance end of the scale, indicating acceptance of hierarchy, inequality, and privilege. Sweden is at the small power distance end, indicating equality, interdependence, democratic management values, and avoidance of privilege. Italy scores on strong uncertainty avoidance, indicating such attitudes as 'what is different is dangerous' and an emotional need for structures and rules, even if they do not work. Sweden, on the other hand, scores for weak uncertainty avoidance; what is different is curious, and there is a minimum of readily changed rules. Both cultures score high on individualism, which would indicate an equal amount of energy in defending a position. Italy is high on the masculinity index while Sweden tops the femininity index—thus pitching, for example, assertive performance against intuition and consensus.

So Hofstede certainly offers much food for thought. Using his dimensions, both explanations and background can be found for the kinds of difficulty that arise when OD practitioners move from their cultural context to another, or to support clients across cultural borders. For travel to work in a new culture, Hofstede's simplest book, *Cultures and Organizations* (1991), is an indispensable guide to general attitudes and behavioral tendencies in a new culture. It also serves as a reminder that OD practitioners are themselves a cultural product, carrying attitudes and behavioral preferences that are not necessarily the result of deliberate individual choice and rational, tactical value, but rather acquired as naturally as the language one uses (and also deeply embedded in that language).

At the same time as Hofstede's work is supportive, it explains and somehow justifies cultural differences without offering solutions to such dilemmas as those Liam's client Adam faced. Using only Hofstede would leave Adam in some sort of so-what situation. When in Italy, do as the Italians do. But then Adam is not Italian, and changing cultural values and behaviors is no easy task.

Indeed, a useful cross-cultural exercise when training Swedish managers is to ask them to try a thirty-minute experiment: 'For the next half hour, make statements that are not honest, boast about your professional achievements, and make flattering remarks to and about your colleagues.' Groups of Swedish managers get to about five minutes before the whole experiment is called off. The requested behaviors are so alien to generally accepted Swedish values that they are beyond the capacity of a group, even as a fun exercise. This despite the fact that these same managers, a few minutes earlier, were claiming that 'business is business' and beyond such abstractions as 'culture'; that employees are morally bound to espouse the work ethic of their employers, no matter what; and other such rationalizations. Values such as honesty, modesty, and moderation are so deeply embedded in Swedishness that it becomes impossible to devalue them.

So even though knowledge and understanding of the other culture supports orientation to what is new and different, it does not naturally follow that OD practitioners can—or will want to—adapt their behavior. Knowing that traders in the Old City of Jerusalem, or the Carpet Market in Jaffa, for example, all like to haggle over prices (and expect to) does not necessarily mean that the visitor simply adapts and does the same. It will never be 'the same.' Many foreigners in this situation become so focused on haggling and not being conned that they could spend all day negotiating and walk away without the object they so wanted to have. In other words, changing the behaviors of a lifetime, embedded in our primary cultural context, is no easy task. Even if we try it, we may simply find ourselves second-class members of the new culture, functioning below our capacity.

This leads to the concept of boundaries.

Boundaries

For Gestalt-trained OD practitioners, the concept of boundary is a central theoretical and methodological frame of reference. The contact boundary is where organism and environment meet and exchange influence on each other. Change occurs at this boundary as influence is exchanged, responded to, rejected or integrated. A practitioner is an organism with the client as environment and at the same time is environment for the client as organism. OD practitioners must attend very carefully and with as much awareness as possible to the exchanges at the boundary of practitioner and client, to the flow of influences, and to what supports an appropriately permeable or rigid boundary. Discussion of other boundary issues follows, but first, a brief diversion.

Other Cultural Dimensions: The Issue of Identity

Hofstede—and to a lesser extent Trompenaars—have explored culture and applied their findings to organization and management, but there is still much to be learned from the social psychology perspective. Both Hofstede and Trompenaars include the continuum individualism–collectivism in their conceptual structures. In his more recent work, Hofstede now includes "the family" as a metaphor for a specific combination of scores on his dimensions. This reflects work done from a more anthropological or social psychology perspective, which generally emphasizes three perspectives, all connected to finding and maintaining a sense of identity (Sedikides and Brewer, 2001; Smith and Bond, 1993; Lonner and Malpass, 1994). These perspectives are individualism, familism, and collectivism. Two of them, individualism and collectivism, are also well established cultural constructs. Familism was introduced by Annick Sjögren (1990), a French ethnologist resident, who has conducted research in Sweden for many years. This construct is also used by Marin (1994), though named "familialism." These identity constructs, a brief description of core issues in each construct, and examples taken from the literature of where they apply are shown in EXHIBIT 2.

EXHIBIT 2. DIMENSIONS OF CULTURE AND
CORE ISSUES OF IDENTITY

INDIVIDUALISM: identity is self-defined, also interpersonally defined. Membership of any sort is largely voluntary, and often strategically chosen. (United States, Australia, United Kingdom, Northern Continental Europe.)

FAMILISM: identity is defined by family membership, family status, sibling position, and responsibilities. Other memberships are usually in the context of family. (Jewish tradition, Mediterranean area, Arab cultures, Iran.)

COLLECTIVISM: identity is in group membership, which becomes a 'given'. Group is embedded in the larger social collective. (Japan, Korea.)

EMBEDDED FAMILISM: the family is embedded in other social structures (for example, clan, tribe, ethnic group), which are in turn embedded in the collective of an ethnic group in a defined geographical area. Or the family is embedded in segregated social strata. (West, South, and East Africa, China, India.)

These macro-level constructs are a solid ground for distinctions in cross-cultural attitudes and behaviors in organizations. It is immediately noticeable that the OD industry, both theoretically and through countless publications and training programs, originates in individualistic cultures. People from embedded familistic and collectivistic cultures have, for example, little or no need for training in group membership and leadership along individualistic lines. They behave in cultures where much about groups is given and accepted as the cultural norm. Personal suboptimization in a group setting is also normal, rather than an individual choice in a strategic context as it can be in more individualistic cultures.

Consequently models of, say, group development and dynamics, grounded in one cultural context, may not necessarily be equally valid in others. For example, in working with a multicultural student group, the variety of reactions and competencies displayed when students are assigned project groups is fascinating—and culturally congruent. Any attempt to indiscriminately apply Anglo-Saxon or Western developmental and leadership models fails dismally—and I have tried them all! As a result, I now work from the constructs of individualism, familism and collectivism and find that most students are more able and willing to relate to them.

Identity as a boundary issue

The 'environmental other'—and therefore the shared boundary—varies in subtle and meaningful ways across the constructs of individualism, familism, and collectivism as applied to cultures. It is common in U.S. OD literature to talk of 'levels of system' (see, for example, Huckabay, 1992). They are usually given as individual, interpersonal, subgroup, and group as a whole, and interventions are aimed at a specific level in the context of the work. In familistic and collectivistic cultures, the individual or interpersonal level is not always appropriate. Similarly, in strongly individualistic cultures, subgroup and group-as-a-whole interventions are often quickly individualized. In Denmark, for example, just about all group and organizational issues are quickly focused on interpersonal-level exchanges. People from Denmark can cognitively grasp systemic concepts, but their natural tendency is to personalize and individualize systemic issues.

Clearly, if identity is self-chosen and interpersonally developed, as in individualistic cultures, then the preferred contact boundary is individual and other individual or individuals. In the cultures of familism, there is a private, individual–family boundary. The social and work-related boundary is more likely to be family (member)–environment. The Irish are a culture of strong familism, tinged with colorful shades of individualism. Irish people—especially perhaps men—can therefore find themselves quite at home in Italy, and even more so in Israel.

I have already mentioned my homecoming twice a year to a Milan hotel, where the same staff has been there now for at least seven years. Being part of the hotel family, as a regular visitor with a two-to-three-week stay, confers some privileges (the occasional complimentary brandy in the bar). It also brings obligations not to have too many troublesome requests, and absolutely no demands (a small price to pay for feeling at home!). In Italy there is also a difference between what is said in an office and what is said at the dinner table in someone's home—in a family context. Luigi Barzini writes that anything said in public in Italy is probably not true (Barzini, 1983). However, since all Italians know this, no one is fooled—except perhaps some honest Northern Europeans who are more used to believing and trusting in everything they hear in a business and organizational context.

With embedded familism, then, we may be meeting the family as clan members, the clan as tribal members, and so forth. In discussing work with a Ghanaian colleague, I was reminded of the need to see the family and clan context of any decisions or proposals I wished to make. Similarly, in Iran the family is the primary environmental other, embedded in the rich ethnic tapestry of being Iranian. For example, I was asked out by one of my clients there to have dinner with him, his wife, and their daughter, aged fourteen. My client specifically asked me to speak English with his daughter and help her with her grammar. As we passed a music store, and I asked the daughter to help me choose a CD by an Iranian musician who was popular with Iranians of her age. My client insisted on making the purchase, and from that moment on our relationship became open and sound.

The cultures of collectivism have the group as the core organism or environment. I well remember a Japanese CEO who asked me to work with his management team. I asked him what he wanted to get from the consultancy. He replied: "We need... What we want is ..." His identity lay not in having a distinct, individual opinion; as a CEO it lay in responsibly representing his group.

Before applying this boundary concept to the mini-case, there are two more ingredient to this recipe for cross-cultural OD: context and communication.

Context and Communication

Edward Hall (1973, 1976, and 1990) introduced the concept of 'high context' and 'low context' cultures, specifically in relation to communication. By high context he means cultures where most of the meaning of a communication is in the cultural context; the participants respond to a shared meaning-making. In low context cultures, each speaker needs to be explicit about the intended meaning of a communication. This is highly relevant to international OD work and facilitation in both homogeneous and heterogeneous cultural settings.

In other words, when facilitators work with homogeneous groups from a high context culture other than their own, they can expect that much of what is happening will be beyond their comprehension. This certainly reflects my experience in Italy, and more so in Finland. Who knows when yes actually means yes and not maybe, who knows, not on your life, or even if I feel like it at the time? In Finland, silence is almost a norm. Anything spoken is expected to be meaningful, accurate, and necessary. In the research mentioned earlier by Zander, Finnish leadership style was characterised as 'silent coaching': if your boss says nothing to you, then you are doing fine!

As OD practitioners, we need to remember that our discipline is grounded in low-context cultures of individualism, where being explicit is the cultural norm. Let us not apply this as a universal norm.

Borders, Boundaries, Context, and the Mini-case

We now return to the beginning and explore the case of Adam Svensson in Italy from all of the perspectives brought up in this chapter. The border issue is clear: Adam is in Italy, and this is an Italian company, located in an Italian township.

Boundary issues can now be added to the information previously derived from Hofstede. Adam is individually oriented, tending toward good interpersonal interactions (for example, with his secretary, and—as he tells Liam—with his assistant, an Italian and longtime employee). There is also the boundary of managing up through a somewhat symbolic Italian former owner to a U.S.-based headquarters. This latter boundary would be satisfactorily interpersonal for both Adam and his U.S. manager. Both can also handle low-context communication, though Adam may not be as used to it as his U.S. manager. With his Italian CEO, Adam is a little lost. Strongly paternalistic, very high-context (and the context is Italy), mildly hierarchical—all of these things add up to confuse Adam. He can see them, he is not surprised by them, and he does not know what to say or do in a way that will influence any change.

Adam and Liam had a good relationship. Liam had, at this time, lived in Sweden for more than twenty years, lectured and consulted in fluent though accented Swedish, and worked in Adam's former company for many years as a consultant and trainer. Liam had also previously worked for two Italian companies and was lecturing in master's programs at an Italian business school. These factors combined to give them great permeability at their shared boundary. They could pool their resources and experience and look for creative solutions.

They reached a quick agreement around the fact that, yes, this is Italy, and they both know that this is how Italian organizations tend to be. Likewise, they both know that Adam is used to—and prefers—a more egalitarian, democratic, and personal leadership style. He needs to know 'his people.' He desires casual and flexible access to the factory floor. He requires the sense of hands-on leadership that this gives him. He also knows that this is his Swedishness talking, in an Italian context.

Switching from the border to the boundaries: the border between Sweden and Italy is as it is; the crossing has its difficulties. What boundaries were there for Adam to explore, where influence could be exercised and change could occur?

Liam went for family. His proposal was that Adam, his wife, and their daughter could begin frequenting the restaurants and cafés of the town at weekends. Adam could involve his secretary, and also his assistant, in selecting a choice of places 'where ordinary Italian families eat.' Adam and his wife wanted to practice their Italian, and get to know the customs of the area. Adam and Liam were both well aware that Adam's secretary and assistant would probably recommend establishments run by their relations (at the same time, they would not short-change him). After all, he was formally their superior in a hierarchical structure. Liam's thinking was this: as Adam and family moved around the town, they would inevitably be seen, noticed, and greeted, however briefly and informally, by 'his people.' He would get to know their faces, recognize them at work, and find it easy to make contact with particular people on the factory floor if he had, just the Sunday before, sat at a table adjoining them and their family for lunch.

In terms of communication, Adam now moved to a form that was nonverbal and very high-context: his family was communicating with the environment, in a language (family) that the Italian environment could understand. Adam moved from being a distant figure on the executive floor to a man in the family out for lunch.

Needless to say, the restaurants recommended included one that was frequented by the CEO and family, and another by the assistant and family. Within three months, Adam found that he was well on the way to resolving his dilemma as well as establishing an easier social relationship with his CEO.

So Adam was apparently out of the woods. But probably heading into the trees! Liam's work was not finished. Since Liam already knew Adam's family well from having met socially in Sweden, he arranged to meet them all at their home in Italy.

Liam's concerns were around two main issues. One is that Swedes in general do not easily nor readily mix their private lives with their work. He expected that Birgitta, Adam's wife, had a threshold for how much she would be willing to use family lunches for Adam's business purposes. Adam would support her in this matter. The second was around Adam's capacity, from the ground of his Swedishness, to maintain and develop a delicate balance between social and managerial relationships, which comes so naturally to an Italian.

Liam discussed these issues with Adam, Birgitta, and Cecilia, their daughter. They also discussed the qualitative difference between Adam being a senior executive in the Swedish parent company coming on regular visits to the Italian subsidiary and his current position as a senior executive in a U.S.-owned though otherwise very Italian company, where he was the only non-Italian. They agreed that there was a limit to the extent of the whole family's involvement in his work-related relationships, and that this limit was not far off.

Liam looked at contact boundaries from another perspective with them. He used a simple concept that looks at the various levels or themes of contact in an international context (see EXHIBIT 3).

EXHIBIT 3. CONTACT LEVELS AND THEMES

- Culture
- Organisation
- Function
- Social
- Personal
- Private

They looked at their experience of Italians (and Liam's experience of Swedes). Italians move early and easily to talking about 'in Italy,' so the cultural level or theme is a natural boundary at which to establish contact. Adam was clear that Sweden would not readily be available to him as a theme, though he could sense his curiosity and insatiable thirst for knowledge about Italy. Sweden would be both too abstract and too subjective. Subjective opinions are not highly regarded in a Swedish context. He would feel more at ease at the levels of organization and function, much more 'factual' and 'objective' themes. They then looked at how Adam could combine these with his experience, rather than his opinions. In other words, he could interact around the themes of organization and function, in the 'language' of culture (for example, 'This is how I would structure my division in Sweden; how would that be done in Italy?') and similarly for function.

They could all agree that what was—and probably would remain—most unclear for them was where the distinctions lay between the social and the personal. The private was clear for them, and they shared the view that this is a level of contact that takes time to develop in an Italian context and is often best left to the Italian party to initiate. So their shared view was that the family would pay careful attention to the whole process of contacts at these particular boundaries (the social and the personal)—in other words, everyday public contacts and possible personal friendships.

Liam's interventions supported Adam and his family in being proactive in their exchange of influence at a number of specific and permeable boundaries, as well being aware of alternatives in reacting to their environment. They were now engaged with their environment, rather than confused onlookers or detached observers.

Borders, Boundaries and Race

This chapter has explored implications of the dimensions of national cultural, individual identity, and boundaries for OD practitioners engaged in cross-cultural work. The issue of racial identity and culture is often present in cross-cultural work, generally avoided by cultural theorists, and subsumed under the generic descriptors of national cultures. The people in many nations have experienced centuries of direct colonial oppression by whites and the dehumanization of the oppressed by the oppressor. Added to this are the twin violations of the patronizing and the condescending attitudes of traditionally 'well-meaning' whites toward indigenous peoples and the mutually binding relational consequences that can arise. These interracial experiences have ramifications for the international OD practitioner that cannot be ignored.

Returning for a moment to the earlier references to working in Iran: the borders were clear and mostly explicit—I was Western in the context of Iranian, Christian in the general context of Islam and the particular context of Ramadan, and white in the multiethnic context of the variety of ethnic origins contained within 'being Iranian'. What I found was that placing myself as a representative of a cultural collective and raising my feelings as an Irishman against British colonialism co-created a permeable boundary and a cultural bridge on which my Iranian clients and I could meet. This permeable shared boundary— shared criticism and bad experience of British colonialism—allowed both parties to move beyond the more rigid borders of our differences; we could meet as we explored their cultural values in the context of international business.

On the sensitive subject of race, it is otherwise only in Cuba that I have met such a variety of ethnicity, giving true meaning to the phrase 'people of color'. My sense in both countries is that the issue is not so much that I am white but rather that I am non-Cuban or non-Iranian, evident through my comparative whiteness. In Havana, being Irish in the bars and restaurants of O'Reilly Street is certainly more important than my color; in Iran, being Irish rather than British or American is certainly more important than that I am white. In both countries, the sense of a shared, historical cultural identity is important, as is the cultural identity of the other. Not being a representative of the old colonialism (Britain), nor of the new version (United States) creates the possibility of finding areas of contact.

Incidentally, people from more individualistic cultures may see all this in terms of an interpersonal interaction; that is, that the Cubans and Iranians had gotten to know the individual, Seán. Another perspective is more likely: I had become subsumed into another postcolonial culture. Being Irish, I must clearly share the environments' view of colonial oppressors. Even as I write this, I am supporting four Ghanaian colleagues in dealing with visa refusals into Ireland. I am ashamed to say that the Irish have moved from the oppressed to the casually oppressive and to institutionalized racism in less than a century.

My point here in all of this is that the issue of racial cultures is deeply enmeshed in interracial perceptions and confounded with descriptors of national cultures. Perhaps the only path for the OD practitioner to tread is to continuously work to be aware of his or her own racial (and, yes, racist) attitudes and perceptions; constantly question, explore, and honestly acknowledge any evidence of their existence in the practitioner; and examine and own the possible impact of these perceptions and attitudes on interactions with people of other races.

Conclusion

International OD practitioners can apply the approach, mentioned earlier, of engaging with the environment at chosen permeable boundaries, to become not just proactive or reactive but rather more fully interactive with clients, more fully in a co-created and shared learning experience.

Along with OD training, OD skills, and OD competence, OD practitioners need knowledge of their own culture and awareness about its impact on thinking and behavior; knowledge of the other culture, respect for its impact on clients and their behavior, and awareness about how it may affect us; and knowledge, awareness, and sensitivity to the boundaries where shared themes and mutual influencing are found.

References

Adler, N. (1991). *Organizational Behavior* (2nd ed.). Belmont, CA: Wadsworth.

Barzini, L. (1983). *The Europeans*. Harmondsworth: Penguin Books.

Hall, E. T. (1973). *The Silent Language*. New York: Anchor Books.

Hall, E. T. (1976). *Beyond Culture*. New York: Anchor Books.

Hall, E. T. (1990). *Understanding Cultural Differences*. Yarmouth, ME: Intercultural Press.

Hofstede, G. (1980, Summer). Motivation, Leadership, and Organization: Do American Theories Apply Abroad? *Organizational Dynamics*, pp. 42-63.

Hofstede, G. (1991). *Cultures and Organizations: Software of the Mind.* London: McGraw Hill.

Hofstede, G. (2001). *Culture's consequences* (2nd ed.). London: Sage.

Huckabay, M. A. (1992). An Overview of the Theory and Practice of Gestalt Group Process. In E. Nevis (Ed.), *Gestalt Therapy: Perspectives and Applications.* Cleveland: GIC Press.

Lonner, W. J. and Malpas, R. S. (Eds.). (1994). *Psychology and Culture.* Needham Heights, MA: Allyn and Bacon.

Marin, G. (1994). The Experience of Being a Hispanic in the United States. In W. J. Lonner & R. S. Malpas (Eds.), (1994), *Psychology and Culture.* Needham Heights: Allyn and Bacon.

Sedikides, C. and Brewer, M. B. (2001). *Individual Self, Relational Self, Collective Self.* Philadelphia: Psychology Press.

Sjögren, A. (1990). Doctoral seminar notes, Stockholm School of Economics.

Smith, P. B. and Bond, M. H. (1993). *Social Psychology Across Cultures.* London: Harvester Wheatsheaf.

Trompenaars, F. (1993). *Riding the Waves of Culture.* London: Brealey.

Zander, L. (1997). *The Licence to Lead.* Stockholm: Institute of International Business.

꒜

This chapter was published in *The NTL Handbook of Organizational Development and Change/078797773X.* (2008), pp. 355-369. CA, USA. and is republished here by kind permission of John Wiley & Sons Inc. Editors: Brenda B. Jones and Michael Brazzel.

7.

Gestalt with Groups:

A Cross-Cultural Perspective

ABSTRACT: An increasing awareness of cultural differences (rather than the more politically correct 'diversity,' which is more related to multicultural societies) is raising issues in many fields concerning the inappropriateness of applying concepts undiluted from one culture to another. Post-colonial sensitivities are part of this dynamic. This article explores some cultural concepts in the context of groups and group work, links this to a Gestalt perspective, and raises issues potentially important to Gestalt therapists, trainers, and OSD consultants working internationally.

Setting the Scene: Some Cross-Cultural Incidents in Groups

I am working on a faculty team with a large multicultural group, with self-selected Process Groups. (Both the choice of self-selected groups, as well as the whole self-selection process, are examples of cross-cultural issues.) I am facilitating a Process Group during its first two meetings. At the end of the second session, a Ghanaian man says: 'This group is my family here, you are all my cousins.' He otherwise had been mostly silent, though attentive, throughout both sessions.

Another example: I am working with a multicultural student group that includes a number of Italians. Whenever any of these Italian students asks a question, it is generally either the eldest male (considered and respectful questions), the female from the highest-status family (intellectually challenging questions), or the youngest (playful, light-hearted questions). The same applies to Mexican, Spanish, and Latin

American students. These students ask questions on each others' behalf, the questioner turning towards a fellow student as I respond.

And yet another example: I am working with multicultural Process Groups in which the opening format is to elicit statements beginning with 'I want' and 'We need'. This is to raise awareness with respect to individual and group issues. For North Americans and Northern Europeans, the 'I want' comes easily, and the 'We need' is either a variation on 'I want' or, alternatively, a cognitive statement reflecting the individual's knowledge of group development models. For Africans and Asians, for example, the 'We need' statement often comes first, and the 'I want' statement is a reinforcement of it.

And here is a favorite example of mine: I am working with a group of 21 senior managers in Tehran, Iran. Eleven of them have the name 'Mohammed' printed on their Western-style name cards. It is the second week of Ramadan, and we have rescheduled the program to allow for their prayer times. The atmosphere is warm, friendly, respectful. I risk a remark: 'If I ever get stuck, and don't know what to say, all I have to do is ask, "What do you think, Mohammed?" and I will get 11 people ready to answer.' They all laugh and start talking animatedly with each other.

Background

All of my work—therapeutic, training, organizational and academic—is cross-cultural and in two languages, English and Swedish. I work with culturally homogenous groups of cultures different from my own, and with multicultural groups of up to 80 students from some 20 to 25 cultures.

I have been aware for some time of the inadequacy of culture-bound group theories and models when dealing with diverse groups. The widely-used group dynamics and developmental models are invariably American in origin and certainly Anglo-Saxon in focus, terminology, and exemplification and, increasingly, they seem to me to be so grounded in the cultural contexts of their origin that their applicability in a wider context is limited. As a result, I have been working on finding a less culture-bound ground for exploring group development and the concomitant dynamics for cross-cultural and multicultural settings.

This is the main focus of this article. My hypothesis is that a Gestalt-based model can be the support I need. In other words, a further aim of this article is to examine the cross-cultural aspects of working with groups in the context of a Gestalt approach.

Let me open by establishing some working hypotheses around the construct 'culture'. This section is followed by some thoughts on Gestalt and culture, as well as my own links to both fields—thus establishing some of the cultural lenses that color my view of my environment. I will then move into a more detailed exposition of the main themes of this article.

Culture?

A colleague of mine who researches cross-cultural organizational issues has currently a collection of almost 400 definitions of 'culture'! Since it is not my intention to explore the theme of culture other than in the context of this article, I therefore will attempt to keep such discussions open to the informed amateur, rather than the professional in the field. My focus here is on culture at a national and/or ethnic level, sometimes bounded by a common language.

As such, 'culture' here is definable as recognizable, internalized patterns of behavior internal to a bounded collection of people, and also patterns of behavior used in their external environment. In other words, the behaviors we naturally use within our own cultural environments, and those we expect from others within our own cultural environments, as well as the behaviors we collectively use in relation to other cultural environments. To a greater or lesser extent—itself culturally influenced—a person can exhibit these patterns if behaving in a cultural environment other than their own. To a greater or lesser extent we are, each of us, representative of our original cultural environments. Typically, these patterns are more obvious to an other-culture observer than to a member of the culture concerned. In Gestalt terms, culture is a primary introject, and can soon become the ground for our primary collective projections onto other cultures.

At the same time, if alone in another cultural environment, an individual may behave somewhat differently than if he or she were one of a number of members of the same culture in this new environment.

I have noticed, for example, how my own behavior as an Irishman will shift gear when there are other Irish people present, and have seen this happening to others. There is also the interesting observation that, for some cultures, a lone individual is rarely seen: the norm here would be a group from that culture.

Cross-Cultural Context #1: Defining Identity

I have chosen three dimensions or aspects of culture as being particularly relevant to the subject of groups, as well as being readily accessible to a reader not especially well-versed in cross-cultural studies and research. These are *individualism, familism*, and *collectivism*. Two of these—Individualism and Collectivism—are well-established cultural constructs (Hofstede, 2001; Trompenaars, 1993). The third—Familism—was introduced to me by Annick Sjögren (1990), a French ethnologist residing and performing research in Sweden for many years. The term also was used by Marin (1994), though named 'Familialism.' Hofstede (2001) now includes a variation of this perspective as a consequence of specific combinations of his other dimensions.

I will add three sub-constructs, the first acknowledged in the research, the other two more intuitive and grounded in my reading and experience: the sub-construct of Familism with Collectivism, which I call 'Embedded Familism'; that is, Familism embedded in a collective; and 'Bounded Individualism'; that is, Individualism bounded by the family. The variation 'Embedded Individualism' is my attempt to describe and understand Scandinavian cultures, in particular Swedish culture—strong on individual rights and equality issues, and equally strong on individual adherence to collectively-accepted norms and rules of behavior.

Here is a brief description of core issues for each, with suggestions for examples taken from the literature (with the intuitive exceptions of 'Bounded Individualism' and 'Embedded Individualism'):

> INDIVIDUALISM: identity is self-defined, also interpersonally defined. Membership of any sort is largely voluntary, and often strategically chosen. (United States, Australia, United Kingdom, Northern Continental Europe.)

Familism: identity is defined by family membership, family status, sibling position, and responsibilities. Other memberships are usually in the context of family. (Jewish tradition, Mediterranean area, Arab cultures, Iran.)

Collectivism: identity is in group membership, which becomes a given. Group is embedded in the larger social collective. (Japan, Korea.)

Embedded Familism: the family is embedded in other social structures; for example, clan and tribe, which, in turn, are embedded in the collective of an ethnic group in a defined geographical area. Or, the family is embedded in segregated social strata. (West/South/East Africa, China, India.)

Bounded Individualism: identity is in family membership (etc. as above) with family-supported latitude for the family member to individually explore the environment. (Ireland, Israel.)

Embedded Individualism: identity is self-defined, although also defined and constrained by the surrounding socio-cultural environment. (Scandinavia.)

As macro-level constructs, these nevertheless provide a solid ground for distinctions in cross-cultural attitudes and behaviors in groups. It is immediately noticeable that the 'Group and Team' industry, both theoretically and through countless training programs, originates in Individualistic cultures. In the cultures of Embedded Individualism, it is of primary importance that a method or theory is made culturally congruent, or at least culturally acceptable, before individuals will subscribe to them (example follows). In my experience of working multiculturally, people from Embedded Familistic and Collectivistic cultures have little or no need for training in group membership and leadership along Individualistic lines. (Something similar—though distinctive—applies to people in Familistic cultures; more later.) They behave in cultures in which much about groups is 'given' and accepted as the cultural norm. Personal sub-optimization in a group setting is also normal, rather than an individual choice in a strategic context, as it can be in more Individualistic cultures. As a consequence, models of group development and dynamics, grounded in one cultural context, may not necessarily be equally valid in others. This is certainly my experience. For example, working with a multicultural student group, the variety of reactions and competencies displayed when students are assigned project groups is fascinating—and culturally congruent. Any attempt to apply Western developmental and leadership models fails dismally—and I have tried them all! As a result, I now work from the above constructs, and find that most students are able to relate to them.

Cross-Cultural Incidents Revisited

To return to the end of the second Process Group session, when a Ghanaian Ashanti man says: 'This group is my family here, you are all my cousins'—and otherwise, he had been silent, though attentive—this latter behavior fits well with the description of an 'intelligent person' amongst the Yoruba, another West African tribe:

> *First, there is the admiration for the individual who does more listening than talking... (who) is believed to be taking in the issues under discussion... (this) wise person listens patiently and speaks only when all views... have been expressed. Second, there is the respect... given to the person who... can respond by placing the issue in its proper cultural context* [Durojaiye, 1993].

I know and respect many Gestalt colleagues who would have intervened around this man's silence—as seen from the perspective of Individualism. Seen through the lenses of Embedded Familism, his behavior is admirable. A further point: working on the same program, an older and much-respected colleague of mine has been called 'Grandfather' and I 'Uncle' by younger South African women.

Regarding the student group and the Italians, these behaviors are typical of Familism, with patterns of sibling position.

As to the different behaviors with respect to 'I want' and 'We need,' this would seem to confirm the research referenced in Triandis (1994):

> ...*[W]e asked various samples of individuals in different parts of the world to complete 20 sentences that start with 'I am'... we found that in colflectivist cultures many of the sentence completions implied a group. For example, 'I am a son' clearly reflects family; 'I am a Roman Catholic' clearly reflects religion (group). On the other hand, such statements were rare in individualistic cultures... (where) people referred mostly to personal traits and conditions, e.g., 'I am kind' or 'I am tired.' If we take the percent of group-related answers obtained from Illinois students as the basis, we found students of Chinese or Japanese background in Hawaii giving twice as many group-related responses, and students in the Peoples' Republic of China giving three times as many such responses.*

Again, imagine the impact of any intervention with only an Individualistic focus. My own work in such a group raises awareness concerning the two perspectives—the individual and the group—and supports mutual respect.

With respect to my 11 Mohammeds, the issue was beautifully, warmly, and humorously resolved. The morning after my comment, one of the two group 'mediators' (who was best in English, and most experienced in working abroad) said that one of the Mohammeds had something to say. The oldest man in the room, and most senior company chairperson, rose and said: 'Professor Seán, about what you said yesterday. When you say "what do you think, Mohammed?," then I, Mohammed the Elder, will stand up and point to him, Mohammed the Youngest, and say—you, answer the professor!' The whole room erupted into loud laughter, and happy conversation. 'Families, you know', my mediator said to me. 'That's exactly how it works here.'

Cross-Cultural Context #2: Communication

Edward Hall (Hall & Hall, 1990) introduced the concept of 'high context' and 'low context' cultures, specifically in relation to communication. By 'high context' he means cultures in which most of the meaning of a communication is in the cultural context—the participants responding to a shared meaning-making. In 'low context' cultures, each speaker needs to be explicit about the intended meaning of a communication. This is highly relevant to group facilitation in both homogenous and heterogeneous cultural settings.

The usual examples are:

HIGH CONTEXT	LOW CONTEXT
China	Switzerland
Japan	Germany
Korea	North America
Latin America	Denmark
Mediterranean	
Sweden	
Finland	

In other words, working with homogenous groups from a high context culture other than our own, we as facilitators can expect that much of what is happening is beyond our comprehension. This certainly reflects my experience in Italy, and more so in Finland. A favorite moment with a multicultural group in Italy was when, with the assistance of the Italians, we arrived at 15 ways of saying 'yes' ('sí'), only one of which actually meant 'yes' in the sense that, for example, U.S and German participants could understand! The Italians had no difficulties distinguishing among them—we others were regularly perplexed. The meaning of 'sí' is contextual, and clearly dependant on the perception of the Italian listeners and their natural ability to make the appropriate shared meaning.

Another favorite was the occasion I worked myself to a standstill for two days with a group of silent Finnish managers, who ended by saying (through their CEO) that their sessions with me were 'okay'—which I know to be about the highest praise possible from a group of Finns.

We need to be mindful that Gestalt, in its German and Jewish origins and American development, is grounded in low context cultures of Individualism/Bounded Individualism, in which being explicit is the cultural norm. Let us not apply this as a universal norm.

Cross-Cultural Context # 3: Boundaries

In my cross-cultural teaching, I often use Lewin's (1948) model of a distinction between Americans and Germans, focused on the individual's boundaries between the private and the public. If Americans and Germans were avocadoes, then the American would have a lot of permeable flesh around a small, hard and almost impermeable kernel. The German would have a smaller amount of permeable flesh, and a larger kernel. Lewin's point was the distinction between the boundaries of the public and the private between the two cultures.

I recently read a fascinating piece of mini-research in the cross-cultural field. Shamir and Melnik (2002) propose 'Boundary Permeability as a Cultural Dimension,' referring in their article to Lewin's work (see above). They distinguish between permeable and rigid boundaries, and relate their model to the seminal cross-cultural work of Hofstede (2001), Trompenaars (1993), and Hall and Hall (1990). Taking the essential cultural dimensions from each author's model, they apply their boundary concept ('permeable' versus 'rigid') to each end of the proposed dimensional continuum. They find that there is a sufficient match to be able to support their proposal. In other words, they present a model of cultures based on boundary issues in relation to both the internal and external cultural environments; that is, a recognizable collective pattern of behavior.

This resonated with my experience, and supported the notion of a relatively culture-free group development model. To clarify this point, let me return to the cross-cultural model I presented earlier, and add the boundary dimensions for each.

INDIVIDUALISM:	person/environment
FAMILISM:	person/family; family/kith and kin; kith and kin/socio-cultural environment
COLLECTIVISM:	person/group; group/other groups; group/socio-cultural environment
EMBEDDED FAMILISM:	person/family; family/clan; clan/ ethnic group; ethnic group/ environment

BOUNDED INDIVIDUALISM: person/family; person/environment
EMBEDDED INDIVIDUALISM: person as member of a socio-cultural
environment/environment

A further aspect is that, in the cases of Familism, Collectivism, and Embedded Familism, the person generally represents most or all of the other levels, even in that person's boundary, with any environment; for example, family honor, clan loyalty, ethnic tradition. I recently experienced an expression of this: I was working in Toronto, and received a present from a Ghanaian Ashanti colleague of a woven scarf with his tribal motif on it. Later in the week, a taxi pulled up in front of me and the driver jumped out and greeted me joyously. He recognized the motif, was from the same tribe, and simply wanted to meet me. When he heard that my colleague was nearby, he dropped everything to meet him. I felt that I had been greeted by the whole tribe.

The idea of boundaries as a cultural dimension reinforced my thinking that a group developmental model, based on contact modalities at any and all of the group boundaries, could be the culture-free perspective I was looking for.

The Cross-Cultural Roots of Gestalt

From any number of perspectives, Gestalt is a synthesis of cultural influences: from pre- and post-World War I academic Germany, to apartheid South Africa, to post-World War II USA, and then back to its European roots; a strong Jewish tradition flavored by theistic and atheistic European Existentialism, as well as Yoga and Zen from India and Japan; and the sweeping universalism of: '…[W]e believe that the Gestalt outlook is the original, natural undistorted approach to life; that is, to man's thinking, acting, feeling'. (Perls, Hefferline & Goodman, 1951). Added to this is the absence of any central and hierarchical Gestalt organization as 'keepers of the truth'. Each Institute forms its own figure from what was once one of two grounds—the original New York Institute and/or Fritz Perls later doing his own, very accomplished, thing. Out of the meetings of the various American Gestalt organisms with the environments of Western Europe and Latin America, for example, there emerged new figures in the various cultural contexts involved. Both American and Western European Gestaltists are now active in training institutes in Eastern Europe and beyond, where the same organic process of mutually-influenced figure formation is alive and well.

Groups: An Introduction

My working hypothesis for 'what is a group' is three or more people: a) defined by the environment as a group, and/or b) defined by themselves, individually and/or collectively, as a group. The group development process is essentially the self-definition process of a group. The smaller the group, the more explicit this process can be, expressed in the dynamics at the individual, interpersonal, and sub-group levels of the group as system. There is general agreement among theorists that up to eight members is a small group, from eight to twelve or fifteen is a median group and, beyond that, a large group. The larger the group, the more likely it is that the dynamics are played out at a sub-group level, sometimes expressed through what may appear to be interpersonal issues. Culturally homogenous groups of any size are likely to support behaviors congruent with the shared culture. In multicultural groups, cross-cultural sub-group issues are likely to be evident. Where the self-defining development process is concerned, culturally homogenous groups will have established patterns. In multicultural groups, these patterns will exist at the cultural sub-group level which, in turn, will influence the direction, pace, and dynamics of the developmental process. In other words, the developmental process of the group-as-a-whole will be a function and/or a synthesis of a variety of sub-group processes.

Again, my hypothesis is that models that are congruent with one cultural context may not necessarily be relevant in another. Also, these models are inappropriate to the complexities of multicultural groups.

Gestalt with Groups

Apart from the widely-known synthesis of developmental models by Tuckman (1965), working from a Gestalt perspective in and with groups has inevitably led to proposals compatible with a Gestalt approach.

Four models predominate, those of Kepner (1980), Huckabay (1992), Schutz (1958), and Yalom (1975). Here is a summary:

Tuckman: Forming   Storming Norming Performing Adjourning
Kepner: Identity   Influence Intimacy
Schutz: Inclusion   Control Affection/Openness
Yalom: Orientation Conflict High Cohesiveness

Tuckman and Schutz are widely known, especially in organizational and educational settings. Indeed, Schutz's model is the basis for a standardized group leadership training program, and is particularly popular with defense forces. Kepner and especially Yalom are often cited by Gestalt therapy groups.

Group Development Models and Culture

I have stated earlier that I am doubtful of the applicability, or even relevance, of American/Anglo-Saxon group development models to a multicultural world. The next section deals with this issue, specifically from the perspective of models generally favored by Gestaltists.

I need to be explicit about my distinction between the relevance of these models to the cultures from which they emerged, and their wider applicability. It is clear to me that people from the culture of 'I' actually need support and training in group membership, group leadership, and team-building.

This section necessarily will be somewhat compressed and highly generalized, and is not intended as anything other than an overview and general presentation of the connections among the themes of this short article.

Let me begin with a brief comparison among the proposals of Tuckman, Kepner, Schutz, and Yalom, respectively:

Forming   Storming   Norming   Performing   Adjourning
Identity   Influence Intimacy
Inclusion   Control   Affection
Orientation Conflict   High Cohesiveness

The similarities are striking, especially in phases 2 and 3, in which even the constructs are almost synonymous with each other.

From a cultural perspective, these can be interpreted as expressions of Individualistic, Low Context cultures. There is an opening phase in which the individuals meet, establish who's who at a social level, sort out who's in and who's out, and get an individual sense of what's going on. This is followed by a phase in which individuals jockey for position, becoming increasingly explicit (Low Context) in relation to each other, getting the pecking order straight, establishing informal leadership. If all goes well, and if there is the time, space, interest, freedom, and choice, then the individuals may become a self-defined group.

From a Familistic perspective, age, sibling position, gender, and family status will all play a part in the opening phase. It is as if the group members are establishing family relationships. As such, there may well be an early phase of some sibling rivalry with respect to leadership—generally between eldest brothers and/or eldest sisters, or family status in the culture concerned. Much of what goes on will be implicit (High Context) and, therefore, private. There is likely to be a strong 'us/them' relationship to other groups—unless there are family relationships between groups. Thus, there are some similarities in terms of phases 1 and 2 above, though expressed differently in the internal dynamics of the group. A third phase in line with the above models is unlikely. My experience of such cultures is that groups tend to function in a distinct and semi-permanent variation of phase 2 as outlined above. Again, the linear, sequential models do not match, nor give meaning to, my experience.

From a Collectivistic perspective, almost nothing of the models applies, except perhaps that such groups are likely to begin with a 'High Cohesiveness' phase, and maintain it. Identity is a given, as is Inclusion, and Orientation to group membership is a way of life. Influence and Control are also givens—the internal hierarchy is naturally established. Conflict is probably a breach of cultural norms. Terms such as Intimacy and Affection are also culturally inappropriate, both as constructs and as public behaviors.

Groups from a 'Bounded Individualism' perspective are relatively easy to extrapolate from the above—and are too easily confused with 'Individualism'. 'Embedded Familism' is the most complex, combining as it does the 'High Cohesiveness' of the Collective with the internal dynamics of a family structure. Again, the Western models presented above do not apply.

One further point: In Western contexts, the distinction between a group and a team is both clear and useful. In Collectivistic cultures, the distinction is not particularly relevant. Any 'group' naturally becomes what Westerners would call a 'team'. For example, staff of a Western company department might well be called a group. From this, some may be designated a team, and be expected to function differently than the group. In Japan for example, the department staff will naturally function as a team, maintaining this sense of themselves in both organizational and social settings.

Implications

As I sometimes say to my students, 1.3 billion Chinese can't be wrong—a culture with a recognizable history of some 4,000 years and a Confucian social psychology since 600 BCE. With the re-emergence of the Eastern European cultures, increased access to and exchanges with Asian cultures and the Indian sub-continent, as well as the post-colonial tragedies in much of Africa and the Middle East, it is no longer possible to confine or even limit our understanding of groups and teams to the ethnocentric models of one region. We have a lot to learn from others—and an opportunity to use our existing knowledge and experience more appropriately than to simply add it to the colonial burden we impose on others. Living and working cross-culturally as I do, I have found that my Gestalt training, knowledge and experience have been invaluable supports both personally and professionally. What follows is what works for me. It may even work for other Gestalt practitioners, in whole or in part.

I began some years ago by working on observing to what extent Gestalt concepts could be used to parallel and replace the constructs of the standard group dynamic models. The main opportunity was with the Swedish and Danish Gestaltists who participated in my '3 × 3 day residential' on Group Processes. There is enough of a cultural difference between these geographic and linguistic neighbors also to give me the opportunity to explore the cross-cultural aspects of my model. Sweden can be regarded as Individualistic, with leanings towards Collectivism and High Context. Danes are more clearly Individualistic, and more Low Context: at the slightest opportunity, Danes are likely to propose the excitement of interpersonal encounters in a group setting, and regard most 'work' as intrapersonal. Swedes, on the other hand, are known for their conflict avoidance (Daun 1989), typical of High Context cultures. As a result, while they value individual freedom (Individualism), it 'should' be within the framework of social harmony (Collectivism).

Interestingly, the Tuckman synthesis mentioned earlier can take on a culturally specific form in Sweden. While working with an international MBA Class, 25 percent of whom were Swedes, I was fascinated to see the following, in one of the Project Team rooms with a Swede as informal leader:

TUCKMAN'S GROUP MODEL

Forming	Norming	Performing

In another group, also with an influential Swede, Schutz's FIRO had become:

Belonging	Finding your Role	Togetherness

When I raised this issue in class, other Swedes thought that the Tuckman variation could better be expressed as:

Forming	Performing	Done

No matter what, 'Storming' had disappeared! As had 'Control!' This is fully congruent with Swedish cultural attitudes and behaviors.

At the same time, I was working with Gestalt groups in Ireland (Bounded Familism, High Context in a 'family' setting, Low Context when functioning as individuals) as well as with groups in other cultural settings, as mentioned earlier.

My focus was on the contact modalities (Salonia, 1992), both internal to the group and between the group (as organism) and me (its environment), as well as between me (as organism) and the group (my environment). I began by pairing the contact modalities into possible polarities, or ends of a contact continuum. This gave the following, with simplified exemplifications:

Egotism (being apart from) – Congruence (being a part of)
Introjecting (open to influence) – Deflecting (closed to influence)
Projecting (putting out) – Retroflecting (holding in)

On further reflection, and with the experience of working with the groups, I began to view the Egotism–Confluence continuum as the structured ground from which the other modalities emerged as supporting figures. Out of awareness, Deflecting and Projecting unattractive characteristics, as well as Retroflecting possible Projections of attractive characteristics can support a basic stance of Egotism; likewise, Introjecting and Retroflecting, as well as Projecting attractive characteristics, out of awareness, can support a basic stance of Confluence.

Also, there is enough of a match between Egotism and Individualism on the one hand, and Confluence with Familism/Collectivism on the other, for this particular continuum to be applicable cross-culturally. Members of a particular culture will intuitively pick their spot on the continuum as a group meets for the first time. For example, Individualist members are likely to move towards Egotism, with an openness to negotiated, strategic, and aware Confluence. There is likely to be a tendency towards a high level of Deflecting, both of each other as well as of the facilitator and, similarly, Projecting, whether silent, verbalized, or acted out.

A group from a Collectivist culture is likely to move naturally towards Confluence. This is easily supported by habitual Introjecting, both of each other and of the facilitator (if he/she is culturally congruent or aware), as well as Retroflecting in the service of group harmony.

A group from a Familistic culture will swing a little between the two until the internal relationships are settled, with all modalities in action from the start.

Awareness

What would Gestalt be without awareness? And it is one of Gestalt's Eastern roots, so it straddles the cross-cultural bridge. There is, however, a cultural difference in self-awareness, and that which is raised by another type of awareness. Here, the whole issue of 'face' comes into play, including the issue of how self-disclosure on a facilitator's part can create difficulties for other-culture group members if it is culturally inappropriate in their culture. In other words, as cross-cultural facilitators, we need a high level of sensitivity and, therefore, selectivity when intervening with any aspect of awareness about ourselves, or the group.

Our self-awareness—in the context of this article—can be about our culture. For example, as an Irishman, I come from a strongly Familistic culture, with equally strong tendencies towards Bounded Individualism. I am High Context in my extended family setting, polemically Low Context in my Bounded Individualism. As such, I understand, feel quite at home, and can function both socially and professionally in Israel, for example. Sweden—despite my 30 years of residence and fluent Swedish—is still a dilemma for me. I need to keep aware of such connections, and keep my sense of multiple realities alive and well at all times.

In terms of the Contact Modalities, I can swing between Egotism and Confluence, depending on the social context. When feeling secure (as in a family), I can Introject and Retroflect to maintain High Context harmony; otherwise and generally, I will Project and Deflect, keeping—as it were—my choice of the co-created contact-boundary fairly impermeable, influencing somewhat more than being open to influence, thus supporting my Egotism. Awareness helps me distinguish between what is what and who is who in my meetings with cultural environments other than my own.

In other words, a Gestalt-based, relatively culture-free model of group development and dynamics would have the Egotism–Confluence continuum as ground, with Deflecting–Introjecting, and Projecting–Retroflecting as the emerging figural continua of the interactive dynamics, both among group members, and between members–facilitator at all levels (individual, subgroup, group as a whole). In a culturally homogenous group, the ground will be structured around shared tendencies towards and acceptance of a position on the Egotism–Confluence continuum, expressed appropriately through the dynamics of the remaining contact modalities. In multicultural groups, sub-grouping is likely in terms of the structured ground, expressed again through choices (habitual or otherwise) of contact modality dynamics. As a facilitator, I need to be open to supporting these dynamics and raising awareness with respect to them, thus allowing the group the opportunity to change and, therefore, develop.

Concluding Remarks

'When in Rome, do as the Romans do,' to the extent that is possible for you in your integrity and cultural values. Be aware of how this affects you as a non-Roman, and sensitively and selectively raise the Romans' awareness of their behavior patterns, thus allowing them an opportunity to change to whatever extent is culturally appropriate. The Gestalt contact modalities offer a cognitive and dynamic map for the facilitator, applicable across cultures. A group will change and develop as its awareness with respect to these modalities increases, both internally for its members, and externally to its environment, so that a wider range of modalities becomes available. At the same time, the perspective proposed here allows for culturally congruent change/ development processes to emerge and be respected.

This is our work: to be fully present in our own fullness of person and culture, and to selectively and sensitively share our awareness with our environmental other, respectful both of our own cultural context and that of the other, and the interactional dynamics at the contact boundary between us. As Gestalt practitioners—whatever our cultural background and values—we have a stance, an approach, a theory, and a methodology that can be applied, culturally congruent, and attuned, in cross-cultural and multicultural settings.

References

Daun, Å. (1989). *Svensk Mentalitet*. Stockholm, Sweden: Rabén & Sjögren.

Durojaiye, M. (1993). Indigenous Psychology in Africa. In U. Kim & J. W. Berry (eds.), *Indigenous Psychologies: Research and Experience in Cultural Context* (pp. 211-220). London: Sage Publications.

Hall, E. T. & Hall, M. R. (1990). *Understanding Cultural Differences*. Yarmouth: Intercultural Press.

Hofstede, G. (2001). *Culture's Consequences* (2nd ed.). London: Sage.

Huckabay, M. (1992). An Overview of the Theory and Practice of Gestalt Group Process. In E. Nevis (ed.) *Gestalt Therapy: Perspectives and Applications* (pp. 303-330). Cleveland: Gestalt Press.

Kepner, E. (1980). Gestalt Group Process. In B. Feder & R. Ronall (eds) *Beyond the Hot Seat* (pp. 5-24). New York: Baunner/Mazel.

Lewin, K. (1948). *Resolving Social Conflicts*. New York: Harper & Row.

Marin, G. (1994). The Experience of Being a Hispanic in the United States. In W. J. Lonner & R. S. Malpass (Eds.), *Psychology and Culture* (pp. 23-28). London: Allyn & Bacon.

Perls, F., Hefferline, R. H. & Goodman, P. (1951). *Gestalt Therapy*. New York: Julian Press.

Salonia, G. (1992). From We to I-Thou: A Contribution to an Evolutive Theory of Contact. *Quaderni di Gestalt, 1*(1992), 31-42.

Schutz, W. C. (1958). *Firo*. New York: Holt, Rinehart and Winston.

Shamir, B. & Melnik, Y. (2002). Boundary Permeability as a Cultural Dimension. *International Journal of Cross-cultural Management, 2*(2), 219-238.

Sjögren, A. (1990). Workshop notes.

Tuckman, B. W. (1965). Developmental Sequence in Small Groups. *Psychological Bulletin, 63*(6), 384-399.

Triandis, H. C. (1994). Culture and Social Behaviour. In W. J. Lonner & R. S. Malpass (Eds.), *Psychology and Culture* (pp. 169-174). London: Allyn & Bacon.

Trompenaars, F. (1993). *Riding the Waves of Culture*. London: Nicholas Brealey.

Yalom, I. (1975). *The Theory and Practice of Group Psychotherapy*. New York: Basic Books.

Commentary I:
BRIAN O'NEILL

> *There are wholes, the behavior of which is not determined by that of their individual elements, but where the part-processes are themselves determined by the intrinsic nature of the whole.* W. Wertheimer (1925, p. 2).

The present state of physics (Einstein and Infield, 1938; Bohm & Hiley, 1993; Lightman, 2000) tells us we live in a world in which we are both matter and field, particle and wave, individual and collective. We are paradoxically separate and in union, so that our identity is fluid, whatever we might individually or collectively determine.

Seán Gaffney's article addresses this duality of our identity and the differences in group process that exist culturally. There is a clear distinction between those that are individualistic cultures (particle-focused) and those that are collective (wave/field focused). In essence, Gaffney offers (in physics terms) a relativistic quantum perspective of individuals in groups.

His work also reminds me of cross-cultural psychiatry and the work of Westmeyer (1985), who identies disorders that are culturally specific (Emic) and those that are universal (Etic). As Gaffney addresses the Emic, I am led to wonder what is Etic or universal in groups, such as the notion of the whole being more than the sum of the parts, or the whole determining the parts (Wertheimer, 1925). Are groups culturally specific and humanly universal? These seem useful questions to pursue now in the light of Gaffney's work. I also had wondered about the possibility of 'Bounded Familism', embedded in Gaffney's own definition of himself as Irish. I would use this term to describe Irish people and also Australian Aboriginal people. Many Aboriginal people (or Koories in NSW) commonly use the terms 'Cus' (cousin) and Auntie when talking about each other. They are 'family' and part of the land.

This cultural difference of Bounded Familism explains what is called the 'Stolen Generation'. The English, including the clergy, thought that the aboriginal children were being abandoned and put one third of the children into orphanages, never to see their parents again. This is such a painful part of Aboriginal identity on the East Coast that working with the aboriginal culture requires an attunement to this as part of any mental health intervention.

Gaffney provides a framework and detailed language to talk in an attuned and intelligent way about these differences. The nexus between culture and group work, particularly Gestalt group work, is now more clearly defined in our literature, and the heuristic nature of this article will be felt, I believe, for many years to come.

References

Bohm, D. & Hiley, B. J. (1993). *The Undivided Universe*. London: Routledge.

Einstein, A. & Infield, L. (1938). *The Evolution of Physics*. New York: Simon and Schuster.

Lightman, A. (2000). *Great Ideas in Physics*. New York: McGraw-Hill.

Wertheimer, M. (1925). Gestalt Theory. In W. Ellis (ed.), *A Source Book of Gestalt Psychology*, 1938, reprinted 1997. New York: The Gestalt Journal Press.

Westermeyer, J. (1985). Psychiatric Diagnosis Across Cultural Boundaries, *American Journal of Psychiatry, 142*(7), 798-805.

⨌

Commentary II:

Talia Levine Bar-Yoseph, MA

Seán Gaffney's concluding remarks start with the immortal phrase: 'When in Rome, do as the Romans do'. He adds, '... to the extent that is possible for you in your integrity and cultural values. Be aware of how this impacts you as a non-Roman, and sensitively and selectively raise the Romans' awareness of their behavior patterns ...'.

A thin line runs between one's integrity and cultural values and the other's potential imposition on them. It takes an artist in the profession of human relations to keep close enough to that line to conduct a dialogue. To be compassionate to the culture you come from, to adhere to your core values, to listen openly for what is the same in the other culture, to listen to the differences, to then meet yourself, to come back into the in-between and meet the other, to identify where the points meet...what a list, and most likely not even a complete one. We are looking at a demand that, at times, reminds me of a well-trained circus team all in one human being. Yes, it is a co-created field and yet, the therapist/consultant is in that situation for a reason. He or she was asked to contain the situation to contribute to a change. Most of the time, that consultant is expected to deliver change.

I enjoyed reading Gaffney's article. The first reason is that he addresses organizational work, which we read less about in our professional journals; the second is his attention to culture, which is close to my heart and important to constantly hold in mind; the third is his simple, inviting way of writing.

Reading through his article, I felt interested to engage in a dialogue with him, agreed and disagreed, and often regretted that he moved to the next point and did not stay longer and deeper with the previous one. I felt invited to a dance in which the music changed before the end of the song. Hence, I am left with curiosity and a number of unfinished Gestalts.

In Gaffney's reference to visiting Rome, there is an invitation to meet the other where he/she is, while maintaining respect both for 'other' culture and one's own cultural values. Dialogue can occur; a meeting between two people can come to fruition only when each party is as fully as possible in contact with self in that moment—meaning that they have a heightened awareness as to who they are and to the fact they are meeting one another, whatever this means to them. The particulars of the other's cultural values, framework, and behaviors can be learned and explored. Without the dialogic stance and a wish to respect the other's context as well as one's own, a meeting would not be possible.

As true as this is about any meeting, it is essential for the facilitator, therapist, or coach to be able to hold onto this stance, and maintain the discipline. Indeed, Gaffney touches a couple of times on the danger in assuming the position of the expert, of the knowing trainer/consultant. In one place, he mentions Western arrogance. I wish he had taken longer to delve into this important stumbling block. There is a need to pay extra attention to the fact that, when coaching others, while we are asked to add value, we are only asked to add value in a specific area. The difference between adding value by having something that the other would like to learn, and being a better person is often blurred.

It is an interesting co-creation: the need for the knowledge and the provision of it. Too often, I have witnessed admiration for knowledge transformed into an admiration of the person who has it. More often than not, the consultant/therapist has a lot to learn, too. I am thinking about the Western consultant who comes from a culture based on individualism, such as the USA, who thus comes with a track record of success in working with North American organizations. She/he arrives at a newly expanded North American organization in countries whose culture is based on collectivism. There is a great deal to learn about the new composition of the company yet, at the same time, there is an expectation to have the knowledge immediately. It takes a lot of internal strength and humility to hold onto all the polarities and still add value for the client.

Transference? Yes. The joy one has in being in this position—countertransference? Yes. Dangerous? Very. In other words, there is a locked agreement in which we observe the expectations the group has of the one with the knowledge, to the point that it disowns what group members do know, and the introjecting of the admiration—neglecting to define the difference between having something the other does not have, and being someone better than the other one is.

'Conflict is probably a breach of cultural norms', writes Gaffney. A lovely, fresh, and beautifully simple configuration of the nature of conflict. This way of thinking, of understanding the nature of conflict, invites a positive ground, and in fact sets a positive ground for a dialogue between those who are divided. It not only helps one hold onto one's own cultural context through the lack of any value judgment as to right and wrong, it creates a positive infrastructure for the meeting. The acceptance of this type of perception is a fantastic starting point, free of blame, for a dialogue.

Gestalt is a school of thought, a philosophy of relationship, a theory of 'meetings'—meetings between human beings, and between human beings and what's around them. Gestalt theory, for me, is a philosophical understanding of the relationship between the inherent, the given, and the other, from a kind perspective towards both human ability and limitations. Even though there are some models, on the whole the most profound contribution that Gestalt offers to the understanding of difference is its stance, discipline, and philosophical underpinning, rather than 'instructions for use.' The latter is for practitioners to figure out in their own creative manner. As long as they adhere to the fundamental understanding of the nature of being, they are invited to be as creative and as diverse as they wish.

Seán Gaffney highlights this point, however covertly. He looks at other models of group behavior and group development, and slowly brings the reader along towards his way of understanding groups, which is much more diverse and open to different cultures and cultural diversity. He adheres to his basic division of three dimensions, or aspects of culture: individualistic, familism, and collectivism. By so doing, Gaffney invites the reader to address group development and cross cultural work from three points of view, from three different starting positions, from a 'no one way of working with groups' stance.

This perspective implies that one model for understanding groups would not be sufficient. An adaptive way of working based on philosophical guidelines is more likely to be effective with the sum of what constitutes humanity's differences in any situation.

We could play with the more general idea that different models arise from different psychological schools of thought, and each contains the nucleus of its cultural system. That the Gestalt way of looking at groups is the one open to diversity—in the modality, as well as in having a variety of perspectives—is no surprise, or indeed, that it adheres to a philosophical stance in looking at groups, which requires that we approach a group within the context of its existence.

Gestalt practitioners are required by the Gestalt approach to address the phenomenological field of the participants. The starting point for a dialogue is the acceptance of differences between individuals and their cultures on the part of the practitioner.

Now, let us return to the use of the word 'kind', above. Understanding conflict as a breach of cultural norm is kind, a positive way to look at conflict that lacks any value judgment. I am not sure that Gaffney would use the word kind when describing Gestalt; however, his configuration of conflict speaks for itself, which in itself is a fundamental component of the Gestalt philosophy: live the value rather than talk about it.

Gaffney adheres to another 'Gestalt expectation'. He keeps his thinking about the issue vibrant and creative, as well as staying attentive to the given situation. By not having a fixed model, but rather holding onto a perception of guidelines, he stays open to the changes which naturally arise from the diverse starting points of a group, regardless of whether it is mixed culture or single culture, or which of the three aspects among individualism, familism, or collectivism is more dominant. 'Single culture' can only occur in the ethnical national sense; otherwise, groups are a mixed culture inherently.

In this paper, Gaffney writes about the national, ethnic aspect of culture. Sadly, he does not address other distinct cultures defined by other parameters such as gender, status, and religion that are present in any group situation. 'In Gestalt terms, culture is a primary introject, and can soon become the ground for our primary collective projections onto other cultures…' claims Gaffney. As much as I agree with that statement, it is somewhat unfinished. Culture is more complex than being a set of primary introjects. Culture is a set of norms, values, and behaviors that are a product of a collective history, relationships, experience, and meetings (or the lack of them) with the different, with the other within and without its domain. It is what has seemed to work ever since a particular culture existed and, at face value, it need not change. It is the set of rules that creates a boundary that defines what is in and what is out, who is in and who is out. In using the term introject, we are in danger of assuming that there is no assimilation of the cultural component within awareness. Gaffney takes the reverse journey. He defines culture in general similarly to the latter, and arrives at the first sentence above which, in his eyes, defines culture from a Gestalt perspective. Actually, 'allowing' a specific culture its own set of norms and values in its own context and within its boundaries is at least as consistent with the Gestalt spirit as using the interruptions to contact such as introjection and projection. The latter, these days, is a source of theoretical challenge and new developments in the field.

The beauty of Gaffney's approach to the three aspects of groups is that he is practicing the very basic concepts of Gestalt theory—the phenomenology of what is, the respect for the other, the perception of conflict as an expression of difference, the awareness to oneself, and the openness to a dialogue.

Gaffney gives quite a lot of weight to the contact styles of the individual and of the culture, and this choice limits his discussion somewhat. Again, within the context of his use of contact styles, or the interruptions to contact as some call them, there is a world of concepts and perceptions: the way one configures the field, his/her phenomenology, the cultural bounded way in which he/she meets the other, the dialogic stance or the lack of it—the individualistic, familistic, and collectivistic fashion in which the organismic self regulation process was impacted.

My willingness to comment on Gaffney's paper was immediate. He writes about culture and organization. For me, it was enough to read the title of the paper. My determination to look at the positive in his writing enabled me to find it and to enjoy most of what I read. In my writing, I chose a few points to elaborate on a bit, and a few on which I would have liked Gaffney to elaborate. He gave me the feeling that there is a lot more where all this came from.

I thank you, Seán, for taking the time to write this paper, and Joe Melnick for giving me the opportunity.

ॐ

Commentary III:
Mark Fairfield, LCSW, BCD

I would like to congratulate Mr. Gaffney for his reevaluation of Gestalt group development and group dynamics models. His reference to multi- and cross-cultural phenomenological data convincingly critiques the ethnocentric shortsightedness of the primarily individualistic sensibilities embedded in our traditional prototypes. I have discussed parallel concerns about the prescriptive use of group development and group dynamic models, a practice that tends to narrow rather than expand awareness of field conditions in group work (Fairfield, 2004).

What I find peculiar about this piece is the conspicuous absence of any overt reference to field theory. While Mr. Gaffney is clearly describing broad field conditions, bringing his contextualist bias to a world often dominated by a stricter systems perspective, he persists in speaking the familiar language of contact modalities and the Cycle of Experience. The model we have inherited is ethnocentric … period. I do not see how we can achieve a 'culture-free' model by merely rearranging its parts to more adequately fit with different cultures.

I think Mr. Gaffney's thinking is brilliant and his assumption that a culture-bound model is inapplicable in other cultural contexts is right on the money. From here, however, I would urge Mr. Gaffney to move to a more radical field-theoretical position, one that recognizes contextual issues—whether cultural, economic, ecological, or otherwise—as continually modulating and organizing boundary processes in various potential ways. I would push for a total deconstruction of the sequential group development models in favor of a thoroughly phenomenological, contextualist approach.

Despite my belief that Mr. Gaffney merely stops short of the level of genius to which his thinking is bound to take him, I would still underscore the importance of his work and, in particular, the well-articulated examples of lack of fit between our traditional models and the actual identity formation, communication, and boundary phenomena encountered in other cultures. I especially appreciated the distinctions made between explicit and implicit communication. Here is a perfect example of a cultural bias embedded almost in the very root of our theory, that vivid figures and clear expression are directly linked with health. Mr. Gaffney successfully recasts the trajectory of healthy development within variable contexts of culture. Perhaps the question left unanswered is whether Gestalt practice in multicultural groups could lead us to an approach to group work that does not need to rely on any orthodox model of group development.

Reference

Fairfield, M. (2004), Gestalt Groups Revisited: A Phenomenological
   Approach. *Gestalt Review, 8*(3), 336-357.

ॐ

Commentary IV:

BUD FEDER, PHD

When I began reading Mr. Gaffney's paper on cross-cultural groups,
I was immediately impressed by the clarity and perspicacity
of his effort. This did not surprise me since I found reading his last
paper in this journal to be a delightful experience. So, in the interests
of transparency, let it be known that I am one of his biggest fans.

My next impression, getting back to the paper, was this: although
the paper is convincing and groundbreaking, what has it got to do with
me? When it comes to broad geographic group therapy leadership, few
can match me for provinciality. I have lived all my life in the suburbs
of New York City, so what care I for the Arab cultures (Familism) or
the Korean culture (Collectivism) or the Chinese culture (Embedded
Familism)? All of my clients, like me, are suburban New Jerseyans.

Yet, what about Don—whose father was born in Lebanon? Or
Thaddeusz, who grew up in Poland? Or Dina, who grew up in Roma-
nia? Or Bienvenido, who came here from Puerto Rico at age 10? Or
Ramecesse, who came here at age 18 from Haiti? I could go on listing
present and former clients who were either born in another culture or
whose parents were.

So as I continued reading, lights began to flicker. For instance,
Don, of Lebanese background (Familism), defers in group to others.
Is this, at least in part, owing to the influence of a culture in which
great attention is paid to sibling position? Is Thaddeusz's exquisite
sensitivity to perceived slights and injustices a result, at least in part,
of a culture that emphasizes low context communication?

These and other questions were provoked in me by Gaffney's paper.

For instance, can every group, as homogeneous as it might seem culturally, still be accurately called multicultural since each member is a culture in her/his own right? Perhaps each group member can be usefully considered in the light of Gaffney's categories. By 'usefully considered,' I mean considered with implications for understanding the client and for therapeutic focus and effort and goals.

At this point, for me these questions are puzzling and provocative, and a bit confusing. And this, for me, is one of the indications of a paper worth reading and re-reading. I hope to see how I can apply these concepts to my work, which after all is the point of it all—the work. How can I use this in my work? I hope to find out.

༈

Commentary V:

CARL W. HODGES, MSW

As Gestalt becomes global, broader, and deeper, differences in culture inevitably arise. That is a good thing. Part of the issue is having concepts that apply cross-culturally. Seán Gaffney's article is, therefore, timely, and I agree with his conclusion that Gestalt has a stance, an approach, a theory which with attunement can be applied in cross-cultural and multicultural settings.

In particular, his 'three dimensions'—Individualism, Familism, Collectivism, and their sub-constructs—seem useful tools for looking at various possible organizations of the organism/environment field: what is figure in a particular culture, and by implication what is ground (e.g., 'personal sub-optimization'). These tools help us organize our thinking. The notion of High Context and Low Context cultures was also a good map, so that we don't get lost in taking things too personally, or blaming 'them' for things that are just part of the culture. Gaffney's work helps to correct this.

My own background (New York Institute) and training (Gestalt Field Theory and process, NTL, SCT) are different than Gaffney's and I have some differences in outlook which I hope will build on what he has written. To me the contact boundary is not 'between us' (a space, a barrier), but rather the contacting boundary is a boundary of meeting and connecting, a boundary of relationship (no space between). Novelty—difference—is inherent in contacting (!) All contacting is here and now.

Therefore, the group only exists here and now. My definition of group is more stringent than Gaffney's, and more strange. He defines a group as three or more people given an identity (traits) 'by the environment' or 'by themselves', but to me this is a 'grouping' rather than a group, and it leads to a blurring of the distinctions among tribe, reference group, department, a group, and a team. For me, a group is three or more people in here-and-now interaction (verbal or non-verbal) who perceive themselves to have a common fate, history, or purpose.

Therefore, the Leader, Trainer, Visitor is always part of the group, and with him or her present this is a new group, with a visceral change in the possibilities, exciting and terrifying, embraced or avoided. This is what can make a group a 'portal' to an almost sacred space, where that which is beyond words can be contacted, felt, spoken, and shared, together; where, with support, the horrific can be held and contained, together; where the unknown can be explored and apprehended, together, changing the experience. This is the magic and beautiful strangeness possible in group.

However, all groups need not make that journey. It depends on the agreed upon goal, which vectors and delimits the work, and on the context and the 'stage' of development of the group. For a short-term group whose goal is the teaching/learning of specific skills and information, there is no need to go beyond the 'second' or 'Authority' stage of group development: Teacher/Student is a familiar structure that is effective and efficient and doesn't (usually) require questioning or exploration, given the goal. In a longer-term experiential or therapy group, or a mature training group, in which the goal is to work on and explore the selfing issues to be met in each field configuration—Authority, Intimacy, and Termination—the group may develop further and deeper, although also be shaped and formed by the cultural ground.

We must have our tools and maps and modalities to orient us, while not forgetting that our maps are not blueprints, that our contact is not with the tools but with the each other, with the experience. Gaffney says it best:

> [W]e need a high level of sensitivity and therefore selectivity when intervening with any aspect of awareness about ourselves, or the group... [And we need to keep our] sense of multiple realities alive and well at all times.

This article is a valuable addition to the literature and, I hope, the continuation of a global discourse regarding cross-cultural issues.

⟶

Commentary VI:

Mary Ann Huckabay, PhD

In his article, 'Gestalt with Groups: A Cross-Cultural Perspective'. Seán Gaffney has set an exciting and ambitious agenda: to challenge the cultural bias of the prevailing (American) models of small group development; to present some alternative lenses in use today through which group behavior in a variety of cultures might be better understood; and to link Gestalt contact modalities (the resistances) to cultural differences in behavior at any/all of the small group's boundaries which, in turn, shape the course of a group's development over time.

I was particularly interested in Gaffney's point that, along the lines of Shamir and Melnik[1] (2002), we might be able to explain a lot about differences in cross-cultural interaction by using the lens of boundary phenomena.

First, some delimiters. Any type of 'category' or 'lens' or language used to explain differences in people (e.g., Hofstede's oft-cited large empirical work[2] [2001], following the fieldwork and theory of anthropologist Clyde Kluckhorn) is problematic. Assigning a category begins to objectify the cultural subject under study. Would Margaret Mead's Papua-New Guineans recognize themselves as she described them? I doubt it.

All categories, even language itself (Lakoff and Johnson, 1999), arise from a specific cultural context and, as Gaffney says, 'culture is a primary introject, and can soon become the ground for our primary collective projections onto other cultures.' So one problem is that any lens we use is a projection. A second problem is that most frameworks for understanding cultural differences, despite their apparent explanatory power, aspire to be politically neutral, thereby skirting the knotty but centrally important dominant – non-dominant power dynamics that profoundly influence any discussion of culture, let alone cross-cultural interaction itself. Indeed, what prevails as the current 'multicultural wisdom' comes down to who has the power to define reality for most people.

Still, choosing a more behaviorally dynamic 'process' lens rather than a more abstract and static structural one gets us a lot closer to a phenomenological, here-and-now understanding of cultural dynamics and the challenges of cross-cultural interaction. For example, describing one culture's tendency toward retroflection, such as Japan, or another culture's penchant for 'egotism'/nonconfluence, as in the United States, versus analyzing how differentiated a culture's sex roles are or how power is distributed, moves us a step closer to understanding embodied culture-in-action. And while Gestalt is by no means culture-free (even the awareness function—what we attend to—is culturally embedded, as Gaffney points out), it nonetheless has contributed a powerful and rich body of theory about organism/environment behavior at the contact boundary. And Gaffney takes Kluckhorn and Hofstede's powerful but static structural notion of collectivistic-familistic-individualistic social

---

[1] Shamir and Melnik explain interaction difficulties between Israeli and American managers in Silicon Valley on the basis of differing levels of culturally defined permeability in four kinds of boundaries: expressive boundaries—how much gets said and at what decibel level; temporal boundaries—how strictly time limits are adhered to; bureaucratic and role boundaries—how much functions and roles are compartmentalized; and where the boundary is drawn between work and non-work activities.

[2] Hofstede's study found that the variance among cultures can be best described by looking at five dimensions: power distance between people, ways of dealing with/avoiding life's uncertainties, individualism vs. collectivism, masculinity vs. femininity, and long-term vs. short-term orientation.

structure and turns it into a lively set of dynamic cultural polarities:

1. Egotism (being apart from) – Confluence (being a part of)

2. Introjecting (open to influence) – Deflecting (closed to influence)

3. Projecting (putting out) – Retroflecting (holding in)

These three sets of polarities above suggest the following sets of boundary functions shown diagrammatically below:

1. Egotism – Confluence: how separate?

2. Introjecting – Deflecting: how permeable?

3. Projecting – Retroflecting: how much gets bounded in/out?

In creating his set of dynamic cultural polarities, Gaffney demonstrates how Gestalt lends to yet another domain (the universe of multicultural understanding) a breath of fresh phenomenological sensibility by showing how someone from an individualistic culture might bound themselves differently from someone embedded in a collectivistic culture. Gaffney moves us a step closer to understanding 'culturing' instead of 'culture'.

References

Hofstede, G. (2001). *Culture's Consequences* (2nd ed.). Thousand Oaks, CA: Sage Publications.

Lakoff, G. & Johnson, M. (1999). *Philosophy in the Flesh: The Embodied Mind and its Challenge to Western Thought*. New York: Basic Books.

Shamir, B. & Melnik, Y. (2002). Boundary Permeability as a Cultural Dimension. *International Journal of Cross Cultural Management*, *2*(2), 219-238.

༄

Commentary VII:

Isabel Fredericson, PhD

In our world, teeming as it is with xenophobia, Seán Gaffney's work with groups in multicultural and cross-cultural settings is groundbreaking and critically important. The breadth of his experience and knowledge is wide and deep; it provides a frame for his thoughts about the effect of culture on group behavior. Concluding that the usual theories about group development are American/Anglo-Saxon-oriented, and not appropriate to groups from other cultures, Gaffney has developed a model that is more appropriate. He used a number of different constructs from which to view specific characteristics of different cultures, and integrated them with Gestalt principles, a model that can be invaluable in helping both group facilitators and group members better understand themselves and others. Extrapolating to other arenas, I believe that it is only by mutual understanding of one another's cultural ground that we can lessen the xenophobia that is prevalent today.

In addition, I think that these concepts can be useful for those of us working with individuals, couples, and families, as well as with groups. The better we are able to understand the cultural ground of our clients, the more fully we can see them.

This article speaks to me in a very personal way by helping me to understand some of the conflicts that I see in my work with couples. It is now clearer that what appear to be personality differences are often cultural differences. Even more personally, Gaffney's writing has given me a better lens through which to see my multicultural family, which includes at least four different cultures: Japanese, African American, Jewish, and upper-middle class American. Our different religious backgrounds are equally varied, and include Evangelical Christian, Catholic, Buddhist, Jewish, and (hardly a religion) Agnosticism. For the most part, out of love and consideration, we have all learned to be curious about and appreciative of our differences.

Although I found Gaffney's article both intriguing and comprehensive, I also found it dense and somewhat disorganized. I would have preferred the examples to follow the theoretical sections, rather than preceding them. There is a wealth of material squeezed into this one article, much of it calling for expansion. It is worthy of a book, which I hope Gaffney writes soon.

ॐ

Commentary VIII:

Joseph H. Handlon, PhD

Stemming from the author's obvious years of experience working with groups from many different countries, Seán Gaffney offers us a cornucopia of new ideas, concepts, a new theory, plus some remnants of old theories. His motivation for doing this is a dissatisfaction with the prevailing, widely-used group dynamics and developmental models which he sees as: 'invariably American in origin, and certainly Anglo-Saxon in focus, terminology and exemplification and, increasingly, they seem to me to be so grounded in the cultural contexts of their origin that their applicability in a wider context is limited.'

Gaffney begins by defining culture using well-known psychoanalytic concepts, saying: 'In Gestalt terms, culture is a primary introject, and can soon become the ground for our primary collective projections onto other cultures.' To my ear this statement has a certain Jungian ring to it as well. He then goes on to present a complex model of Cross-Cultural Contexts 'particularly relevant to the subject of groups' without making clear (at least to this reader) any obvious connection to Gestalt theory.

Part of what makes Gaffney's theory particularly complex is his tendency to connect it to others' concepts and theories, as if to make them part of his own. Here are some examples:

Within Gaffney's Cross-Cultural Context #2, Communication, he invokes Edward Hall's notion of "high- versus 'low-context' cultures. He then presents examples from his experience with different specific cultures.

Within Gaffney's Cross-Cultural Context #3, Boundaries, he makes use of the Lewinian notion of the degree of permeability of such boundaries, also considering the work of Shamir and Melnik.

Gaffney also makes use of the polarities of the contact modalities suggested by Salonia: egotism–confluence; introjecting–deflecting; projecting–retroflecting.

It is these above accreditations which have been added to Gaffney's basic theory that could easily lead to some confusion on the part of the reader—a question, perhaps, of losing the beauty of the overall forest for the tangle of the trees within.

Along this same theme of forest versus trees, Gaffney goes on to present a brief section on the cross-cultural roots of Gestalt, followed by an 'introduction' to groups, relating behavior in groups to the culture in which each group is imbedded. He then presents in some detail the group developmental models of Tuckman, E. Kepner, Schutz, and Yalom, criticizing them, as was indicated above, for their lack of cross-cultural relevance.

Finally, there is a brief discussion of the basic notion of awareness in Gestalt related to cultural differences. Gaffney links this notion to the sticky matter of self-disclosure and how this is connected to the author's model.

With respect to an overall evaluation of what Gaffney has done, although I greatly appreciate the sensitivity and thoughtful creative insight that has gone into building such a complex model, including its several accreditations, I fear that Gaffney has tried to do much too much in this paper. I would have been happier if he had spent more time simply explicating the relevance of his model to groups per se, with more specific, concrete illustrations, and left for another time the matter of its superior applicability to issues of group development over time.

ᴣ

Response

SEÁN GAFFNEY, PHD

My warm thanks to Joseph Melnick and to the commentators for the generosity of their time and effort. I feel honored and humbled by the presence here of some of my friends and/or colleagues and/or Gestalt heroes. And then, isn't that just one of the beauties of being a Gestalt practitioner—the joy of our dynamic, open, seamless, aware, and creatively lively contact?

All communication is embedded in a paradox—the potential differences between the intention of the sender and the perception of the recipient. This is particularly true of written communication; for example, my article: aimed not at a specific other but rather at a generalization of others with only some common denominators (and even those debatable, as is the norm for Gestaltists!) In addition—and fully in the context of my theme—there are the cultural conditions in which both the sender and the recipients are embedded.

O'Neill opens with one of my favorite Wertheimer quotes and thus resonates with my implicit field perspective throughout the article. Further, in naming the Emic/Etic continuum, he explicates the theme of staying with both the here-and-now specifics (cultural and otherwise) of any group as well as being open to the possible shared experiences of human beings in groups—which may be another aspect of the particle/ wave perspective he so usefully contributes to our understanding of individuals in groups. In making the Australian Aboriginals figural in his commentary, he reminds us—certainly me—of the post-colonial nature of our world as well as the relentless cultural imperialism which still insists on its right—usually in the name of God and Democracy— to continue with the subjugation of others. My sincere wish is that we Gestalt practitioners can manage to maintain a respectful relationship to difference and, therefore, desist from actively or passively expecting others to subjugate themselves to our philosophy, theory, and approach.

Levine Bar-Yoseph, editor of a recently published book on culture (Levine, 2005), warms to the cross-cultural perspective—and cools to what I have neglected to mention (gender, religion, etc.). Nonetheless, by choosing to stay with me and my thinking, despite her occasional discomfort and the attraction to themes I have neglected, she manages to give a perfect example of what I am advocating. I appreciate her support for my efforts to broaden and deepen the ground of our work by our being fully open to the behavioral consequences of values other than our own, by owning our difference and its impact rather than imposing it.

Levine Bar-Yoseph accurately pinpoints the phenomenological focus implicit in my approach and the support that our training and Gestalt approach gives us in staying with 'what is,' with our curiosity about difference, our ability to follow a process rather than direct it. And yes—gender and religion clearly have a place in this scheme of things, each worthy of a separate article. Where religion and culture are concerned, there is a wonderful chicken-and-egg relationship in which each is somehow ground for the figure of the other over time in a mutual re-enforcement process.

The Protestant/Catholic divide between Northern and Southern Europe is a case in point: was it the Individualism of the North that was the ground for Protestantism, or was it Protestantism that supported Individualism, as has been suggested? Is the Familism of Judaism, Catholicism, and Islam ground or figure? Is the Collectivism of much of Asia connected to the historical absence of monotheistic religions—or is it the other way around? Levine Bar-Yoseph also appreciatively mentions the shift to an organizational perspective.

Mark Fairfield is as generous with his suggestions for improvement as he is with his support. I regret that that the draft submission/peer review/revision process for my article overlapped with my receipt of Fairfield's (2004) article. Certainly, many of my own students would express the same amazement at the absence of 'any overt reference' to field theory, since it is one of my favorite teaching themes. Then there is the high context issue of 'doing it' versus the low context issue of 'talking about it': I honestly believe that a field theoretical perspective informs my whole article. I felt and feel no need to write 'field theory' in every paragraph. Surely this can be a good example of high/low context communication, where Fairfield and I are concerned! Happily, I can report that the omission Fairfield points to is partially addressed in a later article (2008).

Fairfield adds: 'The model we have inherited is ethnocentric ... period.' I agree completely. My point is, however, that we always start from our own cultural as well as discipline interjects: wherever I work, I am white, male, Irish, Catholic and a Gestalt practitioner, with 30 years in Sweden and 45 years of international work as part of my ground. I am NOT proposing a tabula rasa human being; I am saying that we start with who we are, respecting the other as who she/he is, and explore from there. What I am advocating is that we actively use our awareness of the ethnocentric ground of our Gestalt perspective, bracket it as best we can, and apply our core constructs to generate an open and dynamic developmental model for groups. Field theory and phenomenology provide me with a methodology for group work practice as well as for theory development.

Bud Feder, as one of the editors of the major text on Gestalt with groups (Feder & Ronall, 1980), is an authoritative voice in this field. While 'lights began to flicker' for Feder, his conclusions are brightly lit and illuminating. I thoroughly enjoyed how he shifted perspectives from the individual to the possibly embedded individual, with the cultural ground maybe becoming figural, as well as his openness to seeing each group member as a culture in him/herself. This latter point seems to me to open the way for us, as Gestalt practitioners, to consider our theory as descriptive rather than prescriptive and to provide more freedom and dynamic creativity to our work.

Carl Hodges truly walks the talk of cross-cultural communication: He manages to both fundamentally agree with some of what I write, and equally fundamentally disagree with some of my core issues! And all this without me raising even one combative Irish eyebrow! I feel respected—and respectfully different, and open to a dialogue.

Hodges accurately raises a central point for me—'various possible organizations of the organism/environment field.' It is in exactly this area, its implications and multiple realities, that I am attempting to raise my own awareness, and that of my Gestalt colleagues. Hodges rightly takes me to task for my imprecisions with respect to contact boundary and 'the between', this nonstop grappling with language that a High Context communicator like me has to deal with in more Low Context environments. However, I also trust that he knows what I am trying to communicate.

Our differences are more obvious and less open to interpretation on two issues: what is a group, and leader as 'part' of the group. Since we each have clearly written our descriptions of a group, let us agree to disagree, and hold further dialogues as we feel a need to. I do know that I have learned as much about groups and their self-organizing from people on bus lines, deli counter customers, and supermarket shoppers as I have from reading about and working with groups. However, my difference with Hodges on the second point is, for me, crucial. He writes: '… the Leader, Trainer, Visitor is always part of the group' (italics in the original). For me, the group of group members is a discrete organism and environment. My view is this: the group of members and the facilitator are both together parts of the group/facilitator field, parts whose meaning emerges as the whole field self-organizes. I know that Hodges is not alone in NYIGT in holding this view of the leader as part of the group and, therefore, I am aware of taking a stand for a fundamentally different view. Or, to use Hodge's words for my perspective: the contact boundary is me/group, not undifferentiated us/whatever.

Mary Ann Huckabay, in her closing phrase, effortlessly summarizes my thinking in this article, better than I have been capable of doing myself: 'understanding "culturing" instead of "culture"'. The 'culturing' of any group is the very process to which we attend. In a monocultural setting, this may tend towards the culturally habitual; in a multicultural group, this will tend to be a co-created and dynamic process of a charged field self-organizing around culturally embedded differences. As Facilitator, my own cultural sameness/difference as both organism to the group as my environment, and environment to the group as organism, is the pivotal point of my interventions. Huckabay's clear summaries of the contact boundary issues leave me with a sense that she has read, understood, and reflected on my article with a finely balanced Egotism–Confluence stance, selectively reported with awareness and support.

Isabel Fredericson moves so graciously from the general to the professional to the personal in the space of two pages, that I can fully understand that she finds my text 'dense' and maybe more suited to a book than a journal article! As with Feder, I find her extrapolations and applications to be illuminating of the complex processes with which we work—and live. I am particularly appreciative of Fredericson for having brought the personal and family aspects into focus, as they are very much a part of my ground.

Joseph Handlon takes me to task on a number of detailed issues, and thus focuses more on my 'tangle of the trees' (in his words) than on the forest as a whole. I agree completely with Handlon when he mentions my tendency to combine 'accreditations' from sources other than Gestalt, with some core Gestalt constructs. This was, and still is, a paradox I face: how to create a multidisciplinary or even cross-disciplinary synthesis without it becoming a patchwork quilt of ill-matched patches. For Handlon, my quilt is badly stitched and the color mismatches take away from any possible appreciation or applica-tion of the whole. I take Handlon's comments seriously, inasmuch as such a synthesis of my professional disciplines was my objective. In his case, I have clearly failed, and will re-consider my attempt in the light of his cleanly stated criticisms.

Naturally, I will also take the other commentaries into account, and try to see the forest of the commentaries as well as the trees. I find myself still open to, interested in and, most of all, excited by the prospect of further exploration of the theme of Gestalt with groups in a multicultural, post-colonial world.

Finally, I am reminded of a paragraph by Mark Fairfield (2004):

Jon Frew (1988), who thoughtfully examined how Gestalt therapy had been practiced in groups in its first three decades, concluded that 'the literature of Gestalt therapy would benefit from more written work that defines the possibilities of Gestalt therapy in groups without resorting to lists of oversimplified, all-purpose methods' (p. 93). Not much has been written about groups in the Gestalt literature since then [338].

May I respectfully and humbly suggest that this issue of Gestalt Review, with an article, eight commentaries, and a response from the author, all on the subject of Gestalt with groups, is a meaningful step in the right direction?

References

Fairfield, M. (2004). Gestalt Groups Revisited: A Phenomenological Approach, *Gestalt Review, 8*(3):336-357.

Feder, B. & Ronall, R. (1980/1994). Beyond the Hot Seat—Gestalt Approaches to Group. Highland, NY, USA: Gestalt Journal Press.

Gaffney, S. (2008). On Borders and Boundaries. In M. Brazzel & B. Jones (eds.), *The NTL Handbook on Organization Development and Change: Principles Practice and Perspectives* (pp. 355-369). San Francisco: Jossey-Bass.

Gaffney, S. (2006). Gestalt with Groups—A Developmental Perspective. *Gesalt Journal of Australia and New Zealand 2*(2), pp. 6-28.

Levine Bar-Yoseph, T. (2005). *The Bridge: Dialogue Across Cultures.* New Orleans: Gestalt Institute Press.

సా

This article was published in the *Gestalt Review* (2006), Vol.10(3) pp. 205-219, and is reproduced here by kind permission of the editor, Joseph Melnick.

8.

Gestalt with Groups:

A DEVELOPMENTAL PERSPECTIVE

ABSTRACT: In an earlier article (Gaffney 2006), my figure was the cross-cultural perspective of Gestalt with groups, and a proposal for a group-work model and methodology grounded in basic Gestalt theory, applicable across cultures for the internationally active Gestalt practitioner. Focusing on that figure left me with a lot of structured ground, themes I had chosen to bracket my interest in, and excitement with a charged cross-cultural figure. In this current article, my aim is to revisit and restructure the Gestalt ground of my thinking, and to further explore a number of clear figures where Gestalt with groups is concerned.

Introduction

Over many years, working more and more with Gestalt groups—therapy, personal development, therapist training, Organisational and Systems Dynamics (OSD) training, supervision both clinical and organisational—I have become increasingly interested in finding a working and theoretical perspective more explicitly congruent with the Gestalt theory I teach. I have found it confusing and even unnecessary to use *non-Gestalt* developmental models from group dynamics, psycho-dynamics and other sources when working with Gestalt groups—most especially training groups. I have also found it just as odd to work only from a here-and-now methodology, when change in the group over time is so apparent. My sense is that:

- here-and-now group dynamics are embedded in the then-here-now-next of a group's developmental process.

— this process is the context which can both broaden and deepen the significance of here-and-now dynamics.

These two issues are the core concerns of this article.

With the proposal outlined here, I do not intend to ignore or devalue contributions from group dynamics, psychodynamics, systemic theories or any other source of group theory and developmental models. I am simply looking for a theory-base and methodology that is fully supported by a Gestalt perspective, and can be useful for any Gestalt practitioner, grounded in his/her Gestalt training. I am assuming here that any Gestalt training will tend to cover such core constructs as awareness, contact boundary and contact styles or functions or modalities or interruptions or disturbances, as well as aspects of field theory.

Basics—what is a group?

My working hypothesis is this: three or more people, connected in space and time, who

1. are defined by an environment as *a group* and/or
2. who define themselves—at any or all system levels (see below)— as *a group*.

I propose these as the basic elements—the social group. All other issues, such as shared purpose, task etc. I regard as *added extras* in specific contexts, providing additional complexity and working foci—the work group. Simply put, the smallest unit of a social group is a person; that of a work group is both a person and a functional role, with the latter generally more likely to be in focus. A therapy group, for example, would here be a social group with individual purposes, rather than a work group with an externally assigned shared task with functional work-roles related to the task. A therapist training group might move from one to the other over time depending on the extent to which its members saw becoming therapists as a shared or individual purpose and task.

I am proposing that group development (change over time) is:

1. primarily in the realm of the social group and
2. that this development is an internally generated implicit task and
3. that functional roles may be both assumed and assigned in the implicit response to this task.

Where group development is concerned, *group self-definition* is to me the existential heart of the matter, the process over time of the group self-defining itself as such along with individual group-members' awareness of this process and its impact on them.

The group dynamics are how the process expresses itself at any given moment in group behaviours at all levels of complexity: personal, interpersonal, sub-group, group-as-a-whole, group + facilitator and group/environment (and, where relevant, purpose, task and other specifics of the setting).

To understand and relate to the group, I use two constructs: gestalt-of-the-group (or group gestalt for short), as well as *actual group*. The *actual group* is the specific gathering of persons in the room; the *group gestalt* is the wholeness which is more than and different from the sum of the persons, the wholeness that gives meaning to the parts in Gestalt psychology.

In other words the developmental process of the *group gestalt* over time gives meaning to the in-the-moment dynamics of the *actual group*. This is elaborated on later in this article.

Gestalt theory and groups

First, I will give a very brief and necessarily limited review of Gestalt theory as I see its relevance to groups. Because of space restrictions, this section assumes prior knowledge by the reader, both of the concepts referred to, and their sources. (Please see under *Recommended Reading* for further details.) I will then propose a mixture of a developmental model and methodology.

(When teaching, I usually use the heading '*as if*' above all models and theories. It is *as if* this or that model says something concrete or meaningful beyond its value as a metaphor for lived experience. What metaphors may lack in theoretical stringency, they more than compensate for with the creative freedom we can take with them without losing a recognisable core of shared meaning. So, please feel free to read what follows *as if*—in other words, not so much as accurate statements of abstract theorising, more as metaphors for the rich complexity of our work.)

Organism/environment

- contact boundary
- change occurring at the contact boundary
- contact modalities

From one perspective, the facilitator is organism, with the group gestalt *and* actual group as environment; from the other, the group gestalt and actual group are the organisms, with each other and the facilitator as environments.

They meet and exchange influence on each other as they co-create their contact boundary, by and in their interactions. This leads to change for both. The Gestalt contact modalities (and/or styles/functions etc.) are the interactive dynamics of the organism/environment field. Some of the full complexity involved here is treated under the next heading.

Field theory

- the life-space
- $B = f(P + E)$
- forces of the field
- self-organizing around the 'need'

I see the life-space construct as another perspective on organism environment. The behaviour (B) of both facilitator and group-as-a-whole (*gestalt/actual*) is a function (f) of who they are in the moment (P) in relation to the other (E). The interplay of the forces of the field thus created is the dynamics of the relationship. Given space and time, these forces will continually self-organize around whatever need is emerging as figure from the ground of the relationship.

At the same time, there is the full complexity of each person in the *actual group* having—

1. each other person

2. each dyad/triad or subgroup

3. all others together

4. the *group gestalt*

5. the facilitator and

6. external others, as the environment of their personal life-space.

Each person in the group is thus involved in the intertwining complexities of multiple life-spaces at any one time. In addition, there are the sub-group and inter-sub-group dynamics—the social life-space—which are the key to understanding the change process of the group. Dynamics at individual, interpersonal and sub-group levels of group both co-create and represent the forces of the field of the group, around which this self-organising internal to the group occurs. Tracking the forces of the field of the group is an essential aspect of group facilitation from this perspective, as well as tracking the forces of the facilitator/group field.

This also means tracking the shifting energies of the *what is* of the actual group (= the group dynamics) in the context of the continuous *becoming* (need?) of the *group gestalt* (= the developmental process). In doing this, the *time-space* continuum (see below) may also become figural as I make sense of the journey from here-and-then to here-and-now and await the here-and-next shift towards a new here-and-now.

Levels of system

- group-as-a-whole + leader + environment

- group-as-a-whole + leader

- group-as-a-whole
- sub-group
- interpersonal
- personal

The group as a system can be related to at each, any and all of the above levels of complexity. Gestalt practitioners traditionally focus on the personal and interpersonal, and there is some confusion about what is meant by group-as-a-whole. While this term is generally used in group dynamics and systemic models to denote the collective of the group participants, such established Gestalt practitioners as Bud Feder (undated) and Carl Hodges (Hodges 2006) include the facilitator in this construct.

Based on a) my proposed definition of a group and b) the organism/ environment construct and my use of it—both outlined above—I see the participant collective as the *group-as-a-whole* and the group thus defined + facilitator as a discrete field, in which both the group-as-a-whole *and* the facilitator are embedded. From this perspective, the facilitator is a force of the group/facilitator field rather than a part of the group.

My proposal is, further, that sub-group dynamics are those to which we as facilitators need to attend to more intentionally, and also that what can present as personal or interpersonal may just as easily be sub-group dynamics. Sub-groups are both explicit and implicit, visible and invisible, voiced and silent. Whatever occurs in the group, members respond to in some way. They agree, support, disagree, are indifferent to, don't notice—whatever, but respond they do. These responses become the structured ground from which figures emerge as energies of the field, and support the possible emergence of both implicit and explicit sub-groups.

Figure/ground

- the structured ground
- figure formation/destruction

The actual collection of persons in the room is the ground from which the figure of the group gestalt emerges. With any specific collection of persons, there will be a structuring of the ground specific only to them. The emerging figures will also be specific, both in the dynamics involved as expressions of the group gestalt developmental process, and that process itself. At the same time, the developmental process may have sufficient similarities from group to group to support the proposal of a generic Gestalt group developmental model. This latter point is the main focus of this article.

Contact cycle/cycle of experience

   –   as ground/figure/ground model

The cycle begins with withdrawal/rest from a previous gestalt formation and destruction cycle, to a new contact/change process, to another withdrawal/rest, or, in other words, from ground to figure to ground— now enriched by the resolution of the figure in the action of contact/ change. The structured ground of the group now carries the experience and impact of previous group figures. When the contact/change process around any figure is *finished* (possibly meaning change and resolution), then that particular figure is unlikely to re-emerge, unless in an energised variation in the cyclical group development process. If the contact/change process is *unfinished*, then the ground may structure around supporting its energised re-emergence, or alternatively, around the energised figure of not finishing the contact/change process of the *unfinished* figure.

Space and time

   –   here and then

   –   here and now

   –   here and next

   –   there and then

   –   there and now

   –   there and next

The *group gestalt* is always, in its becoming, both here-and-now (present) and here-and-next (immediate future), probably attracted by there-and-next (possible future). The actual group, its sub-groups and members, can choose to be anywhere and everywhere on the then-now-next and here-there continua. Sub-groups can sometimes represent different space/time dimensions, with the field of the group organising around these as forces. This is one of the natural tensions between the actual group (these persons in this room), and the *group gestalt* as the becoming possible wholeness. (For an example of this in action, see later under *The model in practice.*)

Self and its aspects

- personality

- ego

- id

The *group gestalt* is another way of saying *group self*. A group has a personality, certainly an ego, and much that is outside of its awareness at any and all system levels (id). The wholeness (self) emerges dynamically at the facilitator/group contact-boundary, influencing all aspects of the self just as explicit changes in any aspect will influence the wholeness of the group self.

Awareness

Awareness for the organism is sensory/proprioceptive. This I call *sensory awareness*. There is an energy shift as a figure emerges from the ground, impacted by to what extent this figure is self-energised (figural awareness). For a group, awareness of its own process as a whole is generally retroactive (*reflective awareness*) through the meaning its members make of shared recent experience, including the multiple realities of personal experiences. The facilitator's sensory and figural awareness at the facilitator/group contact boundary is likely to differ from that of any individual or individuals of the group, especially when the group gestalt, as well as the actual group, is perceived as the environmental other of the facilitator.

Openly sharing and exploring these figures is a core aspect of the proposed methodology, and this will be more fully treated and exemplified later in the article.

Contact

Contact occurs dynamically at the co-created boundary of organism/ environment, or person/environment, or self/other, or I/not I—all metaphorical variations on the same theme.

Contact *resistances* and/or *interruptions* and/or *styles* and/or *functions* and/or *modalities*—while Gestalt practitioners may make distinctions between each of these perspectives, there is at least some consensus around what *they* are: PHG (1951/1994) proposes confluence, egotism, introjection, retroflection and projection. The Polsters (Polster E. and Polster M., 1973) proposed deflection, which became widely accepted.

Awareness and *contact* are core Gestalt concepts, and my proposal is based on making connections between them. What if each contact modality is seen from the perspective of the *awareness continuum* (Laura Perls, 1992). I take this to mean a continuum from *out of (or before) awareness* to *with awareness*. My awareness-in-the-moment presupposes my preceding out-of-awareness. So, for example, I move from confluence out of my awareness to a choice of confluence or not with awareness—and in a relationship of any kind, I may well choose to be confluent with the other, with awareness of and responsibility for my choice and my behaviour. The same applies to each of the contact modalities.

In addition, I looked at how the modalities relate to each other, and propose the following contact continua, with very simplified exemplifications:

Egotism (being apart from)	–	*Confluence (being a part of)*
Introjecting (open to influence)	–	*Deflecting (closed to influence)*
Projecting *(voiced praise/criticism,* *other as object)*	–	*Retroflecting* *(silent praise/criticism,* *self as object)*

My experience—and proposal—is that the egotism-confluence continuum is the ever-present structured ground, supported figurally and behaviourally by the remaining modalities. I call the egotism-confluence continuum *the existential dilemma* for any group member a preferred or habitual or in-the-moment chosen position. Being in a group continuously tests, influences and possibly changes this position. It is difficult for any two people to be at some *middle point* of this continuum in relation to each other, especially since both parties are also relating in a complex field of other group relations. For example, A's voiced praise (projecting) of B might upset C, and therefore the A-C as well as B-C relationships, so that the voiced praise becomes a choice for A of projecting or retroflecting.

(This is not to deny or question the always possible emergence of an *I-thou* moment in Buber's sense (Buber 1970), which would be hypothetically at some fully present, fully mutually aware and cleanly contactful in-the-instant still point in the *middle* of any continuum. I regard such evanescent instants to be a rare and rewarding joy of our work and, by definition, not in any way to be either expected, encouraged, held as some ideal and certainly not planned for.)

Out of awareness, deflecting the other, retroflecting attractive characteristics of the other and projecting unattractive characteristics onto the other, generally support egotism; introjecting, retroflecting unattractive characteristics and projecting attractive generally support confluence. From this perspective, it is as if introjecting, deflecting, retroflecting and projecting are the dynamic expressions of the process of dealing with the basic existential stance on the egotism–confluence continuum. Heightened awareness supports choice around how *apart from* or *a part of* the group as environment any member is at any given time, always with the proviso, mentioned earlier, that figural awareness is always preceded by out of/before awareness.

Application to group development

Contact is the essence of group life, both at the member/member, member/sub-group, sub-group/sub-group boundaries and at the group/facilitator boundary. The group, therefore, has internal boundary dynamics and, at all levels of system, external boundary dynamics with the facilitator and other environments. Any Gestalt-grounded model for groups will necessarily focus on boundary issues—in other words, on the contact modalities.

Contact and awareness—the heart of the matter!

A Gestalt group development model—a proposal

I start with the egotism-confluence continuum, the *existential dilemma* being as an individual somehow apart from others, yet acknowledging the inevitable presence and availability of the choice of being a part of others—and that their choice is also involved. People tend towards one or other end of the continuum, and it requires a high and constant level of awareness to be open to the existential choices this awareness engenders.

Being in a group raises this issue, and I propose that

1. it is the foundation of any group process, and

2. it is always structuring the ground of that process.

As forces of the field, the egotism–confluence continuum can be seen as the structured ground for emerging figures around the development of the group, as well as its in-the-moment dynamics. I see this continuum as the core attractors of the field of a group. This continuum is relevant at all levels of system, from how the individual relates to others, how sub-groups form around introjecting others (internal to the sub-group) and deflecting others (external to the sub-group), to how the group self relates to its environmental other, such as the facilitator. In many non-western cultures, for example, the confluence end of the continuum would be the congruent place to be, and notions of individual freedom of choice are not particularly influential, as may be the case in many western cultures.

The group development process can therefore be seen as the continuous resolution of the tension of choice and response to the tendencies towards/away from either egotism or confluence. Awareness is central here. It could be said that a group develops towards a greater awareness around this continuum and its impact on the group's dynamics. This is a learning process, grounded in the experience of the group of its process and dynamics. This is learned experientially in and by the group at all levels, rather than taught, and this learning process is supported by in-the-moment facilitator interventions and also retroactive facilitator and (again at all levels) group reflection. In other words, a group of group-process experts will still have to experience their process, rather than simply apply their knowledge as some kind of checklist guaranteed to remove all the natural dynamics of any group.

As mentioned earlier, these dynamics are expressed through the contact modalities of introjecting, deflecting, retroflecting and projecting. In a sense, these are the figures which emerge from the structured ground of the egotism-confluence continuum. All are of course available at all times. At the same time, I propose that they are likely to emerge as a specific modality continuum—introjecting with deflecting, and retroflecting with projecting—as the dominant modality emerges as figure. This provides the facilitator with some notion of where the group is in its egotism-confluence process.

In other words, as group facilitator I may choose not to work with, for example, what may seem to be out-of-awareness projecting as such, rather see it as an expression of a stance of egotism or confluence in the context of the group's process. That is, not as an individual behaviour necessitating intrapsychic or interpersonal work, rather a force of the field of the group. How is it being responded to by others? Support? Challenge? Silence? How can I creatively intervene at sub-group or group level to support the group's experience and awareness? To what extent may implicit sub-groups have been formed around agreeing with, disagreeing with, being indifferent to or even not having noticed, the possible projecting?

To put this into a developmental perspective, let me propose the following as a Gestalt group development model. The apparently linear and maybe even sequential presentation is, of course, misleading if taken seriously—please read further after the model to get a better sense of what I mean. (I will be eternally grateful to any reader who comes up with a proposal for a better visual presentation!)

Gestalt group development

WITH AWARENESS

Retroflecting Attractive Characteristics	Projecting Attractive Characteristics
Projecting Unattractive Characteristics	Retroflecting Unattractive Characteristics
Deflecting	Introjecting
EGOTISM	**CONFLUENCE**
Deflecting	Introjecting
Projecting Unattractive Characteristics	Retroflecting Unattractive Characteristics
Retroflecting Attractive Characteristics	Projecting Attractive Characteristics

OUT OF / BEFORE AWARENESS

I ask you to imagine the group's developmental process as a meandering line moving up and down, backwards and forwards, round in circles, roughly from the bottom and towards—though not necessarily reaching—the top. That is, from contact modalities supporting and maintaining a basic, opening stance on the egotism–confluence continuum out of/before awareness to the same modalities with increasing awareness and a new egotism-confluence equilibrium. Think, if you will, of a group in your recent experience, and trace its path. How was its journey through the contact modalities as group behavioural figures? And where was it as the group closed?

I have distinguished earlier between the group's developmental process over time, and the group dynamics, which are expressions of how the group deals with its internal affairs as it changes and develops in its process. The construct for the process is the *group gestalt*—the wholeness which is greater than and different to the sum of the members. From the perspective of Gestalt psychology, it is seeing the triangle rather than three isolated dots; it is understanding the parts through first seeing the whole. In practice, this means being open as facilitator to seeing the dynamics of the actual group (expressed through introjecting, deflecting, projecting and retroflecting) as the parts which are given meaning by the development and becoming of the group gestalt.

The group/facilitator contact boundary

The next issue is that of the facilitator/group contact boundary. First a word about context: in a therapy group of previous strangers, the facilitator/group boundary can be *more or less* the core context. A Gestalt training group will also have contact-boundary issues with the core trainer, with other training groups and with the training institute for example. The trainer may be perceived, or present him/herself, as part of these systems—or as independent of them. In an organisational setting, the facilitator may be perceived as an extension of management, or a two-way messenger. Awareness of these issues will support the facilitator in choosing interventions.

The model is the same. There is now a shift from the contact boundaries internal to the group, to the contact boundary group/facilitator, and then the co-created contact modalities which emerge over time.

Here, facilitator awareness around the experience of being introjected or deflected, or projected upon, or being the *object* of retroflection, as well as his/her responses to each of these, is essential. For example, for those of us with a tendency towards confluence, being introjected is an invitation to confluence; being deflected is an invitation to experiencing a group keeping *apart from* its environment—us! Those of us with a tendency towards egotism may well be tempted to deflect the group's introjecting of us. Experiment if you wish with *your* preferences and experience in groups, both as member and, if applicable, as the facilitator.

A group moving towards internal confluence can either invite confluence, through introjecting us, or retroflecting for example its criticisms of us. At group level, internal confluence can lead to a move towards egotism as a stance at the group/facilitator boundary, and support deflecting us or projecting upon us, in order to maintain internal confluence.

A group with a high level of internal individual egotism can, curiously, become collectively confluent about maintaining the individual freedom of internal egotism, and is likely at group level to deflect any intervention which contains a hint of regarding them as a group; or project incompetence upon us (a very subtle deflection) to make our interventions of less value to them.

A reminder: awareness at group level is retroactive and develops and emerges more readily as the developmental process continues. This is part of the facilitator/group relationship, emerging partly from the awareness of the facilitator and his/her ability to time disclosure of what is figural at the contact boundary in a way that is supportive of the developmental process *as it is occurring with any specific actual group*. This is *not* a prescriptive or normative proposal—there is no ideal group phase, other than awareness of *what is*.

A comment here: whilst contact modalities internal to the group are likely to cover most of any contact continuum—represented by individual and/or sub-group differentiations—the modalities at the group/facilitator boundary are likely to be more one-dimensional, that is, at one or other end of any continuum. This is an important distinction between the internal dynamics of the *actual group* and the becoming, integrated *group gestalt* as the latter relates as organism to the facilitator as environment. When, as facilitator, I sense a polarised contact with me, this can be an indication that may also relate to the internal dynamics of the group. This is a choice-point: do I choose an intervention at group level, to support the actual group to further explore the themes and—if the intervention is appropriate—raise awareness? Or do I choose to report on and explore my experience at our shared facilitator/group gestalt contact boundary? My own choices are as much as is possible (I am, after all, only human!) driven/drawn spontaneously by what is figural, are always therefore experimental, and have no predictable outcomes.

Context is important here: what is the environmental other as boundary co-creator as perceived by the group? The facilitator? The institute or organization etc? If the group is struggling with the impact of its shared learning, is this new information being externalised into an environmental other? The facilitator may have to test some intuitive ideas here, based on the experience of the contact modality at the group/facilitator boundary.

Also, as awareness becomes more available at all levels, the polarising of contact modalities gives way to aware choices in the moment. In other words, there is a shift from any contact modality continuum towards the out of—with awareness continuum. As facilitator, I will need to slow down my interventions in order to give the group the freedom of finding its own way to an aware choice of how to relate to me. The facilitator/group relationship is thus becoming more grounded in a developing mutuality, and my previous role is being replaced by my person.

The group gestalt and the actual group —process and dynamics

I have previously mentioned the *group gestalt*, and likened it to the *group self*. I have contrasted the *group gestalt* with the *actual group* (that is, the specific gathering of people involved), and implied a correlation with the personality, ego and id of the Gestalt theory of self. These are described in PHG (op cit) as the *partial systems* of the self as the wholeness of these sub-systems.

In my proposed model, the group gestalt is the wholeness (gestalt) of the collection of persons related to as an entity. This is always in the process of becoming, emerging from its past and moving towards its future through self-organisation, and now is a fleeting wisp of experience instantly becoming *then*. The group as organism is meeting, creatively adapting to, and changing in relation to its environment, creating and confirming a growing sense of identity. This is that indefinable something we can sense when we meet a group, and often use a single word to describe—flat, energised, difficult, willing or whatever.

The actual group is the specific collection of people who form a particular group. As the developmental process of the group gestalt emerges, the actual group expresses the dynamics of the process, at all levels: individual, interpersonal, sub-group and the collective as that specific group. The actual group is likely to have a number of behaviours and opinions analogous with the partial systems of personality and ego, including the fixed gestalts of those systems. The id is, of course, that which is ground to the actual group and out of awareness.

Another point: it is *as if* the developmental process and the dynamics associated with it are supporting a possible meeting of the group gestalt and the actual group. I believe I have witnessed this, and it is a powerful experience. As I write these words, I particularly remember the second-last day of a 3 × 3 day group training programme with Gestalt practitioners. In an open session, some members were making clear statements about their learning, about themselves, about relations with specified others in the room, about the sense of belonging to a vague *something* in the room.

Others continued in the same vein. The comments became briefer and quieter, with longer intervals between speakers. The whole process slowed down into a long, relaxed silence. We sat in silence for some time... then the cook put some music on in the adjoining kitchen, his usual signal that dinner was almost ready. We all broke out into hearty laughter, and spontaneously began leaving the room in twos and threes. Group members still recall that evening, some eight years later.

The model in practice

In the proposed approach, the facilitator works with the process of the group gestalt through the dynamics of the actual group as indicators of that process, as well as with the group gestalt as the becoming environmental other for the facilitator as organism, the becoming organism for the facilitator as environmental other.

This perspective and methodology pre-supposes a high level of selectivity in proposals for experiments from the facilitator, where both the proposed intervention and the group response are part of the experiment. In this sense, all facilitator interventions are experiments. I also want to distinguish here between an experiment emerging in-the-moment as figure, and any off-the-shelf exercises.

In some cases, a previous experiment can become figural in a different group. I always first check my experience in such cases: am I uncertain, or bored, or restless? Am I being tempted to get myself off the hook of staying fully present, or *keeping the group happy* by giving *them* something to *do*, rather than *be*? If any of these apply, then an off-the-shelf experiment/exercise will be out of the question, and reporting on my process can become the intervention. There will also be times when the figure of a particular previous experiment returns with clear energy. When this happens, I will generally share my process and then propose the experiment. So any intervention mentioned here is not being offered as an off-the-shelf intervention for general use, rather simply as an example to support and clarify my work.

Example 1

On joining a group, a person needs to find a place on the egotism–confluence continuum. Some will tend towards one or other end of this continuum. Obviously, cross-cultural aspects will play a part here. Whatever the ground of, or awareness around, the tendency, it is likely that much of the initial phase of the actual group's life will be taken up with this question. Language plays a part here in highlighting the issue: the ease of use of we or I can give the facilitator an idea of the dynamics involved. Incidentally, insisting for example on the use of I statements during this phase is counter-productive from the perspective of my proposal, as it unnecessarily interferes with the organic dynamics of the group, especially in cross-cultural or multicultural contexts.

> *Adam arrived late for the first of three Thursday lunch – Sunday lunch residentials, reluctantly made a minimal introduction of himself, and kept to himself during breaks, then declared later during this first module of a programme on personal and professional development that he had no interest in endless, chit-chat process or particularly small-group work—he would only promise to attend focused process sessions, theory and application sessions (negotiated membership—even if somewhat unilateral). Another person voiced an opinion about how 'we' as group members 'should' behave. Yet another spoke to freedom of choice, as long as it doesn't affect 'us' and the programme. The remaining nine people were silent, some looking towards me.*
>
> *I suggested an experiment, and described it as I designed it in my head. No one protested, and no one showed much enthusiasm (introjecting? deflecting?). So I continued. I asked the three who had spoken to seat themselves in different corners of the room, briefly repeating their words. The fourth corner was for 'don't know or don't mind'. I asked the 'speakers' to repeat their perspectives,*

and invited the others to join the corner they felt most agreement with. I then invited people to speak for their perspective from each corner, and suggested that everyone was free to move freely as the spirit moved them. Some took up positions between two corners. Some changed opinion from one corner to another.

By the end, Adam had been joined by two others—one who admired and lacked his courage, one who supported him in principle and felt strongly about it. From the perspective being presented here, the group had now explored how the egotism-confluence continuum was being played out in the moment, with all its nuances. Adam found himself—and was seen to be—a member of a sub-group. The actual group now had a greater awareness of a central group issue—being 'a part of' and 'apart from'—at group level, rather than at an individual/interpersonal level (Adam/the rest of the group).

I can't help reflecting to what extent scapegoating in groups would be lessened if sub-group dynamics received more focus.

Example 2

I am here applying an exploration of the field of the group through work on a member's dream:

In the morning session of the second of three days, Birgitta mentions and briefly reports on a dream she had during the night. She is on the platform in a train station, and discovers she has far too many suitcases. There is no way she can manage to get them all on board by herself, the train is soon leaving. Maybe she should leave some suitcases behind? Or re-pack everything, taking only what she needs? Or quickly buy some new, more functional, suitcases and re-pack into them? Will she miss the train if she delays deciding? As the train starts moving, she grabs what she thinks might be the most essential suitcases, and jumps aboard, looking out the window at the remaining cases piled on the platform. She sits in silence.

Charles starts with his input for the morning session. Denise cuts across him to ask Birgitta if she was really finished, and whether she wants to work on her dream 'the Gestalt way'. Birgitta says that she can come back to it if there's time, and looks at me. Charles expresses his irritation at being interrupted by Denise—if Birgitta wanted to work on her dream, then she had the chance to say and do so. Denise responds by saying to Charles that he is always too fast to get into his own stuff. Charles and Denise exchange comments to and about each other. Eric breaks in to say that maybe Birgitta's dream was a 'group dream', and that we should work on it as such.

There is a silence, during which many group members look towards me. I ask if there is anyone else who has something to say. No one responds. I ask Birgitta if she is interested in, and willing, for me to do some work in the group around her dream. She is.

So I ask her to recount it again in the present tense, and ask the others to simply listen and notice whatever happens to them as they do so. As she finishes, I ask if anyone is resonating to any aspect of the dream, and if so, to be that aspect, in the present tense.

Eric says 'I am a platform at a train station. People use me to come and go. No one stays on me, unless it is Birgitta's left-over luggage. I am for comings and goings and left-overs and peoples' overflowing rubbish in the trash-cans. Any train that stays beside me is always empty and it's night-time and dark and cold'.

Then Frida: 'I am too many suitcases, too much. Some of me will be chosen to travel with, some of me left behind. If I go on the train, then I don't know where I'm going…but maybe that's better than being left behind. I just don't know, and it's not my choice anyway. Someone else always decides'.

Then George: 'I am indecision…will I, won't I…what if I choose wrongly, make a mistake…I hate regretting my decisions, so I usually don't decide anything'.

Then Charles: 'This is crazy. It's Birgitta's dream, not mine or anyone else's. Let her say how she understands it'. Harriet speaks: 'I always have too much with me. Can you imagine, here I am on an intensive residential course, and I have two books for my studies, a novel I'm in the middle of reading with a bad conscience because I should be studying, and some papers from work that I have to go through and report on next week. If the train is this course, then I might miss it or get off at the wrong station'.

> *There is some general conversation about the richness of the various perspectives. As this dies down, I ask Birgitta what she would now choose as a theme to explore in the present. She chooses the train: 'I am a train at a platform in a station. I don't know where I am, or even where I am going. Anyone who doesn't mind not knowing where I'm going can come on board. I'm going to wherever I'm going, anyway. Yes, that's it. I always need to know everything in advance, especially on a course with some people I don't know. I want to know exactly what I'm going to get—in advance. Not this time. I'll leave all my old suitcases on the platform and just see what happens. Thank you, everybody.'*
>
> *I asked if there were any more inputs. A number of people spoke to the richness of the process, and how absorbing it had been.*

I suggested a coffee break, which was welcomed! Since this was a training group, there were some questions that had arisen during the break about the methodology of working with dreams. These I addressed, careful to maintain a focus on curiosity and experiment rather than bald statements about *individual* versus *group* dreams—any response charged enough to resonate for someone is always worth exploring, whatever it happens to be. Everything that happens is a valid part of the dynamics of the group. I asked them to reflect individually on their sense of what had happened and what that meant to them, and then to share this with others in pairs and trios. This was followed by a whole-group sharing of what was figural for each. This gave everyone access to the themes and energies of the morning session, as well as the full richness of individual and shared meaning-making.

Example 3

This is a continuation of Example 2. The time/space continuum had been figural for me during the coffee-break as I reflected on the dream session. I decided therefore to create the opportunity for some experiential learning around this theme, as well as explore the theme as energies of the field of the group.

I first presented the time/space continuum:

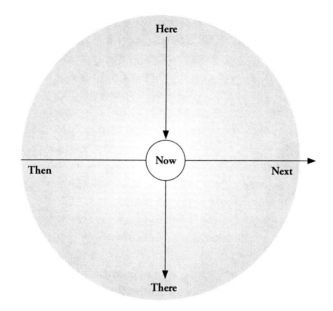

To exemplify, I used the following: we all came here from *there and then*. Depending on how strong and figural some aspects of that were for us, we may well have moved to *there and now*, or even *here and then*. On and off, we may have been *here and now* or even *here and next*. Some may have thought about next week, and been *here and next* or *there and next*— depending on how vivid an imagination we have!

I asked each person to reflect on the morning session, and as best as possible track their passage through time and space, using the above model as a guide. Again, this was followed by sharing in twos and threes, exploring patterns and distinctions.

The following is a brief summary of the group discussion: Birgitta had brought us all to the *there and then* of a dream last night, and the *here and then* recounting of the dream in the past tense. This was followed by some *here and now* exchanges, as well as the *here and now* of Birgitta's present tense recounting. We were then brought on a journey through time and space as each person resonated first with Birgitta, and then each of the other dream themes as they were presented. And also: *here and next*—this room and us and where are we heading? As well as *there and next*—people seeing applications of their learning at work and at home, following the residential days.

Transitional sub-phases

Transitional sub-phases are also involved here. A transition occurs when the central theme of a particular phase—for example, the probable opening dynamics of the egotism–confluence continuum—is reaching some form of resolution at whatever level is appropriate for the actual group at the time. As this resolution becomes figural, the first clear signs of the becoming theme begin also to emerge. Sub-groups, or individuals as the voices of explicit/implicit sub-groups, carry and express the transitional dynamics. This is an important point: as the group develops, its internal dynamics become more and more those of inter-sub-group dynamics, rather than individual sub-group/group.

So, for example, the transitional themes of the current resolution of the egotism–confluence continuum are likely to be expressed through *I* and *we* statements, in various ways. *I* can be expressed either as acceptance of a negotiated and re-negotiable *membership*, with both rights and responsibilities; or, as some form or other of *being on the margin*—either put there by others, or as a personal choice. *We* can be expressed as acceptance of the group as a valid entity, with all that involves of individual sub-optimisation; or as some form of close-knit *we-ness*, The out-of-awareness transitional themes are likely to precede the themes with awareness, as mentioned earlier. In the example with Adam, he found himself able to move from marginalising himself (and maybe being marginalised) to membership of a respectful and supportive sub-group, itself an accepted part (member) of the whole.

The *becoming contact theme* will also emerge. For example, obvious introjecting and/or deflecting behaviours, internal to the group, will be a sign that this is the next developmental phase—or voiced projecting and silent retroflecting. A transition is also likely to give rise to forces for change (the new phase) and forces for sameness (the almost previous phase) as the field of the group, as it organises around the changes at all levels of the group as system. This self-organising can take the form of a general choice of the almost previous phase, or a general choice of the emerging phase, sub-group tensions or ambivalence and uncertainty. The facilitator's role here is to support the group wherever it happens to go—the group really does know best.

At the group/facilitator boundary, the egotism-confluence phase internal to the group is likely to present as the group—in general—introjecting the facilitator. This can be active, or in the form of passive acceptance. Deflecting is likely to be passive, or even playful. The group will also retroflect in various ways, and, of course, project upon the facilitator. However, the dominant figural modality is likely to be introjecting. Note-taking, supportive questions, paraphrasing of the facilitator's utterances, laughs at his/her jokes etc—all support introjecting. Participants on the egotism end of the continuum may well show some token signs of autonomy, often to the discomfort of others—so such signs may well be followed by a public introjective behaviour by another participant, in support of the facilitator.

At the facilitator/group boundary, the transitional sub-phase may well be marked by a shift (in the example above) towards signs of deflecting from the group—breaks somehow start taking a little longer than agreed, interventions are mildly misunderstood and so on. There may also be the occasional voiced projection onto the facilitator, in itself a subtle form of deflecting. There is a slight shift in the group–facilitator relationship: it is now the facilitator begins to feel that this is work! And that there is more work on its way!

For me, these dynamics all point to the clear emergence of the group gestalt in its own right, as organism to me as environment; as environment to me as organism; as a self in contact with my self at our mutually created boundary. I feel influenced and changed. Whatever certainties I may have had initially evaporate: I am in the unmapped no-man's-land of the dynamic contact boundary of a deepening relationship, where the former social norms of our roles as facilitator and participant begin to change from the general to the specifics of this particular time and place.

Conclusion

We have a base in Gestalt psychology's perspective of the whole defining the parts, of figure/ground and figure formation/destruction. We have the richness of such concepts as organism/environment, the contact boundary, field theory, self, awareness and contact modalities. In this article, I am proposing these as the basis for a Gestalt approach to groups.

In addition, I have developed a model as a version of this approach, in plain English and easily translated, for use with groups where teaching Gestalt constructs is not an objective and English not the first language. I and others have tested this in educational and organisational settings, with very encouraging results—(and the foundation of another article!).

I believe that the model proposed here, as a theoretical foundation for a methodological practice, is more than enough to support a Gestalt group approach. I further believe this is particularly applicable in a Gestalt training setting.

References

Buber, M. (1970). *I and Thou*. New York: Charles Scribner's Sons.

Feder, B. and Ronall, R. (undated). *The Group as Fertile Ground for Growth*. Unpublished manuscript.

Gaffney, S.(2006). Gestalt with Groups—A Cross-cultural Perspective. *Gestalt Review*, *10*(3), pp.205-219.

Hodges, C. (2006). Commentary on Gaffney's article. *Gestalt Review* (in press), Cape Cod: Gestalt International Study Center.

Perls L. (1992). *Living at the Boundary*. New York: Gestalt Journal Publications.

Polster, E. & Polster, M. (1973). *Gestalt Therapy Integrated*. New York: Random House Inc.

Further Reading

GESTALT WITH GROUPS

Feder, B. and Ronall, R. (Eds.), (1980). *Beyond the Hot Seat—Gestalt Approaches to Group*. New York: Brunner/Mazell, Inc.

Phillipson, P. and Harris, J.B. (1992). *Gestalt—Working with Groups*. Manchester: Manchester Gestalt Centre.

Woldt, A.L. and Toman., S.M. (Eds.), (2005). *Gestalt Therapy—History, Theory, and Practice*. Thousand Oaks: Sage Publications.

Field Perspectives

Agazarian, Y.M., and Gantt, S.P. (2000). *Autobiography of a theory*. London: Jessica Kingsley Publishers.

Fairfield, M.A. (2004). Gestalt Groups Revisited: a Phenomenological Approach, *Gestalt Review,* 8(3). Cape Cod: Gestalt International Study Center.

Wheelan, S.A. (1994). *Group Processes—A Developmental Approach*. Boston: Allyn and Bacon.

Comparative Perspectives

Houston, G. (1993). *Being and belonging—group, intergroup and Gestalt*. New York: John Wiley and Sons.

۶

This article was published by the *Gestalt Journal of Australia and New Zealand*, (2006), Vol. 2(20), pp. 6-28, and is reproduced here by kind permission of the editors, Richie Robertson and Nickei Falconer.

The following commentaries were solicited by the author, following the pattern in *Gestalt with Groups—a Cross-Cultural Perspective*, and were published in his PhD thesis. They are included here with kind permission of the writers.

۶

Commentary I

Jon Frew

Sean Gaffney has taken on the ambitious and noble task of developing a model for groups that is 100% proof Gestalt, not distilled by adding the 'impurities' of other models from, for example, group dynamics, psychodynamics or systems theories. Although the paper is a bit 'thick' in places and will be a challenging read (particularly outside the Gestalt community), he does a laudable job of reconstructing pieces of Gestalt theory that are relevant to groups into a model he calls 'Gestalt Group Development.'

I was particularly impressed by his focus on the egotism-confluence continuum as 'the foundation of any group process' (p. 14). I have witnessed the power of this rather universal polarity in every group I have lead for the past thirty years and agree with the author that it is a major influence of emerging figures at all levels of system. I also appreciate that culture was included as a factor on this continuum to account for a skew toward individualism or collectivism.

Sean's statement that 'the group development process can therefore be seen as the continuous resolution of the tension of choice and response to the tendencies towards/away from either Egotism or Confluence' (p. 15) is quite provocative and unfortunately quite inaccurate as phrased. Non-Gestalt group development theories have made a compelling case for other 'players' being in the group development game (e.g. desire for power, need for orientation). None the less, this model is being offered as a proposal and as such the author has the license to make such a statement and to provide supporting evidence from Gestalt therapy and his own group experiences.

Another highlight of the paper is how the author integrated the other boundary phenomena (deflecting, introjecting, retroflecting and projecting) with egotism and confluence and yes, a better visual representation would be very helpful!

The description of the model in terms of its execution by the facilitator (pp. 16-19) was difficult to fully track. The appearance of the examples, the model in practice, was timely in that regard and the reader can begin to see how a facilitator would work using this model as a frame.

My compliments to the author for developing a model that stays within the borders of Gestalt therapy and will provide those of us who lead groups from a Gestalt perspective some very practical and theoretically sound ways of reading the complex map of group work.

ॐ

Commentary II

CLAIRE ASHERSON BARTRAM

Good Gestalt work is analogous to Aikido, a martial art which I trained in for several years. I was impressed with the ability of those experienced in the art of Aikido who had the ability of producing affect with minimal movement. A gifted Aikido artist appears untouchable; when attacked he or she can move a hand or manoeuvre their body and the attacker will fly away, flipping and somersaulting to the ground. The whole movement of attack and defence is as one and is beautiful to watch. The skill is a combination of an alert and aware state of mind and physical responsiveness supported by knowledge of how the body works and an understanding of balance. This enables energy put into an attack to be deflected back to the person attacking. Without understanding the how of Aikido works what happens when it is practiced looks like magic.

I was similarly impressed by Seán's group work, which I witnessed when I worked with him as a co-leader for process groups at an AAGT conference in Amsterdam. This was a small group of eight people who met four times. Our remit as leaders was to encourage participants to use the space to bring whatever the conference material had evoked for them. After introducing ourselves and the purpose of the meeting, people started talking; Seán sat back in his chair his eyes closed, apparently musing, possibly asleep. One of the participants (x) said that he had learnt something important at the workshop he had attended at which point, Seán opened his eyes and drew attention to a gesture that x was making. Immediately x moved into contact with his emotions and began a deep exploration that involved everybody in the group.

In the following four meetings Seán worked in a similar way. Eyes closed, he would become alert with a comment or an intervention that elicited deep, responses and spontaneous exploration. His interventions were minimal and non-directive however they inspired individuals to become involved in experimenting with new (to them) forms of contact in the group. He was able to tune into the dynamic currents of the group and this was the skill that seemed akin to that of the martial artist. From the first meeting this group felt bonded and people explored areas of personal importance, quickly and with extraordinary depth; I attribute much of this to Seán's facilitation.

I was therefore delighted when Seán asked me to write in response to his article on groups and I looked forward to gaining some insight into his work. However, when I received the article and started to read I immediately got sleepy which is often my response to finding theoretical writing difficult to understand. In this regard his writing is in good company; among numerous books that 'put me to sleep' is Gestalt Therapy by Perls, Hefferline and Goodman (1951). I understand my sleepiness as being my way of escaping the work I need to do in order to engage with theory that I am not managing to grasp—superficially I'd rather go shopping, potter about in the garden or play the flute. It therefore took me a while to get through the article as I had to read it a page at a time, and go through it several times before I began to make sense out of what I was reading. The third time, I wrote my comments on each section on what was being said and it began to fall into place.

This brought me to reflect on the irony of theory being conceptually complicated and hard to express when practice can be so alive, fluid and immediately exciting. It seems that there is a real difficulty in describing complicated ideas in a communicable form. The book 'Gestalt Therapy' (from now on PHG) is a good example. Paul Goodman's text is for many people dense and hard to assimilate. It contains many gems, beautiful language, compelling philosophy and powerful descriptions and it also contains paragraphs that elude understanding and where the language seems archaic and quasi scientific. The experience of reading it is for me like travelling through a landscape of verbal and intellectual clouds whilst encountering rays of sunshine, awesome vistas and bewildering fogs along the way. At the heart of the journey is Gestalt's fundamental theory of experience and contact that is, when transferred to practice such a compelling model.

I am not alone in finding PHG hard to engage with. I come across people who have not ventured into the second part of the book but have worked through the exercises that constitute the first part, where they are able to involve more than their intellectual faculties in understanding what is being presented. However, to really understand the thinking that underpins Gestalt practice it is necessary to grapple with the theory, otherwise how can we understand as practitioners why we do what we do; how can we inform our interventions without thinking about theory, what it means, whether we agree or disagree, whether it is born out in practice etc. So that we take it in, change it and contribute to it.

'But' a voice within me pitches in at this point, does it have to be so difficult, couldn't the language be easier, couldn't it be explained more clearly? And another voice answers that the difficulty is lodged both within me and within the theory. In order to understand theory I need to be open to thinking about it, if what is being described is complicated, then its nature is hard to grasp and difficult to describe. Gestalt concepts are very complicated in that they are 'boggling', like tricks of perspective, and like Jewish law continue to be argued in minute detail by practitioners with a philosophical bent. Language is a challenge, when writing new concepts words become used in new ways and acquire new meaning. The words and meanings attached to them become bound up in our thinking so that it becomes structured by the language that is given. It is then hard to break away from those words in another context. Thus in order to describe the theory of Gestalt, words are used that have specific meanings belonging to that theory. Also, this particular article attempts to condense several complicated ideas into a relatively short article; this gives the article a dense quality.

I now turn to the content of Seán's article which presents a Gestalt theory of the complex process that is a gestalt group. While assuming his audience are already familiar with Gestalt concepts he extends the thinking and language to group development in Gestalt terms. He is not the first person to write about groups from a Gestalt perspective. Among others, Bud Feder et al wrote a collection of essays 'Beyond the Hot Seat' (1980) in which Elaine Kepmner presents developmental stages; Gaie Houston wrote 'The Red Book of Groups' (1984) which focuses on technique and exercises more than theory, and also 'Being and Belonging' (1993) which describes group issues in depth through a construct that allows perspective from different orientations including Gestalt. Seán's offering is purely Gestalt theory and he explicitly is not attempting to integrate or discuss other perspectives.

A group is an incredibly complex phenomenon, involving multiple processes taking place on both an individual and collective level. At any time, a group members' behaviour and experience has different meanings according to the perspective from which it is looked at. Within a group simultaneous realities exist, as many as there are members of the group, each of which is equally true. The same information differently configured contributes to each reality or 'meaning', which while co-existent with each other, cannot be viewed at the same time. (Various 'Gestalt' pictures demonstrate this in particular the old woman/young woman).

Adding to the complexity is the plethora of different models both within and without the Gestalt world. Seán shows that there are many boundaries or perceived formations within the collection of individuals that constitutes a group which exist simultaneously, although like the classic pictures demonstrating figure and ground, cannot be held perceptually at the same time. For example there is the group of individuals and the facilitator, the figure being those people present, the physical space—the group room and the time frame, the environment being the rest of the world—or perhaps the different lives of the different people. It is also possible to view the actual group as the participants who are figural with the facilitator as environment, all held within a larger field that contains both, or for the facilitator to be figural with the participants as environment. Therefore, the sections of this article which supply (briefly) a description of the perspective from which Seán is viewing a group are essential as a means of orientation to his approach. However I did find his definitions confusing and spent some time checking what was meant by 'the group as a whole' and 'the actual group'. I'm still not clear I've got this straight.

Much as an individual who has developed to a point where they are aware of themselves, where many aspects of themselves are available to them so that they can chose responses, a group can reach a point where the members become individually and together aware of group processes, their responses as a whole and interact together accordingly. Seán describes dialogue which takes place in the 'actual group' as an expression of an aspect of the group gestalt, which in his model is where the whole meandering process is moving towards, so that a mature group may get to a place where there is integrity.

Part of how this happens is through the facilitator's attention to the voices of individuals which Seán views as both self-expression and also an expression belonging to the 'group gestalt'. The facilitator chooses interventions based on observing how the individual speaks for a sub-group of the whole group. Sub-groups may be covert, however skilful intervention can bring them into awareness and dialogue can then take place between them. It is dialogue on this level that can support the group to develop so that it has an integrity that has an inclusive quality of the difference contained within it.

I enjoyed Seán's live examples and his description of a meeting between 'the actual group' and the 'group gestalt'. This came across as a moment of vibrant integrity within the group he described, when all felt more than who they were at the moment. This was for me the point where the theory and writing became alive and I could understand more of what was being said.

It is important to note that, while acknowledging alternative per-spectives, Seán is looking at group and facilitator as separate beings with both as part of a wider field; there is a contact boundary between facilitator and other participants. The facilitator is an 'agent of change' through interventions with 'the actual group' (the actual individuals present) but with an eye on the development of the group which rests in 'the group gestalt' (the group as a whole which is greater than the sum of is parts and which includes the facilitator). And the group gestalt is analogous to 'the self' of the group which correlates (to my satisfaction) with something I wrote a few years ago.

> 'Just as we make meaning of visual and aural stimulus and of emotional material, we also make meaningful configurations of the groups we belong to. That meaning is a whole, a group which operates as an organism itself, with the people who make it up as cells, each with their own agenda and each operating for the existence of the whole group, often in ways of which they are not fully aware. Thus a Gestalt view of a group might be one of individual organisms within the boundary that defines the group, and working both for their own personal meaning and in the service of the group. Perls, Hefferline and Goodman[1] state that 'experience occurs at the boundary between organism and

the environment' and that self is ' the integrator, the synthetic unity'[2]. A group can be viewed as operating in a similar way as an individual, with the boundary between that which is within and that which is without being the definition of the group. It can be seen that the group is meaningless without a field in which the boundary is the contacting element, the divider between inside and outside, the semi-permeable membrane, the point of containment, absorption and resistance; and that there is such a thing as group self, an integrating element within the group, which each group member lives and is an element of.

An aspect of the facilitator's reading of the group process is the movement between seperateness or egotism of individuals and together-ness/being one of a group or confluence which forms a constant flow. The dilemma between being an individual or one of a collection is a constant dynamic of humankind in groups. In the Gestalt therapy group, a facilitator is not exempt from this process but is simultaneously both part of, and separate from the group-as-a-whole.

I like thinking of the group as having some form of self in that there seems to be an integrity that is served by the separate members, sometimes out of awareness. This was brought home to me in a group I attended. On the final afternoon of the group, in the same city, a mass demonstration against war was taking place and several group members felt conflicted. The group resolved this by appointing those members who felt they must go to represent the group and gave them presents, good wishes etc. In this way the integrity of the group was preserved, even though some people had left.

This also demonstrates Seán's point about confluence and egotism in that there was a clear movement between these within the group and that the resolution allowed for both—a separate action that al-lowed difference between group members and yet which preserved a 'confluent' whole. The discussions where some people wanted to leave, others didn't, fear of the group disintegrating etc. formed the ground

---

[1] Perls, Hefferline & Goodman, Gestalt Therapy, Part One Introduction, 1. The Structure of Growth 1: The Contact Boundary

[2] ibid 11: The Self and its Identification

from which emerged the figure of our final decision. This manifested in a moving ceremony where gifts were given to the group emissaries so that they carried something of the group with them. It felt powerful, satisfying, graceful etc.; the qualities of a healthy Gestalt.

Conclusion

Overall, I see this article as providing a thorough and exciting model of Gestalt group development and facilitation. I found the language difficult, perhaps because it was 'Gestalt' language and concepts, and because it was assumed that I—the reader—was familiar enough with them for it to have meaning. This was a drawback in regard to appreciating what was being said. Therefore my preference would have been for more illustrations from actual groups.

When I did understand, I saw a correlation between this model for groups and Kepner & Brien's model for Gestalt Therapy 'to develop more "intelligent" behaviour; that is, to enable the individual to act on the basis of all possible information and to apprehend not only the relevant factors in the external field, but also relevant information from within' (1970, p. 43).

In that the Gestalt group is seen as developing towards an integration and awareness that belongs to the whole group. Each member becomes more fluidly a part of a whole at the same time as maintaining a personal integrity. In this way the group becomes a vehicle for personal development and for dynamic 'belonging'.

References

Feder, B. & Ronall, R. (1980). Beyond the Hot Seat: Gestalt Approaches to Group. New York: Brunner/Mazel.

Houston, G. (1984/1993). *The Red Book of Groups: And How to Lead Them Better*. Rochester, NY, USA: Rochester Foundation.

Perls, F. S., Hefferline, R. F. & Goodman, P. (1951). *Gestalt Therapy: Excitement and Growth in the Human Personality*. Middlesex: Penguin.

Kepner, Elaine & Brien, Lois, (1970) Gestalt Therapy: A Behavioristic Phenomenology, *Gestalt Therapy Now*, Harper Torchbooks.

ᢙ

Commentary III

Philip Brownell

I appreciate this opportunity to read a paper by Seán Gaffney and regard it a privilege to comment on one. I am responding specifically to 'Gestalt with Groups: A Developmental Perspective.'

Seán Gaffney identified his focus almost immediately in his paper —something that was clear and appreciated. It helped orient to what he was doing. He stated:

> *I have also found it just as odd to work only from a here-and-now methodology, when change in the group over time is so apparent. My sense is that:*
>
> *— here-and-now group dynamics are embedded in the then-here-now-next of a group's developmental process.*
> *— this process is the context which can both broaden and deepen the significance of here-and-now dynamics.*

Seán identified these two issues as the core concerns of his article, but then he obscured them with a recitation of various tenets of Gestalt therapy theory. He went on to describe what a group was, organism-environment, field theory, figure-ground dynamics, cycle of experience, self and its aspects, awareness, and contact. He also listed a couple of things many Gestalt therapists would not accept as core to Gestalt theory: levels of system and space and time. He would also often introduce novel suggestions for how to consider these various tenets. For example, he suggested continuums, or polarities between contact interruptions/styles. He further proposed that the main contact consideration is the dimension defined by the gradient between Egotism (being apart from) and Confluence (being a part of).

All of this was somewhat distracting to what had been so clearly stated as the focus of the paper. Then, Seán claimed that the continuum between egotism and confluence is the structured ground for the emerging of figures around the development of the group. I'd like to halt the momentum right there. I do not see any such continuum as actual structured ground. I see it as a theoretical construct, and as such is one potential consideration among many others—as evidenced by all the various tenets Seán listed leading up to this moment. I like many of his ideas, such as the dimensional scaling he suggested with these continuums. I have suggested a similar approach in an article on psychological testing in Gestalt therapy, which appeared in the British Gestalt Journal, so I think Seán and I are on the same track there. Yet, that constitutes 'another story' as compared to this issue of what structured ground might actually be.

Structured ground is the residue of experience that forms the architecture of one's life space. As such, it is not a potential; it is an actuality. This brings up what I believe is the necessity in moving from terms developed around the experience of an individual organism to the application of those terms in group work (the experience of several organisms interacting over time with shared figures of interest, investments of time and energy, and mutual influence with respect to each one's field). How does a group have a consciousness of past experience? Would not, instead, the individuals in the group have various senses of that? If there is a group self, how does that come into being and how does it differ from the individual self of any given member of the group? Merely applying Gestalt terminology to talk about groups is not satisfying to me; I would like to see how such applications might be justified. I believe at times they can be justified, but I also believe Gestalt practitioners would benefit from seeing how that is rather than being forced to make those connections on their own, on the fly so to speak, as other things are happening in a paper, workshop, or training session.

Here is another point. My experience of reading this paper was one of sorting my way among what I could latch onto as recognizable and helpful on the one hand and what I could not accept or recognize on the other. For instance, instead of accepting that a continuum between Egotism and Confluence becomes reified as the dominant group consideration, I was attracted to the simple statement that instead of seeing projection as a signal that intrapsychic or interpersonal work needed to be done, one could observe it taking place as a force in the developing field. I found that quite helpful as a simple observation. I also liked the observation that in terms of a group development, the emergence of sub-groups is a healthy signal.

My experience of reading the paper was at first one of finding myself critiquing rather than enjoying. In a sense, I was acting out the structure Seán suggested, by keeping myself distinct from him and his ideas in an egotism. It was not until I reached his examples and case illustrations that I moved along that dimension more toward a relaxed 'entering into' the experiences he described, which could be seen as a more confluent response. I am realizing this as I write. I am also realizing that I seem to be responding to a series of points that might be otherwise disjointed. It can't be helped.

I was drawn to the distinction between 'Actual Group' and 'Group Gestalt.' I understood the actual group to be comprised of individual members (or parts), meeting in one venue, somehow structurally or intentionally configured as belonging together, but not necessarily dynamically/relationally invested in one another. The group gestalt, on the other hand, I understood to be the whole that, in Gestalt therapy vernacular, is larger than the sum of its parts. I further understood this group gestalt to be potential, in that it was always developing. Thus, I have two points about these observations.

First, using the terms of emergence and supervenience, I understand the group gestalt to be dependent upon the actual group such that any change in the actual group will result in a change in the group gestalt, that the group gestalt is dependent upon and determined by the actual group, and that the group gestalt emerges from the contact dynamics of the parts/members of the actual group. The group gestalt is not the same thing, or identical with the actual group, and the group gestalt exerts a 'downward' causality on the actual group. It is this downward causality (which is not Gestalt therapy language, but is an experience-near way of describing what is going on), which comprises the 'other' of the group identity, to which any given group member (at the level of actual group) works out his or her egotism – confluence polarity.

Second, since the group is always developing, that is, it is always alive and dynamic, the here and now is all one actually has both in terms of the actual group and the emergent group gestalt. It may, indeed, be a wisp, as Seán has said, but it's all one has. His example experiments illustrate how he works in the here and now to, paradoxically, understand/affect the there and then. Thus, I would think that group 'self' (to use one other way of talking about these things) is the level of creative adjustment, paradoxical change, uncontrollable result and direction of contact, and that one cannot target and grasp that any more than one can target an I – Thou moment. Thus, if a facilitator wants to work the group, it seems best to work at the level of the actual group, leaving the developing group gestalt to the realm of mystery.

I have enjoyed the opportunity to read Seán's thinking on group development. It was not a futile endeavor as it has impacted my understanding of groups. I doubt that I will conduct any group, or participate in any group in the future without thinking of what he has written here. I would suggest, however, that he focus more and leave out the distracting references to other Gestalt therapy constructs (unless they can be seen as directly relevant in the discussion of actual group and group gestalt), and I would also like to see more of the discussion put into common vernacular, as he has claimed to have done in the conclusion of the paper. (The terms 'egotism', 'confluence,' and so forth are not common terms.)

ॐ

Commentary IV

ANNE MACLEAN

If you are interested in Gestalt and particularly if you are a member of a group, a trainer or facilitator of any type of group then here's an article that will remind you at the very least of some of the things that you have learned so far. Here Seán Gaffney lays out in detail his proposal model for Gestalt group work and the parts of this model remind us of what we learned or will need to learn to allow us to become capable facilitators. He has written out of his considerable experience so different angles and facets of the model are highlighted along with the original Gestalt concepts.

The way in which the article is laid out begins with a short introduction, followed by the basics of *What is a group?* and then, *A brief
and necessarily limited review of Gestalt theory as I see its relevance to
groups.*

In setting out this development model he states that:

— *here-and-now group dynamics are embedded in the then-here-
now-next of a group's developmental process.*
— *this process is the context which can both broaden and deepen
the significance of here-and-now dynamics.*

Here lies an invitation to consider in more breadth and depth the
ground and the dynamics of a group. While on a first reading I was
somewhat startled and a little skeptical, on a closer look I found I
was adding more through these simple statements to my awareness of
group process. As the article proceeded I became aware of each section
adding more information about group process and the group itself, as
well as the facilitative role.

The way in which this writing is structured reflects group process.
The beginning lays out the ground, the Gestalt concepts which un-
derpin this developmental perspective. The starting work for a group
is the 'working ground' where the process begins and allows the group
to know the parameters that will generally govern the work and any
central, specific concepts being given figural place within this process.
Then as the article develops, work within a group setting is reflected
in both the theoretical ideas and the practical examples.

There is a simple layout to begin each concept and then, often in
only three or four sentences, a richness of expansion. He invites exploration and wonderment, as if we might engage in a direct conversation
each sharing our own experience—'I disagree with you—how do you
get there?' 'Is this accurate?' 'Oh, say some more. I do this when I
facilitate.' Any one of these sections could be taken and commented
on, explored and expanded.

From an overall point of view and central in his proposals are contact
and awareness and making connections between them. He ask *what
if* the resistances, interruptions, styles or functions were viewed as
points on the *awareness continuum*—confluence, egotism, introjection,

deflection retroflection and projection. He states that his *awareness-in-the-moment presuppose my preceding out-of-(or before) awareness to with awareness.* Thus moving from unconsciousness of an introjection to a consciousness of the choice of introjecting or not introjecting.

In *A Gestalt group development model* he argues for the egotism-confluence continuum being the starting point, and he goes further and names this as the key component and more influential than the others. This is the ground on which, out of which, the other styles emerge. I am in agreement with him based on my own work in groups and he follows on with a very clear description making the links to contact and awareness.

> In addition, I looked at how the modalities relate to each other, and propose the following contact continua, with very simplified exemplifications:

> Egotism (being apart from) – Confluence (being a part of)

> Introjecting (open to influence) – Deflecting (closed to influence)

> Projecting – Retroflecting
> (voiced praise/criticism, (silent praise/criticism,
> other as object) self as object)

> My experience—and proposal—is that the egotism-confluence continuum is the ever-present structured ground, supported figurally and behaviourally by the remaining modalities.

> Contact and awareness—the heart of the matter.

A facilitator needs to be aware of where they are and where each person is as they work within and as a group; so analyzing group process in terms of these three grouped polarities is a good way of explaining the dynamic interactions. In facilitating there are layers to awareness, and he goes on to support this by broadening the impact of using these three opposing modalities on the group and the usefulness of this to the facilitator. This continuum invites a return to a conscious awareness of the parts, the details offer new and different perspectives to be considered, offering a chance to review how you work, and the possibility that something new to you will be useful in that work.

> *The actual group is the specific gathering of persons in the room: the group gestalt is the wholeness which is more than and different from the sum of the persons, the wholeness that gives meaning to the parts in Gestalt psychology.*

The ideas under *The group gestalt and the actual group—process and dynamics* highlight the development process. Over the life time of a group, the group gestalt, which is the wholeness, and will, of course be different from and more than the sum of the persons will also reveal and give meaning to the actual group's *in-the-moment* dynamics.

On reading the section on Field Theory I wanted to bring one aspect mentioned into a fuller perspective, in relationship to the gestalt group; I wanted more explanation.

> *Dynamics at individual, interpersonal and sub-group levels of group both co-create and represent the forces of the field of the group, around which self-organizing occurs. Tracking the forces of the field of the group is an essential aspect of group facilitation from this perspective, as well as tracking the forces of the facilitator/ group field.*

I would like more information about what Seán means by ‘*Tracking the forces of the field of the group*….’ He lists and mentions the intertwining complexity contained within a group which allow understanding of how a group changes. These multi-level dynamics in the forces of the field need to be tracked, i.e. individual, interpersonal, and sub-group levels, and will provided a greater understanding of what is happening and are potentially there to work with. What exactly does he mean as he tracks the forces of the field of the group and the forces of the facilitator/group field. He also mentions shifting energies and I would be unwise to assume that he and I would mean the same thing when we spoke of them, or the forces or tracking. So, I'm left with a curiosity about what else might be there if his own process was included.

This article offers development out from the core concepts of

Gestalt. Each section is given coverage, with an overall sense of working through to a gathering of a whole developmental model of Gestalt with groups—a sense of a completed Gestalt. This article provides a theoretical explanation that is based on reasonable assumptions, and is in accord with practical experience. I appreciate when theory and practice are linked, so there is a living-sense made through the considering or experiencing, or both. Very satisfying—I like that congruence enormously for the confirmation of the model is born out at more than a surface level.

Name the work as supervision, psychotherapy, training or group facilitation, the training begins with the person who will do the training of others. In this case, only when he knows how the work manifests, both as a group member and as a facilitator, will he then be able to teach the chosen material with competence. Oh yes, you may argue that these are skills that can be learnt, and there is more. This is about the integration and the discipline of intimate involvement with what will be taught not just through words, but in an osmotic process of being. Here in this article Seán offers an invitation and a chance to be excited as a facilitator as consciousness is given the chance to evolve. His examples from working situations support and give clarity to this proposed model.

If *contact and awareness are the heart of the matter* then here is offered an excellent Gestalt model. Each time full expression is experienced, on any matter in the process of a group, the heart of the matter is touched and held more consciously by everyone.

Unless I read with awareness, make lively contact with the ideas, integrate and am touched through this process, then nothing in me changes. May you be alive and changed when you have finished reading and pondering the ideas in Seán Gaffney's writing—*Gestalt with groups—a development perspective.*

౸

Conversation

with Peter Phillipson on Gestalt with Groups: a Developmental Perspective

Extracts from the article in plain type
Peter and Seán's responses in italics

Abstract: In an earlier article (Gaffney 2006), my figure was the cross-cultural perspective of Gestalt with groups, and a proposal for a group-work model and methodology grounded in basic Gestalt theory, applicable across cultures for the internationally active Gestalt practitioner. Focusing on that figure left me with a lot of structured ground, themes I had chosen to bracket in my interest in, and excitement with a charged cross-cultural figure. In this current article, my aim is to revisit and re-structure the Gestalt ground of my thinking, and to further explore a number of clear figures where Gestalt with groups is concerned.

- when change in the group over time is so apparent. My sense is that:
- here-and-now group dynamics are embedded in the then-here-now-next of a group's developmental process.
- this process is the context which can both broaden and deepen the significance of here-and-now dynamics.
- **Peter:** *Sometimes it broadens it, sometimes limits it and makes it more shallow.*

Seán: *Hmmmm… well, yes and…no, in the sense that WHATEVER happens is ONE way in which the process is optimized for any group…I need to think this one through a bit further. Thanks.*

Basics—What is a Group?

My working hypothesis is this: three or more people, connected in space and time, who

1. are defined by an environment as 'a group' and/or
2. who define themselves—at any or all system levels (see below) —as 'a group.'

PETER: *I like the breadth of your definition.*

SEÁN: *I'm glad YOU do—Carl Hodges doesn't! I included this in the article that Carl did a commentary on for the Gestalt Review. Carl wants task and goal as part of the definition, and my next paragraph is an attempt to cover his views without radically changing my own*

⁂

I propose these as the basic elements—the social group. All other issues, such as shared purpose, task etc., I regard as 'added extras' in specific contexts, providing additional complexity and working foci —the work group. Simply put, the smallest unit of a social group is a person; that of a work group is both a person AND a functional role, with the latter generally more likely to be in focus. A therapy group, for example, would here be a social group with individual purposes, rather than a work group with an externally assigned shared task with functional work-roles related to the task.

PETER: *There could be said to be functional work-roles in maintaining the group as a therapeutic setting for themselves and each other.*

SEÁN: *I fully agree—and will get this point into my later drafts. Clearly, this section is deserving of more full treatment, which the delimitations of journal articles just don't allow…even if I made a little attempt to cover it in the following sentence!*

A therapist training group might move from one to the other over time depending on the extent to which its members saw becoming therapists as a shared or individual purpose and task.

Where group development is concerned, 'group self-definition' is to me the existential heart of the matter, the process over time of the group self-defining itself as such along with individual group-member's awareness of this process and its impact on them.

PETER: *I think this can be true, and I know that the groups I ran over a long time developed a wisdom that could be passed to new members. However, it could also be defensive, avoiding the difficult areas, and becoming more social/friendship groups than therapeutic, encouraging each person to risk being more themselves.*

SEÁN: *Peter, this is an issue where we seem to be coming from different perspectives and with different objectives. For me, what you call 'defensive' is not a description I would use. Indeed, even if I did, my interest would not be in the defensiveness in itself, but rather in the dynamics of how 'it' came to be...*

Field Theory

    – the life-space
    – $B = f(P + E)$
    – forces of the field
    – self-organizing around the 'need'

I see the life-space construct as another perspective on organism/environment. The behaviour (B) of both facilitator and group-as-a-whole ('gestalt'/ 'actual') is a function (f) of who they are in the moment (P) in relation to the other (E). The interplay of the forces of the field thus created is the dynamics of the relationship. Given space and time, these forces will continually self-organize around whatever 'need' is emerging as figure from the ground of the relationship.

PETER: *How does this fit with your 'there and then', if the way that 'there and then' is experienced is also a function of who they are in their environment now?*

SEÁN: *If I were not already white-haired, I would have become so as I wrestled and battled with this point. No doubt that a 'there and then' memory occurs in the current environment—though may be experienced by the person as 'being there and then' ALSO. Clearly a tricky and maybe moot point, well worth further discussion!*

⁂

Based on a) my proposed definition of a group and b) the Organism/ Environment construct and my use of it—both outlined above—I see the participant collective as the 'group-as-a-whole' and the group thus defined + facilitator as a discrete field, in which both the group-as-a-whole AND the facilitator are embedded. From this perspective, the facilitator is a force of the group/facilitator field rather than a part of the group.

PETER: *The logic of your definition of group is that both group-with-facilitator and group-without-facilitator are possible groups, and it is more which one you want to focus on rather than which IS a group.*

SEÁN: *NICE POINT! SHIT!! And yes, you are quite correct. I need to be clearer here that I am making a choice. The distinction I would like to make is that between the group-of-participants, and field of facilitator/ group. So: more clarity!*

⁂

My proposal is, further, that sub-group dynamics are those to which we as facilitators need to attend to more intentionally, and also that what can present as personal or interpersonal may just as easily be sub-group dynamics. Sub-groups are both explicit and implicit, visible and invisible, voiced and silent. Whatever occurs in the group, members respond to in some way. They agree, support, disagree, are indifferent to, don't notice—whatever: but respond they do. These responses become the structured ground from which figures emerge as energies of the field, and support the possible emergence of both implicit and explicit sub-groups.

PETER: *The person who comes to mind here is Yvonne Agazarian. See her Systems-Centered Therapy for Groups, pub. Karnac Books, 2004. She is a group analytic therapist, but associated with the New York Institute for GT, where I met her, and an influence on Carl Hodges. Her whole approach is as you describe, round subgroups.*

SEÁN: *YES! I have read all of her books, and some articles, and she appears more fully in a draft introduction to the theme of Gestalt with Groups in—dare I say it?—my possible and very eventual thesis!*

⸰⸰

Self and its Aspects
  − personality
  − ego
  − id

The 'group gestalt' is another way of saying 'group self.' A group has a personality, certainly an ego, and much that is outside of its awareness at any and all system levels (id).

PETER: *We have recently had a long discussion of 'self of group' in the New York Institute, and come to the conclusion that it is not a viable extension of the self theory. Specifically, we couldn't find a way to incorporate ego functioning into group. The function of ego in an individual is to bring focus, unifying perceptions, into a clear owned figure of contact. If a group did this, it would be because they were in confluence, subordinating their individual interests to a group figure, rather than a sign of good functioning.*

SEÁN: *Ah well—fools rush in etc! Dan and I have been debating this point back-channel, and I am becoming clearer about my need to more*

strongly emphasise the more metaphorical than substantive perspective
I am bringing to bear here. So maybe 'self-of-group' rather than 'group
self'…I have a lot more to do here!

꙳

Awareness

Awareness for the organism is sensory/proprioceptive. This I call
'sensory awareness'. There is an energy shift as a figure emerges from
the ground as well as to what extent this figure is self-energised ('figural
awareness'). For a group, awareness of its own process as a whole is
generally retroactive ('reflective awareness') through the meaning its
members make of shared recent experience, including the multiple
realities of personal experiences.

PETER: *I would follow PHG and call this kind of meaning-making, delay*
etc. egotism rather than awareness. Again the health of a group is where
it facilitates multiple possible awarenesses in its members, rather than
pushing towards a single awareness or meaning, and that is a major way
a group is different from an individual and from self process. I know you
make a lot of egotism later on, but I can't understand what you mean by
it, possibly a synonym for 'isolation'.

SEÁN: *For me, 'isolation' might be Egotism without awareness, with*
'insulation' as a possible expression of Egotism with awareness…And I
know that I have a lot more work to do here with the whole contact is-
sue…in retrospect, this is where I could have usefully started, rather than
going for the group jugular! Shit—more bloody work!

The facilitator's sensory and figural awareness at the facilitator/group
contact boundary is likely to differ from that of any individual or
individuals of the group, especially when the group gestalt, as well
as the actual group, is perceived as the environmental other of the
facilitator.

PETER: *I agree with you there!*

SEÁN: *Thank you—this is important to me.*

Openly sharing and exploring these figures is a core aspect of the proposed methodology, and will be more fully treated and exemplified later in the article.

PETER: *Yet part of the difference is that, more than anyone else, what the facilitator says can be taken up or disagreed with by the group members for very complex transferential reasons, nothing to do with its wisdom or otherwise.*

SEÁN: *Sure—and still grist for the mill, since I am of the opinion that ANYTHING can be taken as a function of the organizing of the field in that moment.*

Contact

Contact occurs dynamically at the co-created boundary of organism/ environment, or person/environment, or Self/Other, or I/Not I—all metaphorical variations on the same theme.

Contact 'resistances' and/or 'interruptions' and/or 'styles' and/ or 'functions' and/or 'modalities'—while Gestalt practitioners may make distinctions between each of these perspectives, there is at least some consensus around what 'they' are: PHG (1951/1994) proposes 'confluence', 'egotism', 'introjection', 'retroflection' and 'projection.' The Polsters (Polster E. and Polster M.,1973) proposed 'deflection', which became widely accepted.

'Awareness' and 'contact' are core Gestalt concepts, and my proposal is based on making connections between them. What if each contact modality is seen from the perspective of the 'awareness continuum' (Laura Perls, 1992)? I take this to mean a continuum from 'out of (or before) awareness' to 'with awareness.' My awareness-in-the-moment presupposes my preceding out-of-awareness. So, for example, I move from confluence out of my awareness to a choice of confluence or not with awareness—and in a relationship of any kind, I may well choose to be confluent with the other, with awareness of and responsibility for my choice and my behaviour. The same applies to each of the contact modalities.

PETER: *For me, if you rename 'contact interruptions' into 'contact modalities', you lose the meaning of 'contact' in GT. Oftentimes the movement from developing interest to clear figure formation to final contact to assimilation and withdrawal need no interruption, sometimes they are interrupted to support their better completion in the next moment, and sometimes they are interrupted habitually as a defensive manoeuvre.*

SEÁN: *As I said earlier, 'fools rush in!' more work, more work!*

In addition, I looked at how the modalities relate to each other, and propose the following contact continua, with very simplified exemplifications:

Egotism (being apart from) – Confluence (being a part of)

PETER: *How does this fit with the Gestalt description of 'egotism'? 'Isolation' maybe.*

Introjecting (open to influence) – Deflecting (closed to influence)

PETER: *Again, for me this misses the point. In one way, introjection and deflection are opposite, in another they are both similar, being ways to avoid the need to assimilate/use teeth, in Perls' imagery. In introjection, you are not influenced but taken over, not tasting the bits of the influence that are growthful. In deflection, you avoid letting any influence get too close.*

Projecting	–	Retroflecting
(voiced praise/criticism,		(silent praise/criticism,
other as object)		self as object)

PETER: *For me, praise or criticism would be projection if it was spoken as something wholly about the other, not about my response to the other, or myself as reflected in the other. And it doesn't seem totally a polarity either: the retroflected praise/criticism can be a projection of my own characteristics at the same time.*
You might want to look at John Swanson's 'Boundary Processes and Boundary States' in the Gestalt Journal Vol.XI, no. 2, Fall 1988, and the

dialogue that ensued in that and the next issue. He does something very similar.

SEÁN: *Peter, you hit many nails cleanly on their heads here! When I stood at my bookshelf, and went to lift out the Journal volume concerned, I had a 'there and then' moment! Yes—this is where it all started … or 'I' all started, with my first reading of Swanson etc. So back to my drawing-board!*

My experience—and proposal—is that the egotism–confluence continuum is the ever present structured ground, supported figurally and behaviourally by the remaining modalities. I call the egotism–confluence continuum 'the existential dilemma' for any group member, a preferred or habitual or in the moment chosen stance. Being in a group continuously tests, influences and possibly changes this stance. It is difficult for any two people to be at some 'middle point' of this continuum in relation to each other, especially since both parties are also relating in a complex field of other group relations. For example, A's voiced praise (projecting) of B might upset C, and therefore the A-C as well as B-C relationships, so that the voiced praise becomes a choice for A of projecting or retroflecting.

PETER: *Those are not the only choices. If there is support in the group for honesty even if someone gets upset, and there is support also for the upsetness, or the individual A has outside support for honesty, or even self-support ('I am here to grow in self-knowledge, so I will speak even if it causes immediate difficulties'), more choice is possible. Different cultures would also deal with this situation differently.*

SEÁN: *Yes—the cross-cultural aspects are the focus of the Gestalt Review article, and I agree with your last sentence above. Again, I need more space and fewer constraints of number of pages etc.*

PETER: *In general, I am unclear about your classification. I don't understand what you mean by 'egotism'. Are you talking about plain simple ego functions of identification and alienation?*

SEÁN: *Back again to the heart of the matter! You really are more an English Terrier than a Central European Shepherd! AND I greatly appreciate your capacity for both!*

'Out of awareness', 'deflecting the other', 'retroflecting attractive characteristics of the other' and 'projecting unattractive characteristics onto the other', generally support egotism;

PETER: *Egotism, as described in PHG would involve lots of SELF-commenting, not projecting onto the other. Those could be attractive or unattractive characteristics.*

SEÁN: *Again, I need to more clearly define my frames of reference, and how they differ from a traditional PHG perspective.*

'Introjecting', 'retroflecting unattractive characteristics' and 'projecting attractive characteristics' generally support confluence.

PETER: *Again, my experience is different. People with 'low self esteem' are isolated, not confluent. For example, if you try to give them a more positive evaluation of themselves, they will deflect it instantly.*

SEÁN: *DÉJÀ VU ALL OVER AGAIN!*

⁂

Application to Group Development

Contact is the essence of group life, both at the member/member, member/sub-group, sub-group/sub-group boundaries and at the group/facilitator boundary. The group, therefore has internal boundary dynamics, and—at all levels of system-external boundary dynamics with the facilitator and other environments. Any Gestalt-grounded model for groups will necessarily focus on boundary issues—in other words, on the contact modalities.

PETER: *I wholeheartedly agree with you there.*

SEÁN: *Again, Peter, I am pleased that we have a ground of agreement about core issues like this.*

Contact and awareness—the heart of the matter!

A Gestalt Group Development Model: A Proposal

I start with the egotism – confluence continuum, 'the existential dilemma', being as an individual somehow apart from others, yet acknowledging the inevitable presence and availability of the choice of being a part of others—and that their choice is also involved. People tend towards one or other ends of the continuum, and it requires a high and constant level of awareness to be open to the existential choices this awareness engenders

Being in a group raises this issue, and I propose that

1. it is the foundation of any group process, and
2. it is always structuring the ground of that process.

PETER: *I agree with what I think you are saying here. Existentially, we move between the security of 'being part of' and the freedom of asserting autonomy, and this movement underlies our stances in group situations. My disagreement is in your use of terms. I think you are describing basic ego functions, identification and alienation, and their fixation in confluence and isolation. Or, to use different terms that PHG uses, the stances of spontaneity and autonomy.*

SEÁN: *Peter, as I respond to you, I am becoming more aware of some interesting background: I was trained in the YABC tradition, with such as Jorge Rosner and Tom Munson. Tom pathologised just about everything anybody said or did, always using Fritz as a reference. To this day in the Gestalt Academy, there are therapists/trainers who happily use the words 'contact style' then condemn every utterance as an 'interruption/resistance.' So I can see how this as a context has influenced me... now I need to feel the influence and think outside of it...*

⚸

The group development process can therefore be seen as the continuous resolution of the tension of choice and response to the tendencies towards/away from either egotism or confluence. Awareness is central here. It could be said that a group develops towards a greater awareness around this continuum and its impact on the group's dynamics. This is a learning process, grounded in the experience of the group of its process and dynamics. This is learned experientially in and by the group at all levels, rather than taught, and this learning process is supported by in-the-moment facilitator interventions and also retroactive facilitator and—again at all levels—group reflection. In other words, a group of group-process experts will still have to experience their process, rather than simply apply their knowledge as some kind of checklist guaranteed to remove all the natural dynamics of any group.

PETER: *Yes. I agree.*

SEÁN: *Yes—just think of AAGT!*

As mentioned earlier, these dynamics are expressed through the contact modalities introjecting, deflecting, retroflecting and projecting. In a sense, these are the figures which emerge from the structured ground of the egotism–confluence continuum. All are of course available at all times. At the same time, I propose that they are likely to emerge as a specific modality continuum—introjecting with deflecting, and retroflecting with projecting—as the dominant modality emerges as figure. This provides the facilitator with some notion of where the group is in its egotism–confluence process.

PETER: *I think seeing these as the only possibilities rules out spontaneity, I–Thou, full contacting.*

SEÁN: *I am not seeing them as the only possibilities—I do propose seeing them as constructs which any Gestalt-trained professional will have become acquainted with in some form, and therefore be able to work with to whatever extent they may choose. And certainly, your points of 'spontaneity, I-Thou, full contacting' will generally fall into such a category. However, I also know that PHG IS NOT read in Scandinavia, the only translation is incomplete and long out of print... and this may well apply elsewhere.*

In other words, as group facilitator I may choose not to work with, for example, what may seem to be out-of-awareness projecting as such, rather see it as an expression of a stance of egotism or confluence in the context of the group's process. That is, not as an individual behaviour necessitating intrapsychic or interpersonal work, rather a force of the field of the group.

PETER: *I think you are saying something important here. In my language, the interruptions are not in themselves pathological, but where they become fixed there is something being avoided that needs to be brought to awareness, not the fixation in itself, which is just a sign.*

SEÁN: *Thank you! And maybe this is where GT could do with a clearer construct than 'interruption to contact' which carries all sorts of possible applications to the pathological, or at least the 'unhealthy'—another word I have some problems with!*

Gestalt Group Development

WITH AWARENESS

Retroflecting Attractive Characteristics		Projecting Attractive Characteristics
Projecting Unattractive Characteristics		Retroflecting Unattractive Characteristics
Deflecting		Introjecting

EGOTISM ———————————————— CONFLUENCE

Deflecting		Introjecting
Projecting Unattractive Characteristics		Retroflecting Unattractive Characteristics
Retroflecting Attractive Characteristics		Projecting Attractive Characteristics

OUT OF / BEFORE AWARENESS

PETER: *You might want to look at Will Schutz's 'FIRO-B'. See http://www.afirstlook.com/archive/firo.cfm?source=archther. I think this is somewhere in the same area, though FIRO-B is now more individually oriented.*

SEÁN: *Yes. I do so in the Gestalt review article.*

✢

Example 1

On joining a group, a person needs to find a place on the egotism – confluence continuum. Some will tend towards one or other end of this continuum. Obviously, cross-cultural aspects will play a part here. Whatever the ground of, or awareness around, the tendency, it is likely that much of the initial phase of the actual group's life will be taken up with this question. Language plays a part here in highlighting the issue: the ease of use of 'We' or 'I' can give the facilitator an idea of the dynamics involved. Incidentally, insisting for example on the use of 'I' statements during this phase is counter-productive from the perspective of my proposal, as it un-necessarily interferes with the organic dynamics of the group, especially in cross-cultural or multicultural contexts.

> Example: Adam arrived late for the first of three Thursday lunch – Sunday lunch residentials, reluctantly made a minimal introduction of himself, and kept to himself during breaks, then declared later during this first module of a program on personal and professional development that he had no interest in endless, chit-chat process or particularly small-group work—he would only promise to attend focused process sessions, theory and application sessions (negotiated membership—even if somewhat unilateral). Another person voiced an opinion about how 'we' as group members 'should' behave. Yet another spoke to freedom of choice, as long as it doesn't affect 'us' and the program. The remaining 9 people were silent, some looking towards me.
>
> I suggested an experiment, and described it as I designed

it in my head. No one protested, and no-one showed much enthusiasm (introjecting? deflecting?). So I continued. I asked the three who had spoken to seat themselves in different corners of the room, briefly repeating their words. The fourth corner was for 'Don't know/mind.' I asked the 'speakers' to repeat their perspectives, and invited the others to join the corner they felt most agreement with. I then invited people to speak for their perspective from each corner, and suggested that everyone was free to move freely as the spirit moved them. Some took up positions between two corners. Some changed opinion from one corner to another.

By the end, Adam had been joined by two others—one who admired and lacked his courage, one who supported him in principle, and felt strongly about it. From the perspective being presented here, the group had now explored how the egotism–confluence continuum was being played out in the moment, with all its nuances. Adam found himself—and was seen to be—a member of a sub-group. The actual group now had a greater awareness of a central group issue—being 'a part of' AND 'apart from'—at group level, rather than at an individual/interpersonal level (Adam/the rest of the group). (I can't help reflecting to what extent scapegoating in groups would be lessened if sub-group dynamics received more focus).

PETER: *That is exactly how Yvonne Agazarian works.*

SEÁN: *WOW! So more of her in my next draft!*

Example 2

I am here applying an exploration of the field of the group through work on a member's dream:

In the morning session of the second of three days, Birgitta mentions and briefly reports on a dream she had during the night. She is on the platform in a train station, and discovers she has far too many suitcases. There is no way she can manage to get them all on board by herself, the train is soon leaving. Maybe she should leave some suitcases behind? Or re-pack everything, taking only what she needs? Or quickly buy some new, more functional, suitcases and re-pack into them? Will she miss the train if she delays deciding? As the train starts moving, she grabs what she thinks might be the most essential suitcases, and jumps aboard, looking out the window at the remaining cases piled on the platform. She sits in silence.

Charles starts with his input for the morning session. Denise cuts across him to ask Birgitta if she was really finished, and whether she wants to work on her dream 'the Gestalt way.' Birgitta says that she can come back to it if there's time, and looks at me. Charles expresses his irritation at being interrupted by Denise—if Birgitta wanted to work on her dream, then she had the chance to say and do so. Denise responds by saying to Charles that he is always too fast to get into his own stuff. Charles and Denise exchange comments to and about each other. Eric breaks in to say that maybe Birgitta's dream was a 'group dream', and that we should work on it as such.

There is a silence, during which many group members look towards me. I ask if there is anyone else who has something to say. No-one responds. I ask Birgitta if she is interested in, and willing, for me doing some work in the group around her dream. She is.

So I ask her to recount it again in the present tense, and ask the others to simply listen and notice whatever happens to them as they do so. As she finishes, I ask if anyone is resonating to any aspect of the dream, and if so, to be that aspect, in the present tense.

Eric says 'I am a platform at a train station. People use me to come and go. No-one stays on me, unless it is Birgitta's left-over luggage. I am for comings and goings and left-overs and peoples' overflowing rubbish in the trash-cans. Any train that stays beside me is always empty and it's night-time and dark and cold.'

Then Frida: 'I am too many suitcases, too much. Some of me will be chosen to travel with, some of me left behind. If I go on the train, then I don't know where I'm going...but maybe that's better than being left behind. I just don't know, and it's not my choice anyway. Someone else always decides.'

Then George: 'I am indecision ... will I, won't I ... what if I choose wrongly, make a mistake ... I hate regretting my decisions, so I usually don't decide anything.' Then Charles: 'This is crazy. It's Birgitta's dream, not mine or anyone else's. Let her say how she understands it.' Harriet speaks: 'I always have too much with me. Can you imagine, here I am on an intensive residential course, and I have two books for my studies, a novel I'm in the middle of reading with a bad conscience because I should be studying, and some papers from work that I have to go through and report on next week. If the train is this course, then I might miss it or get off at the wrong station.'

There is some general conversation about the richness of the various perspectives. As this dies down, I ask Birgitta what she would now choose as a theme to explore in the present. She chooses the train: 'I am a train at a platform in a station. I don't know where I am, or even where I am going. Anyone who doesn't mind not knowing where I'm going can come on board. I'm going to wherever I'm going, anyway. Yes, that's it. I always need to know everything in advance, especially on a course with some people I don't know. I want to know exactly what I'm going to get—in advance. Not this time. I'll leave ALL my old suitcases on the platform and just see what happens. Thank you, everybody.'

I asked if there were any more inputs. A number of people spoke to the richness of the process, and how absorbing it had been.

PETER: *Nice example of the intertwining of individual and group processes.*

SEÁN: *Thank you. This is what I am trying to do, so—great!*

⚜

Example 3

This is a continuation of Example 2. The time/space continuum had been figural for me during the coffee-break as I reflected on the dream session. I decided therefore to create the opportunity for some experiential learning around this theme, as well as explore the theme as energies of the field of the group.

I first presented the time/space continuum:

Here

Then   **Now**   **Next**

There

To exemplify, I used the following: we all came here from 'there and then.' Depending on how strong and figural some aspects of that were for us, we may well have moved to 'there and now', or even 'here and then.' On and off, we may have been 'here and now' or even 'here and next.' Some may have thought about next week, and been 'here and next' or 'there and next'—depending on how vivid an imagination we have!

PETER: *I would still want a bracketing statement that all these are ultimately here and now. How the there, then, next… are imagined or remembered is a here and now event.*

SEÁN: *Agree with all of the above… next draft!*

9.

Teaching and Learning in a Multicultural Environment

A Mild Polemic

This chapter combines general background material and practical exercises—all easily facilitated by any teacher—to explore and consider issues related to culture and education. The focus is on how these issues may impact on a class of international students. In addition, it provides an overview of the relationship between individual, group and the class as a whole from cross-cultural and group dynamics perspectives. Throughout, it offers practical exercises at individual, small group and class levels, aimed at generating experiential learning of value to both students and their teachers.

Naturally, these potential 'learning outcomes' are partly dependent upon the reader's interest in the subject itself. For teachers, the outcomes are also linked to the teacher's interest in developing a range of classroom skills of particular relevance to working with international student groups. Finally, I am aware that my own presentation of these themes will also impact on the reader's interest, patience and curiosity.

Introduction

Increasingly, Business School classes at undergraduate, graduate and doctoral levels are intentionally international with regard to their composition. In some cases, this internationalism is based on the nationality of the students. In other cases, it is more culturally based: the students may all be formally of the same nationality while, at the same time, culturally diverse in terms of ethnicity and home environments, as can increasingly be the case in many schools. This can be made further complex by issues which are internal to a particular sociocultural environment. I have met a student who was officially identified by the university as 'Malaysian'. In Malaysia, she is identified as 'Indian'. Within the Indian community in which she lives, she is identified as 'Christian'. As one of her teachers, I needed to learn from her of these complexities in order to relate professionally to her in a manner which was meaningful to her—and therefore supportive of her learning.

I have many colleagues worldwide who regard such information as both unnecessary for them as teachers and even as a problem they can do without. If, on the other hand, colleagues are interested in learning—which I believe is one of the responsibilities of a professional teacher—then the 'problem' provides ample opportunity.

A recent example of my own learning—as a Senior Lecturer on an intentionally international MBA Programme—I had four Chinese students. During my early sessions with the class, it was not unusual for one of them to ask a question or make a comment, followed by a brief exchange between them all in Chinese. These interactions with me slowly faded into a compact silence. My 'exam' for this particular class is in the form of a personal learning paper, reporting on the learning process as it unfolded during the course. Amongst the issues I ask the students to address is to consider what 'cultural aspects' supported or alternatively hindered their learning. One of the Chinese students —explicitly on behalf of the others as well—stated that their learning was hindered early on by the behaviour of a male 'western' student who addressed me by my first name and constantly questioned my input and debated details with me. For the Chinese students, this meant that I would regard the whole class as disrespectful of me, and, in consequence, they—the Chinese group—then felt too embarrassed to engage openly with me.

Whilst this may seem like an issue related only to the Chinese students, in fact it had wider implications. A number of other students in their learning papers referred to the 'distant' and 'uninvolved Chinese'. A behaviour which the Chinese experienced as including them as members of a collective class was having consequences for them which were being experienced by others in a totally different manner. In other words, the social and learning interactions of a whole class were influenced by the experience of four students in relation to the behavioural interaction of one student with 'the professor', and the ripple effect this had on the class as a whole. Part of my learning here is the importance of the issues this chapter addresses, including the classroom exercises—with respect to the example above, this class did not have the opportunity to participate in any of these preliminary exercises. Had they done so, then both the students and I would have had a shared experience and reference for discussing classroom behaviours.

To further focus on this issue, allow me to cite some other recent examples from various MBA Programmes internationally, on which I teach. The names used are fictional in all cases and the nationalities equally anonymous—it is not my intention to provide some checklist of cross-cultural behaviour and teacher interventions, but rather to present issues which the reader can relate to their own experience as a teacher (or even as a student!). As a result, I have deliberately chosen a selection of male and female names in Gaelic (the original language of Ireland and Scotland).

1. Oisín is a member of a project group on an explicitly international MBA Programme. He seems to be under stress during the early modules, and eventually requests a meeting with me. (I am identified as a Gestalt Psychotherapist and Lecturer on the 'Group Dynamics' module). He explains his situation. Oisín comes from a culture where class-group and family loyalty is paramount, though he was born and raised in another country. Having successfully completed his first degree, he quickly got a junior executive position and had been working abroad as a middle-manager. His father had been in constant touch with him, and had recently begun to mention things like 'coming home' and 'settling down'. This had led to a lengthy description of 'suitable' single women within their community. There was, however, a difficulty: the most suitable possible wives had PhDs. Oisín did not. In his father's view, a distinction from a reputable MBA Programme might be a balancing factor. So Oisín was encouraged to find an MBA of sufficient status where a degree with distinction could be used as a bargaining item in marriage negotiations with the parents of suitable daughters

with PhDs. He found himself on what he regarded as a MBA Programme of some status—though where group projects and grades were part of the programme, something he had read about in the prospectus and not thought through. Working in a group deprived him, as he saw it, of the possibility of a degree with distinction as a personal and individual achievement. This was an existential issue for him, and deeply private. It took me an hour of conversation with him to get to this point. His need was for a similar goal for all members of his group—which did not seem to him to be forthcoming.

2. Bríd is an ambitious young woman with some professional experience as a junior manager. The international MBA is her first experience of extensive cross-cultural interaction in an international setting. In her Project Group, she pushes a strong ethnocentric line about how a group 'should' function, how individual members 'must' behave. Any other group member who does not explicitly comply with these apparently obligatory and inevitable 'norms' became the subject of her criticism, both explicit and implicit. She also elicits alliances with other group members around these issues, thus consolidating her ethnocentric expectations into a normative perspective.

3. Eoghan had difficulties from the opening of the programme. Following a day when class members each presented themselves, the faculty introduced the project groups, which had been chosen to ensure a maximum mix of gender, culture, language, academic background, working experience, and so on. The groups were asked to meet and prepare a presentation of themselves as a project group. On the following day, as these presentations were about to begin, Eoghan expressed his frustration at the time-wasting involved—since everyone had already presented themselves earlier, surely this would simply be a repeat of those presentations, in his opinion. As the group work progressed, there were complaints from his group colleagues about Eoghan's behaviour. He did not come to every group meeting about their project. He never came to any social event when, for example, the other group members suggested going out to dinner or for a drink together. On the other hand, he would generally do

any task allotted to him, though not always within the agreed time frame. He had little or no interest in reading anyone else's contribution. If he did read the finished group product, it was generally with a stream of critical comments including how he would have done it had he been left alone to do so.

4. Daragh was slightly older by about five years than any other group member. He also had very specialist knowledge outside of the general economics focus of the MBA. Within weeks, he was openly critical of the comparative youth, lack of working experience and level of knowledge of his fellow group members. He began missing meetings and being openly critical of his group colleagues within the class in general. He refused to participate in contributing to group projects as he was 'not learning anything from the others'.

5. Aislinn seemed to fit in smoothly with her group. Then comments from her group colleagues began to become complaints. She was generally silent during group meetings, turned in work if the guidelines were clearly stated, and only contributed verbally if 'pushed' to do so.

It is all too easy to see these as examples of individual behaviours, requiring individually-based interventions. However, the reality is that, in each of the above cases, the whole Project Group and its dynamics as a working-group were impacted. Sides were taken; groups fragmented; interpersonal animosities became increasingly central. Deadlines were either missed or managed by last-minute individual actions. The issues internal to the Project Groups leaked out into the class as a whole. Over time, other students also took sides; some avoided the students mentioned above. Some blamed the faculty and even the programme itself for disturbing the smooth flow of input and exams by bothering with group projects.

Osín had difficulties sharing his dilemma with others and became increasingly isolated. He finally confided in one other member and thus—unwittingly—created a secret alliance which led to them both becoming isolated in a more and more fragmented group. Bríd finally became a scapegoat in her group and, by extension, in the class as a whole. Eoghan's consistently 'self-focused' behaviours created compact opposition and he faced being expelled from the programme as an increasingly disruptive presence. Daragh managed to polarise the class as a whole around 'being in a bad group', and found a way to switch groups—though the faculty had expressly stated that the essential learning about group dynamics would be best served by working through individual and group difficulties in each of the three sets of Project Groups that would be operative over the programme. In a written assignment, Aislinn explained how difficult it was for her to be in her Project Group. She was the youngest and female. Her degree was not of the same 'quality' or relevance as those of her colleagues. Her English was comparatively the weakest. Her experience of groups in her home culture differed considerably from that of the others. She was used to showing respect for those older and more experienced than she, and only speaking when directly addressed. The cultural change was more than she could understand or handle.

Interestingly, those of the faculty who had experience of teaching in the home cultures of the students mentioned above could recognise the patterns of behaviours which were being exemplified. As such, some of these behaviours could be predicted; at the very least, they were not particularly surprising when they did arise.

These examples of the dilemmas of cross-cultural dynamics in our classrooms are further compounded by the trend towards group-work and Project Groups, and even group grades in many cases. This adds the dimension of group dynamics to an already heady mix. It also raises two other issues: 1) to what extent are Business Schools prepared to admit group dynamics as a practical and theoretical subject; and 2) to what extent are the more academically inclined and therefore content-oriented teachers prepared to tolerate that such dynamics are allowed to play a part in the educational programme as a whole. Interestingly enough, there are cultural contexts at work here. In some cultural settings—USA for example—group dynamics and organisational behaviour would not be unusual as integral parts of an MBA. In many countries in Europe, the opposite applies. Further afield, in many Asian and African environments not over-tainted by a post-colonial heritage, groups might be taken as a given.

There is clearly a link between project and/or group work on international MBA Programmes and the growing awareness in the corporate world of the use of multicultural Project Groups and teams: 'Multinational executive teams are coming of age. The days are passing when major multinational corporations (MNCs) such as General Electric or Matsushita, could operate complex, dynamic industries from the unambiguous cultural base of a home country ... Resources are likely to flow towards MNCs that know when and how to use multicultural teams as business conditions require them (Bartlett and Ghoshal 1989).' (Maznevski and Peterson 1997, p. 61.)

In addition, this complex interweaving of individual, group and class as a whole issues are typical of organisational life—precisely the context for which we are preparing our MBA/Business School students. To offer courses on management and leadership, Business Ethics and HR without acknowledging that our classes, teachers and school management are directly analogous to the realities of corporate life is to miss an opportunity for powerful and realistic learning.

Working effectively with cross-cultural group processes and dynamics in academic settings offers a number of challenges. Does the School Management genuinely support innovative practices in an academic setting, or is it merely talking the talk of competitive Business School marketing? Is there sufficient theoretical and practical support in terms of knowledgeable and experienced academics/group practitioners on the faculty? Can other faculty members, whose focus may be more content and examination-based, accept the inevitable impacts of group dynamics and cross-cultural issues? Can faculty function as an integrated whole when cross-cultural group dilemmas emerge?

Interdisciplinary tensions are a natural aspect of any faculty: the question here is to what extent any faculty is prepared to accept group dynamics' dilemmas as an organic part of any programme. Part of the dilemma is this: that a cross-cultural group dynamics perspective does not have any easy or standard solutions. It has rather a number of in-the-moment issues which require in-the-moment interventions aimed at student and faculty learning rather than the pragmatic removal of anything which 'disturbs' some illusory status quo.

MBA students learn little when potential real-life tensions in work-groups are apparently programmed out of existence by rules and regulations which aim at prohibiting or curbing such totally natural dynamics. The opportunities for true experiential learning—by both students and faculty—are considerably more valuable than an often over-optimistic attempt to pre-empt reality.

The remainder of this chapter will therefore focus on some practical supports for both students and teachers in multicultural educational settings. All of the examples which follow have been part of my work with international groups over the past 30 years in graduate, MBA and Executive Programmes, and, as such, are tried and tested.

Cross-cultural generalisations with a practical classroom exercise

'Culture' as a construct is a generalisation, referring to collectives rather than individuals. Individuals may or not be typical or representative of such generalised values, attitudes and their behavioural expressions—under normal circumstances. Under pressure, many individuals will resort to their instinctive cultural perspectives, as this provides security and familiarity. This would seem to be the case in the above examples.

There are as many definitions of culture as there are researchers into and authors on the subject. My intention here is to sidestep any debates around definitions, and focus on the work of Geert Hofstede (Hofstede 1984, 1994), as he has specifically addressed the impact of a cultural environment on education. What follows is an extrapolation of his work in this regard. Please note that using the model explicated below does not require any special cross-cultural knowledge by the teacher. All that is required is an ability to allow students to learn for and by themselves through facilitating an in-class exercise well within the competence of any teacher.

The model shown below is used in multicultural classes to raise awareness amongst all students of the differences and similarities they may have in their roles as students as well as in relation to the institution and its teachers. I ask them to work in culturally congruent groups where possible, and to explore their reactions to the model—what patterns do they recognise as representative of their experience in pre-school, school and university settings. To increase the interaction between teacher and students, I suggest that this model is best presented on a whiteboard, one column at a time:

TEACHER SEEN AS:	CONTENT SEEN AS:	STUDENT FOCUS 1:	2:
Authority figure	The TRUTH	Me	Success
Expert	The latest	My group	Fairness
A resource	A range of possibilities	All students	Non-failure

Some examples of how I may explicate each of these items: to begin with, the first two are both concerned with a double perspective—the teacher's/institution's and the students'. So where any institution or teacher places themself is one side of the coin. At the same time, since this choice may in itself be culturally congruent, it is always relevant to the situation as a whole. How others perceive us can often be a function of how we see ourselves.

As an 'authority figure' I, as teacher, have power and influence both in and outside of the classroom. Students are likely to open the door for me, or at least wait until I have gone through before doing so themselves. Should I happen to walk into a café/restaurant/bar where students are gathered, those who see me as an 'authority figure' are likely to stand up and greet me formally. Whatever I say is important and is to be taken as the truth—and passing exams means reproducing my thinking, especially my favourite opinions. Alternatively, the café/restaurant/bar scenario could lead to some students seeing my presence as an intrusion on their personal time, and they are likely to leave and go elsewhere.

As 'expert', I am expected to know most and best. I should have the correct answer to any and all questions, and be fully up-to-date with all issues related to my subject. No student should ever be able to upstage me on a point of content. Any student who 'over-engages' with me in class can be seen as depriving others of my planned input and therefore impacting on the course content.

As 'resource', I am available for discussion and debate. Questioning my opinions and requesting my guidance are normal: the norm here would be a collaborative form of classroom interaction, exploring alternatives, delighting in differences of opinion, allowing individualised learning according to interest and ability.

As can be seen, each of these descriptors in the first column is directly related to the 'Content' column, so that the first two headings are interrelated as constructs. As touched upon above (Chinese and 'western' students), these distinctions in student/teacher perceptions of their relationship and its relevance for course content, can and do lead to misunderstandings. An additional aspect is that these first two columns may also be indicative of the ethnocentric nature of the Business School teaching/learning culture. To what extent this is implicit or explicit will also have an impact. Far too many students are being lured to schools by an over-enthusiastic use of the word 'international' in the school's marketing, only to find that faculty and management apply a policy of 'our way or the highway'!

When we move to the 'student focus' area, we are moving into a less obvious—or maybe less acknowledged/acknowledgeable—area. Here, students are generally more able to recognise others than they are at describing themselves. Be that as it may, even considering these options opens up areas for discussion. The student whose full focus is 'me' is generally easily recognised. For 'my group', the implications are more easily known. Generally, students with a shared background— whether national-cultural or social—can be distinguished. This can include sharing notes in exams. The 'all students' dimension is generally recognisable where student unions or student representation through, for example, class representatives are essential and active elements.

Where 'success' is concerned, we need only think of students for whom a distinction is the only valid result, or being class valedictorian, or any other such distinguishing honour. 'Fairness' is characteristic of students whose cultural influences include total honesty at exams, totally honest exams where all questions have been adequately covered in lectures or readings and so on. 'Non-failure' can be described as a situation where students focus on minimum requirements for a pass, and no more.

Such simple, generalised descriptions are usually more than enough for students to begin working on a profile of their 'home' culture and educational environment. Groups can report to the class as a whole, and a rough class profile can be created. Students can be encouraged to elaborate on these patterns, comparing and contrasting with each other.

It is not unusual for students to discover that differences in the first two dimensions do not exclude similarities in the latter two. Or that a value on 'fairness' can lead to explicit condemnation of cheating at exams, which may be more typical of a value on 'my group' and 'non-failure'. An interesting variation can be that 'authority figure' and 'the truth' can be combined equally well with 'me' and 'success', as can 'resource' and 'range of possibilities'.

What is important is that students and teachers share an opportunity to explicate, explore and as openly as possible discuss these issues publicly, so that awareness is being raised on a collective level of some of the underlying and culturally relevant issues in any international class. Issues raised and discussed during an opening session can become a reference when misunderstandings seem to be occurring later.

With an international MBA class, a simple extrapolation can be useful. Replacing the words as follows has an interesting impact. 'Teacher' becomes 'management'; 'content' becomes 'company policy'; 'student' becomes 'career'. Exploring these can add a dimension to the original educational setting, relevant to an international class in any Business School.

From the general to the particular, with a practical individual/classroom exercise

As educators, our interest is in learning. A number of researchers and authors have explored this subject, amongst them David Kolb (Kolb 1984). Kolb correlated his findings on the process of learning with possible 'styles' of learning or preferences, and developed his Learning Styles Questionnaire (LSQ), with 120 self-evaluated items. In England, two management trainers—Peter Honey and Alan Mumford—adapted Kolb's model and LSQ for easy application in executive settings. This led to an 80-item Learning Styles Inventory (LSI), and four simply understood Learning Styles: Activist, Reflector, Theorist and Pragmatist (Honey and Mumford 1992). Naturally, combinations can and do occur.

In order to promote a more interactive process in class than might usually be the result of an individual pen-and-paper exercise, I have developed a 16-item 'quick and dirty' version. Professors Jane Klobas and Stefano Renzi of SDA Bocconi, Milan, Italy have used this in their classes and correlated the results with the use of the 80-item pen-and-paper version. While there are certainly individual nuances in the results, the overall view of the Learning Style subgroups in any class are sufficiently accurate to be of use to both students and faculty. Anyway, here it is:

I draw the following matrix and ask students to copy it. I then give four learning situations, with four alternative learning preferences. First the diagram:

	A	B	C	D
1				
2				
3				
4				

I then go through the following situations and responses.

Situation 1: Learning to Ride a Bicycle

(As a metaphor for learning about a new mobile, computer, camera, computer program and so on).

    A. You get on the bicycle, wobble around a bit, fall off. You get back on the bicycle, adjust your balance and speed of pedalling and start cycling You try to turn, and fall off again. You get back on again, hold your balance, pedal firmly, and turn less sharply. It works! You then get bored, hop off your bicycle, and go on to something new. You have, however, now learned how to ride a bicycle and will always remember it.

    B. You watch A. You notice—with feeling—the dangers of falling off. You note the connections between balance, speed and careful turning. You go home, think it all through, and the following day, carefully mount a bicycle on a gentle downward hill, and start putting your observations and reflections into practice.

    C. You find the best manual you can on 'Riding a Bicycle'. You read it, absorb it. Should you ever need to ride a bicycle, you now know how.

    D. You find an expert cyclist, and ask them to simply and clearly show you how. No theory, just hands-on practice.

SITUATION 2: GROUP-WORK ON A COURSE

To explore this, imagine that each lettered group—A, B, C, D—is represented by five members of that learning style.

A. Before the teacher has quite finished introducing the task, you in your A group are up and running, looking for a public place in which to work. It is important for your group to see and be seen, to hear and be heard. Your group members will manage a task focus for about five minutes before launching happily into a discussion of everything and anything. With five minutes to go before it is time to report back, one member will bring the group to focus on the actual task—this member will probably be the group presenter. The presentation is likely to be highly spontaneous and include many items which others of that group do not explicitly recognise—though agree with as possibilities.

B. You and the other potential members of this group wait until it is absolutely clear that the teacher has no more information to give. You then look for a quiet and private place where you may work in peace. After a couple of moments, you all slowly agree that you are not all fully clear about the task. A reluctant representative is dispatched to find the teacher and clarify the task. Now your group can work! Group B will never be finished on time—it is always too soon to reach a final and safe conclusion. The reporting back will be brief, and focused more on the questions raised than any possible conclusions.

C. You will probably first get clarification of the task, then work with great efficiency to complete it, which you and your Group C colleagues are likely to do with time to spare. You use this time to explore other models and group tasks you have experienced, probably better suited to the current task than that being taught. Your group report will be more about the suitability of alternative models, than the actual task.

D. You will have one question: Why are we doing this? If the teacher answers satisfactorily, then your group will do the task. You are generally finished first, and use the spare time to make phone calls, check mail, watch the news, and so on. Group D reporting will be to the point and practical.

SITUATION 3: ASKING QUESTIONS IN CLASS

A. These are frequent questioners. Any silence can be ended with your questions. You can ask incomplete questions, where the answer comes to you as you ask the question. You can start off with a question which becomes a statement. You can ask the same question twice, apparently unaware that you have already asked it.

B. Asks retroactive questions—on yesterday's class, last week's readings, and so on. Always well-formulated and well-articulated questions (you probably rehearse your questions, to get them absolutely right!).

C. Asks short, concise and analytical questions. You want an answer now—or soon.

D. Your favourite words: 'Why' and 'How'.

SITUATION 4: PRE-COURSE/CLASS READING MATERIAL

A. Received with enthusiasm, fully intending to read it, you manage to find it again immediately before the relevant class, flick quickly through it for a diagram. Come to class with the reading prominently displayed. At the earliest opportunity, you refer enthusiastically to the one diagram you have seen, making intelligent comments about it. Honestly intend to read the material after class, which you never actually do.

B. Experts with highlight-pens, usually green and red or orange. Highlight all texts according to a consistent system. Your course material is always a rainbow of highlights.

C. If the material is clear, logical and complete, you will probably not come to class—too many time-wasting questions, group-works, and general time-wasting.

D. Will check what it is of the material you absolutely must read in order to follow the class. Frustrated if you discover that you have read materials unnecessarily!

When the students have completed the matrix, I ask them to identify as '4A', '3A', '2A', '1A' and so on, through A, B, C, D. They are also encouraged to focus on combinations, for example 2, each of any letter. They form groups around similar profiles. As such, the class has now moved from the culturally homogenous groups of the first exercise, to more interpersonally related groups of personal learning styles in this second exercise.

I then add the specific Learning Styles and some general information on them, as shown in Table 9.1:

TABLE 9.1:   HONEY AND MUMFORD'S LEARNING STYLES

A	B	C	D
ACTIVIST	**REFLECTOR**	**THEORIST**	**PRAGMATIST**
Learns through activity	Learns through observing and reflecting	Learns through theory, models, solid input	Learns through 'hands on' practice
Likes interaction	Prefers listening	Likes structured, focused discussions	Likes realistic exercises
Likes a high tempo	Likes a slow tempo	Expects the 'right' tempo, which they 'know'	Likes varied tempo
Asks questions	Retroactive questions	Concise, logical questions	'Why' and 'how'
'Moves on' quickly	Prefers to consolidate	Moves on when satisfied	Can stick with it until they know how to do it

This is followed by discussion in the Learning Style groups, and then a general open plenary session.

With these first two exercises, both general cultural as well as more specific personal differences and similarities have been explored and explicated around learning—the shared activity of an international student class. Issues of direct relevance to working life in an international career have been explored in the safer and less decisive environment of a classroom—rather than in the stressful and costly world of real business and real organisational life. The next section of this chapter completes this combined learning focus of using the classroom as well as any group projects to provide solid experiential learning of value to both the students and the class during the programme—as well as solid practical training for life after Business School.

Groups and group work, with a practical group exercise

As mentioned above, the use of groups, group projects, group reports and group grading is becoming (or maybe even has become) standard practice in Business Schools. Regrettably, the use of professional group facilitators lags far, far, behind this trend. In what seems like a fit of neo-Taylorism, students are simply expected to be the group robots of trendy faculties. The reality is that people in groups—especially perhaps young, ambitious, career-hungry MBA students—are anything but robots. The Oisíns, Bríds, Eoghans, Daraghs and Aislinns of the opening vignettes are in full focus—including their impact on the groups/classes of which they are members. Cross-cultural and/or interpersonal and/or inter-competence differences are bubbling to the surface. In addition, the development process of any group is also up and running! And this process is particularly complex across cultures, in terms of expectations, attitudes, norms, behaviours and sanctions. This may be the forgotten—or even neglected or disowned—child of international business education.

An additional complexity here is that the most popular models of group development are generally from an Anglo-Saxon perspective and more particularly from an American one. Significantly, in this context, the most commonly-used models are moreover embedded in the dominant WASP (White, Anglo-Saxon, Protestant) and highly individualistic subculture of the USA. As such, these perspectives are fine and fully applicable within the cultures from which they sprung—though less useful in other cultures or with multicultural groups (Gaffney 2006).

My own research has been into testing parameters of group development which may apply cros-culturally inasmuch as culturally heterogeneous as well as homogenous groups can apply the constructs in a manner which supports group development without overt normative elements, other than those projected by members of specific cultures. This latter aspect is one which the proposed model can highlight, thereby providing an opportunity for further process within any group.

First, the Self and Peer Appraisal 'International Group Dynamics Model' (IGDM). This is worked on in two separate steps—Basic Stance and Behavioural Dynamics. It is strongly recommended that the Basic Stance exercise is used as early as the first gathering of a new Project Group.

HANDOUT 1:

BASIC STANCE

A Part of the Group . . . . Apart from the Group

INSTRUCTION: Please prepare to describe what each of these would mean in your home culture; also where you would be most comfortable on this continuum. Indicate the latter with an 'X.'

Then, one at a time, each member describes their understanding of these terms, and where they have placed themselves on the continuum.

The purpose of the Basic Stance self/peer appraisal is to explore the underlying assumptions about being a member of a group which each person brings with them. Further, to contrast and compare these assumptions—and first then to find whatever degree of congruence there may be amongst group members' perception of their positions as self- and—later—peer-appraised.

By about the third meeting, the group can be ready for the next step. Start with a current version of the Basic Stance exercise, as follows:

Handout 2

Basic Stance

A Part of the Group . . . . Apart from the Group

Instruction: Position yourself in this group with an X on the continuum. Use names or initials to position your perception of where the other group members are.

Each member declares their own self-appraised position, followed by listening to each other member's peer appraisal of that member's position.

The teacher can then present the next step, using the Behavioural Dynamics model (Figure 9.1). This step is best done spontaneously in real time. (Please note that the behaviours to the right might be those mostly associated with maintaining a Basic Stance of being 'A Part of the Group', with the opposite applying for those to the left. However, such generalisations will give way to the specific internal dynamics of any particular group, as self- and peer-perceived.)

The model provides an instrument for a) self-appraisal and b) peer-appraisal. Each member of a Project Group, for example, first self-appraises—ascribing whatever meaning to the constructs of the parameters which is relevant to them. They then also do a chart for each of the other members—from whatever perspective the appraiser holds, and whatever meaning the appraiser gives to the constructs of the model.

For example: take the core constructs 'A Part of the Group' and 'Apart From the Group' which here cover an hypothesised universal issue of group membership with a variety of cultural norms and practices. In the vignettes mentioned earlier, it is probable that Oisín, Bríd, Eoghan, Daragh and Aislinn would each place themselves as 'A Part of the Group' from their personal/sociocultural perspectives. Voicing these perspectives and their concomitant self-assessments will open up important issues within their respective groups and allow for discussion of cross-cultural behaviours, their similarities and differences.

HANDOUT 3

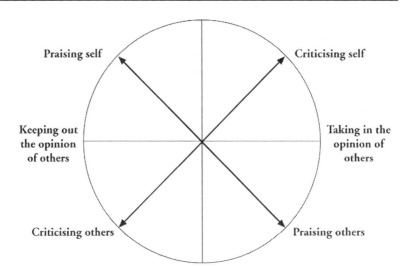

FIGURE 9.1: BEHAVIOURAL DYNAMICS

INSTRUCTION: Do a self-appraisal by indicating with an X where you see yourself on each continuum. Please note that you may find it appropriate to mark 2 X's, indicating some situational aspect of your choice—mostly in one place, though sometimes in another on each continuum.

Now do a peer-appraisal by indicating with names or initials your perception of where each of the others are positioned.

Each member first gives her/his position on each continuum, then receives the peer appraisals.

Discussion

When the full three-step exercise has been used, and each group member has voiced their self and peer assessments, these issues may become dynamic and fertile aspects of life in a multicultural work group. Issues which may hitherto have lain under the surface of the group's dynamics will at least be aired, if not immediately resolved. Resolving such issues in a manner which supports the work of the group can be seen as the 'inner task' of the group. It is the group members themselves who dynamically establish, develop and maintain the norms of that specific group to which they belong, finding a specific equilibrium between the diverse social, professional and cultural forces at work in the group at any time.

What is often referred to in the Anglo-Saxon literature as a balance between group maintenance and task (Adair 1986) is a more complex issue in multicultural contexts. In this latter case, a self-created synthesis of values and behaviours is more likely to be consensually developed and maintained by group members than any externally enforced normative system. Such a system may all too often be ethnocentric in origin and aims, thus allying itself from the outset with some, though probably not all, group members and inadvertently already dividing rather than uniting the group as a working unit with a shared task.

To return a moment to the earlier project group vignettes: in the always possible event that these students found themselves in the same group, the following scenario might well be relevant.

At the first meeting, all would probably place themselves as 'A Part of the Group'. Some would do this because, culturally, they 'ought to/ should' do so; others because they 'must' as part of the course; others because being 'A Part of the Group'—any group—is a cultural norm and expectation. The discussion which followed this first exercise may well support the members to accept and even explore their differences.

By the third meeting, when the self-appraisals meet the peer-appraisals, then core group issues which were either casually or rationally accepted the first time may now become open to distinctions between theory and practice. Wherever members place themselves on the Basic Stance continuum, they are now faced with hearing how others perceive them—which may or may not be congruent with their self-appraisal. For example, Eoghan's on and off appearances and contributions would not influence his cultural perception of—formally—being 'A Part of the Group'. Others may be likely to place him 'Apart from the Group', as they perceive group membership. Aislinn's faithful attendance and obedience to explicit requests may create some confusion: whilst others would place her as 'A Part of the Group' with a touch of 'Apart from the Group', she is likely to place herself firmly as 'Apart from ...' due to her self-criticism around age, experience, contribution, and so on.

These and other issues would become more explicit as the group explored the Behavioural Dynamics exercise in both cases. Eoghan's ability to keep out the opinions of others as well as his generally critical attitude would be up for discussion, as would Aislinn's ability to take in others, be silently self-critical and openly impressed by others' knowledge and experience. Properly facilitated, the discussions that followed this exercise would not only support this Project Group as a working, task-focused unit, it would also provide an invaluable opportunity for all students to experientially learn about group dynamics. This latter would include some notion of the complexity and opportunities of cross-cultural group leadership in the context of international business. Surely such considerations fully belong to the curriculum of any serious international Business School education?

Concluding remarks

I intentionally subtitled this chapter 'A Mild Polemic'. I have far too many experiences of schools, managements and teacher colleagues who hold tightly on to known and proven approaches, while marketing innovation and creativity. Or schools which market 'an international environment' and actually mean the students, not the school. And certainly not the management in its attitude, nor the faculty in either its constitution or attitudes or practices. Neither ethnocentric nor standardised approaches, however explicitly proposed, can fully accommodate or satisfy an international student market. It is my firm belief that, until Business Schools can fully and actively engage in cross-cultural educational practices, then we are not practising what we may like to preach, and certainly not encouraging the very internationalisation of business that we claim to espouse and promote. We are rather continuing the cultural imperialism and dominance that has, in part, created the divided world in which we live.

Concluding recommendations for management and teachers

I am starting with management, as it is impossible for any teacher to attempt anything new without support—both before and after (see 3 below!).

1. Explore the needs of students by encouraging more qualitative programme evaluations rather then the ethnocentric question-naires of today, mostly geared to reinforce your status quo.
2. Pay more attention to younger faculty, who in terms of age and experience, are closer to your students. Balance their views with those of senior faculty who represent the quality of course content in general.
3. Experiment. And remember that a 'failed' experiment in an educational setting has as much to do with the experiment itself as it has with the outcome. Do not be afraid to try again.

For teachers:

1. Remember that you do not need any major cross-cultural knowledge to facilitate the learning of multicultural classes—your classroom skills are often more than enough!
2. Allow multicultural classes/groups to find their own equilibrium. Neither expect nor impose 'your' norms.
3. Learn to enjoy experiential learning—your own most of all!

References

Adair, J. (1986). *Effective Teambuilding*. London and Sydney: Pan Books.

Bartlett C.A. & Ghoshal S. (1989). *Managing Across Borders—The Transnational Solution*. London: Hutchinson Business Books.

Gaffney, S. (2006). Gestalt with Groups—A Cross-cultural Perspective. *Gestalt Review, 10*(3), pp205-219.

Hofstede, G. (1984). *Culture's Consequences*. London: Sage Publications.

Hofstede, G. (1994). *Cultures and Organizations*. London: Harper Collins.

Honey, P. & Mumford, A. (1992). *The Manual of Learning Styles*. Maidenhead, Berkshire, UK: Peter Honey Publications Ltd.

Kolb, D. (1984). *Experiential Learning*. New Jersey: Prentice Hall.

Maznievski, M. & Peterson (1997). *Cross-cultural Work Groups* (Claremont Symposium on Applied Social Psychology). Edited by Granrose and Oskamp. Thousand Oaks: Sage Publications.

ᴦ

This chapter was published in *Teaching and Learning and Business School: Transforming Business Education* (2008), chapter 10, pp.111-125, published by Gower Publishing Ltd. Hampshire, England, and is reproduced here by kind permission of the editors, Par Martensson, Magnus Bild and Kristina Nilsson.

10.

Gestalt in the North of Ireland:

A Blow-in's Perspective

Models of Training in Gestalt Therapy in Ireland' (O'Leary & O'Sullivan, 2003) is the title of a paper in an earlier issue of *Gestalt Review*. The authors provide a brief history as well as a full description of more recent and current developments. The focus is clearly on the Republic of Ireland, with two brief mentions of Belfast and Northern Ireland. One of these refers to the inaugural meeting of The Irish Gestalt Association (IGA) and mentions that 'Gestalt therapists from as far away as Belfast in Northern Ireland travelled south to participate.' As recently, then, as 2003, Belfast was still regarded by some as another country—the United Kingdom of Great Britain and Northern Ireland—and therefore 'far away'. In view of recent political events, and the ever-increasing use of 'the island of Ireland' to denote the geographical whole in which more and more integrated activities are becoming the norm, this is as good a time as any to complete the picture by adding this current paper to that earlier one.

First, allow me to explain the subtitle and thus provide the particular context of this brief paper. A blow-in is a stranger who apparently has taken root to some extent, probably temporarily although possibly more permanently, in an environment other than the one that is na-tive for her/him. As such, I am a blow-in in the North of Ireland in general, and Belfast in particular. I am a Dubliner from the Republic to the south, and a resident of Stockholm, Sweden! At the same time, I spend more time per annum in Belfast than in Dublin, and have done so since 1996...so, yes: a blow-in! Anyway, here is my perspective on Gestalt in the North, vetted by local Gestalt practitioners.

In the late 1990s, I was asked by a local Gestaltist to do a three-day

residential 'Introduction to Gestalt in Organisations' workshop with
a socio-politically mixed group of professionals in the fields of social
work and community development. Having completed the social
preliminaries, I casually asked whether there was anyone with any
previous experience or knowledge of Gestalt. 'Yes,' said a man, 'Gestalt
and battery!' (For non-native speakers of English, 'assault and battery'
is a common criminal charge related to violent behavior.) He went
on to graphically describe his experience of 'a rabidly confrontational
American' Gestaltist in the 1970s who had 'abused' his way through
a Gestalt workshop in Derry, North of Ireland. I was left in no doubt
whatsoever that the slightest hint of any such tendencies in me would
result in at least three people immediately leaving, having first advised
all others to do the same! I am happy to say that the workshop ended
with all still present.

In the intervening period, from the worst excesses of 'Gestalt and
battery' to the beginning of the 1990s, some individuals found Gestalt
training outside the North, either in the South of Ireland, or Scotland, England, or further afield. Two in particular worked with Ischa
Blomberg's Gestalt Trust in Italy: Hilda Courtney and John Leary-Joyce.
Each of them would later become pivotal in the development of Gestalt
in the North of Ireland. In the South, Eleanor O'Leary in Cork and
Joan O'Leary (no relation) with an American, Hank O'Mahony, in
Dublin were offering training programs. These and others are covered
in the 2003 paper.

In 1992, following inquiries from local professionals in youth
work and community development, Hilda Courtney and her colleagues from the Gestalt Trust, Edinburgh, Scotland came to Belfast
to start up a training program and possibly a local Gestalt Trust along
the lines of Ischa Blomberg's fully participative model. Group 1 was
formed and Gestalt training in the Region had formally begun. The
trainers were Hilda Courtney, Flora Meadows, Marea Robertson,
Dagmar Theisen, and Norberto da Silva. Following a chance meeting
at EAGT in Cambridge, in 1995, I was invited to be a trainer in the
program. I came to Group three in 1996, and have been working with
Gestalt in the North ever since, up to twelve weeks a year as of 2002.
Within a year or two of arriving there, I was engaged as a supervisor
by a graduates from Groups 1 to 3 of the Trust's training program.

We negotiated the startup of a Supervision and Training Group with a focus on working with groups and organizations. One of the issues that emerged early in the life of this group was my recommendations about good and relevant reading material regarding Gestalt and society. I was delighted to recommend immediately both of Philip Lichtenberg's insightful books (Lichtenberg,1990; Lichtenberg, van Beusekom & Gibbons,1997). This later led to a small group forming the Gestalt Practitioners' Network (GPN), which invited Lichtenberg to do a workshop in Belfast. Both he and they fondly and regularly recollect that workshop and the strong links they forged. So Lichtenberg's admirable and socially relevant work is alive and well, and contributing to the gestalt of Gestalt in the North.

More recently, Contact Youth, a voluntary organization working with counseling and group work in schools and communities with Gestalt-trained people at the senior management level, invited Carl Hodges (NYIGT) to do a workshop on racism—a growing area of concern in the North, with a large Chinese population and a growing African presence, both overflows from Britain, on top of the existing racism of sectarianism and socio-political polarization. In addition, a voluntary community organization in Omagh, County Tyrone, North of Ireland, invited Bob Lee to do a series of workshops on 'Shame' which he is in the process of doing at the time of writing (2007). Bud Feder, from New Jersey via Berkeley, ran a workshop on Gestalt Group Therapy in Belfast in the summer of 2007.

There is a special significance here in these contributions to the knowledge and skills base of local practitioners. Both Lichtenberg and Hodges were dealing with issues that are directly and fundamentally social in nature. Lee's theme of shame is particularly relevant in a society divided between the guilt and shame syndromes of the Catholic Church at its most conservatively traditional, and those of the Protestant free churches which are especially prevalent in the region. Additional sources of shame in a social context are in the nature of a community's involvement/non-involvement in the violence of the years of conflict since the late 1960s in particular. Feder's theme of group is a recurring focus for Gestalt practitioners here, offering a more socially relevant model than individual therapy.

The fact is that local Gestalt practitioners are deeply involved in social and political issues and in the relevance of their work in that socio-political context. Paul Goodman would feel at home here among the local Gestaltists, as would Eliot Shapiro. Even individual therapy comes under this heading, including the intentional client—choice of a therapist from their own community—or one from the other community. Interestingly, more and more Gestalt individual therapists are moving towards co-working and running both closed and open therapy groups. The socio-political context is always ground here—and sometimes figure. These and other issues mentioned below are more fully dealt with in a forthcoming paper (Gaffney, 2008).

Among us, I believe that Philip Lichtenberg, Carl Hodges, Bob Lee, Bud Feder, and I may have finally put the 'Gestalt and battery' reputation to rest in terms of 'visiting' Gestaltists (I somehow belong to that category: the North is distinctly and proudly tribal. I am, after all, from Dublin in the South and living in Stockholm, Sweden). Our local colleagues have assisted its death, waked it, buried it, and carried on.

Around the turn of the last century, a difficulty arose with the Gestalt Trust training. The Trust was not accredited by the major accrediting bodies in Britain. This led to a choice-point: continue with non-accredited training, or change training institute?

At this point, the Ischa Blomberg connection between Hilda Courtney and John Leary-Joyce became supportive. John was one of the founders and directors of the Gestalt Centre London (GCL), and they had a fully accredited Masters' Programme in Gestalt Psychotherapy with the University of North London, England. On invitation from graduates of the Trust Programme, GCL became the formal training organization. This led to the Masters, Certificate and Postgraduate Diploma programs being offered by GCL in Belfast in which I was a trainer, clinical supervisor, and tutor. The first dissertations currently are being drafted and were aired at the Writers' Conference in Belfast in May, 2007. The GCL faculty that set up and successfully implemented these programs included John Leary Joyce, Gaie Houston, Toni Gilligan, Jane Puddy, and Carol Siederer.

At the same time, I still ran (and run) a group/organization supervision group, a clinical supervision group, individual clinical supervision, management consulting, and occasional organizational development engagements from Belfast.

Other aspects of the development of Gestalt in the North include the seven trainee groups that have been there from Sweden in as many years, the recent (2005) active presence of a truly international Gestalt group, and the EAGT Writers' Support Conferences. The Swedish groups are fourth-year students from the M.Sc in Gestalt in Organisations program at the Gestalt Academy of Scandinavia. They have spent a training week in Belfast, mixing both socially and professionally with local Gestalt practitioners as well as their organizational clients since 1999. The GIC/GISC sponsored Organization and Systems Dynamics International (OSDI) Program spent a week in Belfast in 2005. The 36 participants were from 13 countries ranging from the USA in the West to Singapore in the East with a large contingent from sub-Saharan Africa and the Middle East. A core part of this program is that six-person consultancy teams—chosen by faculty to guarantee the maximum mix of all diversities—do a two half-day, hands-on consultancy to a real organization in the area.

So there were six teams of six people in Belfast practicing Gestalt skills in real time. The impact was amazing. One organization subsequently ran a staff conference in line with its management team's experience of being with a Gestalt team for two half days. Another made a significant policy change. From two others, there have been requests to join Gestalt training programs in the North.

The local Gestalt practitioners have become influential members of the community—socially, politically and professionally. Among their many sources of influencing and supporting change, the following are some of their major areas of work.

Triskele is a voluntary community development agency, located on the Republic of Ireland side of a 'cross-border' area, and serves the local and cross-border communities. This was founded by two Belfast-trained Gestalt therapists, and the agency's first Director was a graduate of the GIC/GISC OSDI Program. A number of Gestaltists have acted as process facilitators to the management and staff since the organization's birth, and its staff are now co-leading groups with Gestalt practitioners from Belfast.

Barnardo's 'Parenting in a Divided Society' Project. Doctor Barnardo's Homes were originally a British-based Protestant home for orphaned or underprivileged children. In the North, Barnardo's became more concerned with child protection and educating parents in parenthood under the banner, 'Parenting Matters'. A Gestalt practitioner from Group 2 of the original Gestalt Trust Scotland training program has worked there as a project leader for many years. The focus of the 'Parenting in a Divided Society' initiative was to work with parents from both of the main communities whose children and whose parenting had been seriously impacted by the years of armed conflict. A Gestalt colleague from Group 1 and fellow member of the Supervision and Training Group was engaged by Barnardo's to co-work the project.

They worked with two groups from each of the most seriously impacted housing areas in Belfast from either side of the community and political divide. Their work was demanding, draining, and filled with anxiety as they carried their own affiliations into their work with each other and, for each of them, 'their own' and 'the others'.

The result is a brilliant display of Gestalt work at its best: daring, respectful, experiential, experimental, and phenomenological. Published as a *Resource Manual* (Keenan & Burrows, 2004a) for social workers across the region, it consists of a main document and five specific workbooks. It was launched with general political support at a premiere location, and the authors have followed up the launch of the *Resource* with a series of one-day and half-day workshops across the North. Apart from the authors having orally and in writing declared themselves to be Gestalt therapists, the *Resource* amply quotes and references such well-known Gestalt authors as Beisser, Kolodny, Lewin, Lichtenberg, Nevis, Phillipson, Wyman, and Perls, Hefferline and Goodman.

Contact Youth: this is a growing voluntary organization that offers and supports counseling services in schools and a 24/7 telephone service and youth groups in the communities' interface areas, and it is now a major participant in a special youth suicide prevention project. This agency also has engaged Gestalt practitioners from each of the major communities as facilitators of an equally mixed interface youth group.

The resulting report, *Do You Think We're Mental* (Keenan & Burrows 2006) where 'mental' is 'psychiatric cases', covers not only the work itself, but also Gestalt therapy theory and practice, as well as lengthy references to and descriptions of field theory using the writings of Malcolm Parlett, and Mark McConville's insightful and Lewinian work on adolescence.

Flying Horse: despite its somewhat poetic name, this is a sprawling estate of mildly substandard housing hastily built in an area well south of the city by the Belfast City Council to house dispossessed families, mainly from the Catholic community. It has long suffered from high unemployment and all its attendant ills: alcoholism, domestic violence, criminality, drug abuse, and high suicide levels. With the active support of a Gestaltist from Group 1, three local Gestalt therapists have worked there in community development and social research with a view to improving services to this underprivileged community. A report has been published, *Out of Town, Out of Sight* (Keenan & Burrows 2004b), and another is on its way (Keenan & Gartner, 2008).

Northern Ireland Childrens' Enterprise (NICE). This is a volunteer organization that works with schools from each tradition, first bringing two parallel classes together, followed usually by parents and teachers. The school children have regular, jointly facilitated sessions together and a two-week residential session each year. As these children grow older, many return to NICE as volunteers. The Programmes Manager is a graduate of the GCL Diploma in Gestalt Psychotherapy Programme, as are many of the facilitators. NICE has also been one of the organizations visited regularly by the Swedish groups mentioned earlier.

Accredited Counseling Training: a Gestalt therapist in the Belfast area and another in the Derry area are engaged as trainers, specifically in Gestalt theory and methodology, in local, professional counseling skills training programs.

Group Work Skills: Originally deisgned and run by one of the first trainers with The Gestalt Trust, Scotland, this accredited training program has been further developed by training 'generations' of Gestalt practitioners, each of whom have left their mark on the materials and methodology. It is one of the best-known and respected professional skills training programs in the Region.

In addition, local Gestalt practitioners are actively involved in organizations that work with rape victims and families bereaved during 'the Troubles' by military, police, and/or paramilitary actions; they also work as group facilitators in political movements and parties as well as in a wide range of volunteer community development organizations. In addition, most of the people concerned have individual therapy practices.

As can be seen, Gestalt is alive and well and developing. However, there are not at present, nor have there been since 2003, any local training groups or training organizations to train Gestalt therapists. For 'foreign' organizations, the travel and accommodation costs along with trainer fees require a specific number of students with the means to make a long-term time and financial commitment, and while these numbers are potentially there, they are not, at present, in practice. Recruiting consumes time, money and energy—which is an added burden for a non-local Institute. Affiliating with established universities, as many of the English institutes do, adds to the expense as well as the administrative burden. And since local practitioners in the North of Ireland formally come under the British authorities in the form of the National Health Service, the Department of Education, and the like, then a connection with an established institute with a university affiliation that offers a path to licensing as a Gestalt therapist is not only desirable, but also is experienced as necessary.

Only time will tell how the further development of this small, thriving and influential Gestalt presence will emerge in the North of Ireland, and thus also make its contribution to the presence of Gestalt throughout the whole island of Ireland.

ৎ

My thanks and appreciation to those members of the Gestalt community in the North of Ireland whose work I have alluded to in these pages: Michael Ahearne, Rosie Burrows, Joëlle Gartner, Bríd Keenan, Paula Keenan, Tom Kiernan, Dominica MacGowan, Gráinne McKenna, Berny MacMahon, Maria MacManus, Joanna McMinn, Mary Kay Mullan, Sonya Murray, Norma Patterson, Marie Quiery, and Fred Williams.

References

Gaffney, S. (2008). Gestalt Group Supervision in a Divided Society. *British Gestalt Journal, 17*(1), pp.27-39.

Keenan, B. & Burrows, R. (2004a). *We'll Never Be the Same: A Resource*. Belfast: Barnardo's Northern Ireland.

Keenan, B. & Burrows, R. (2004b). *Out of Town, Out of Sight: An Action Research Report*. Lisburn: Down Lisburn Trust.

Keenan, B. & Burrows, R. (2006). *Do You Think We're Mental? A Therapeutic Approach to Groupwork with Young People*. Belfast: Contact Youth.

Keenan, B. & Gartner, J. (2008). *Progress Report*. Lisburn: Down Lisburn Trust, in press.

Lichtenberg, P. (1990). *Community and Confluence: Undoing the Clinch of Oppression*. Cleveland: GIC Press.

Lichtenberg, P., van Beusekom, J. & Gibbons, D. (1997). *Encountering Bigotry*. Cambridge, MA: GestaltPress.

Maalouf, A. (2003). *In the Name of Identity*. New York: Penguin Group.

Memmi, A. (1967). *The Colonizer and the Colonized*. Boston: Beacon Press.

Nevis, E. (1987). *A Gestalt Approach to Organization Consulting*. Cleveland: GIC Press.

O'Leary, E. & O'Sullivan, D. (2003). Models of Training in Gestalt Therapy in Ireland. *Gestalt Review 7*(2).

Parlett, M. (2005). Contemporary Gestalt Therapy: Field Theory. In A. Woldt & S. Toman (eds.), *Gestalt Therapy: History, Theory and Practice*. Thousand Oaks: Sage Publications.

Perls, F., Hefferline, R., & Goodman, P. (1951/1994). *Gestalt Therapy: Excitement and Growth in the Human Personality*. New York: Julian Press.

⤳

This article was published in the *Gestalt Review* (2008), Vol.12 (1) pp. 93-99, and is reproduced here by kind permission of the editor , Joseph Melnick.

11

Besides the Hot Seat:
Gestalt in Organisations
—Perspectives and Applications

Introduction

Rick Maurer commented about the validity of gestalt in organizational settings, or OSD (2005, p. 238), and I made the following point in response:

> *The theory and practice of OSD is not necessarily a case of an individual therapeutic modality being used out of the context for which it was intended, and to which it should primarily be applied. It is, rather, a sibling if not a twin to gestalt therapy, one which can stand on its own feet, which always had developed and still is developing its own uniqueness. It was not and is not a distant cousin from an estranged branch of the family. Its core theoretical roots are the same. Its practice makes the same demands on its practitioners, though in the complex environments of groups, larger collectives and the individuals embedded in both of them.*

In this chapter, I will now expand on that proposal, supported by a brief review of the history and development of gestalt OSD, and provide some theoretical considerations, interspersing both of these with examples of applications from my own practice as a gestalt OSD consultant.

Background

Of the collection of radical thinkers who met in New York and founded the New York Institute for Gestalt Therapy (NYIGT), two were known social activists in the USA—Paul Goodman and Eliot Shapiro. While Goodman practiced as a gestalt therapist for a short while, he soon returned to teaching as a form of social action as well as to his richly varied writing—this latter also a forum for his social thinking and encouragement of social change (Stoehr, 1997). Shapiro, radical educator and trade union activist that he was, brought his experience and learning from the NYIGT meetings to his work as a school supervisor (Hentoff, 1966; Wysong & Rosenfeld, 1982).

What had begun as an eclectic collection of influences, ideas, and therapeutic practice originating in the Germany of the 1920s, came by way of South Africa to New York in the late 1940s via Fritz and Laura Perls. On this journey, the holism of Jan Smuts (Smuts, 1926/1996) had been added to an already well-integrated mix of Kierkegaard, Buber, the gestalt psychologists Wertheimer, Koffka and Köhler, the neurologist Goldstein, the early work of Kurt Lewin, and the towering presence of Freud and psychoanalysis.

To all of this was now added the influences of Shapiro and Goodman. Shapiro had already read *Ego, Hunger and Aggression* [F. Perls, 1947], and was using it in his lectures (Wysong & Rosenfeld, 1982, p. 81). Goodman was steeped in philosophy, literature and social thinking.

Amongst the influences now also present, mainly through Goodman, was that of the American Pragmatists—Mead, Dewey, and James (Kitzler, 2006). By the time the notes of Fritz Perls were being transformed into what would become PHG—as it is affectionately known within gestalt circles (Perls, Hefferline & Goodman, 1951)— the overriding theoretical input of Goodman had become increasingly figural.

At the same time, Fritz and Laura Perls, Shapiro, Goodman, and the other members of the band of 'blessed and rebellious outcasts' (Eliot Shapiro, quoted in Kitzler, 2006, p. 58) were practicing these new ideas on each other. The focus here was on the therapeutic applications as this was what the Perlses had brought with them as their core professional competence.

However, as Shapiro and later Goodman showed, the theory and practice of what came to be called 'gestalt therapy' was equally applicable by Shapiro to a chaotic and neglected school system and by Goodman as a sound base for his socio-political thinking and writing.

A good example of the latter is Goodman's *Growing up Absurd* (1956), where ideas that originally appeared in PHG turn up practically unchanged in this later work (Gaffney, 2006, p. 11). Goodman's book is decidedly non-psychotherapeutic, and one in which he is closer to Shapiro than to the individual therapy focus of Fritz and Laura Perls. Goodman's focus is on 'the problems of youth in the organized society,' on exploring a society's influence on and responsibility for whatever disaffection needs to be expressed by any section of that society. Here he has moved to a level of complexity way beyond the hot seat of individual therapy and the hope, perhaps, that psychologically healthy individuals would create an equally healthy society. Goodman's thinking and writing here is truly grounded in a field perspective, in which the wholes are as worthy of examination and change as are the parts: his razor-sharp criticism of organizational, media, educational, and political mediocrity and his support for healthy refusals to submit to them are still relevant and brilliant more than 50 years after his book's publication.

In addition, it is significant to note that, amongst the first programs to be offered by the newly-formed NY Institute was one on education by Shapiro and one on writer's block by Goodman (Kitzler, 2006, p. 56). Interestingly enough, the 2006–7 NYIGT President, Burt Lazarin, was a union activist, as was Shapiro. 'What goes around, comes around ….'

While Shapiro was actively creating a *gestalt* in the school system through his practical work, Goodman, Fritz and Laura Perls, and later Isadore From were asked to train a group of organizational and clinical psychologists in Cleveland who had heard of this new approach at the NYIGT. Many of the Cleveland group had also trained at the National Training Laboratory (NTL), Kurt Lewin's brainchild. This was a group of professionals, politically and socially radical in U.S terms, who wanted to further develop their knowledge base and skills. As such, the NYIGT group, in its various constellations, was preaching to the converted. The Cleveland group included Richard Wallen, Sonia and

Edwin Nevis, Erv and Miriam Polster, Elaine Kepner, and Joseph Zinker, amongst others. Interestingly, both Kepner and Zinker wrote influential chapters in the original *Beyond the Hot Seat* (Feder & Ronall, 1980/2000)—and these chapters are again included in this edition.

The Gestalt Institute of Cleveland (GIC) was founded in 1955, three years after the NYIGT. Originally offering gestalt therapy training, its continued professional activities in organizations led to the founding of the GIC OSD Center in 1973. This branch of GIC offered professional training in a gestalt-centered approach to process consultancy in organizations, as well as training in leadership and work with groups.

This orientation continues in the work of the Gestalt International Study Center (GISC) on Cape Cod, founded by Edwin and Sonia Nevis, with its increasing focus on leadership not just of corporations, but more important of social and political organizations such as police departments, and health and community care agencies, and voluntary as well as statutory organizations dealing with HIV/AIDS. 'Social applications of gestalt' was the topic of a GISC 2006 Conference in Cape Town, South Africa, and the GISC ROOTS III 2007 Conference in Rome. In fact, 'Gestalt in Society' will be the focus for a new book (Melnick & Nevis, (eds.), in press, 2010). There is a sense in which the work and aspirations of many of the 'blessed and rebellious outcasts'—to have an impact in and on society—is once more figural and energized.

So, back to my opening comments and proposal that the practical applications of the thinking which permeates PHG was from the outset open equally to creating a theory and methodology of working with groups, and in organizations and social settings as it was to an exclusively individual therapy focus. I believe that the original Cleveland group's attraction to the work and training of the NYIGT people, as well the ease with which they integrated, developed, and expanded its application, further supports this idea.

As a result, I have chosen to title this chapter 'Besides the Hot Seat' to reinforce the notion that these twin applications—gestalt individual therapy and gestalt OSD—spring from the same theoretical and methodological seeds.

An Illustrative Mini-Case with Reflections: *The Division has a 'Problem,' #1*

On the recommendation of a colleague, I am contacted by Alison (name changed, as are all others) manager of a specialist division of a major publishing company. Over the phone, she tells me of a 'problematic' and 'difficult' member of her staff, who has become increasingly 'disruptive' in her division. She says she is contacting me as a 'last resort' in resolving this issue.

> *Oh, how I rise to the challenge of being a 'last resort'! When all else fails, call for Gaffney! If anyone can fix it, he can! Having luxuriated in this illusory euphoria for a moment, I acknowledge to myself that it is part of who I am in my work. This includes acknowledging to myself how often I have mired both myself and former clients in these treacherous swamplands! I can now return to a more sobering contextual reality. In the region where this work may take place, firing an employee is a long and complex process, often supported by documented evidence of 'having tried everything' to resolve it by other means—including the hot-shot consultant!*

So I move away from a fuller description of the issue over the phone by arranging a preliminary meeting with Alison. She immediately suggests that Brian—the 'problem'—also be present. I demur regarding Brian, explaining that this preliminary meeting is essentially to explore whether I believe that I can be of use to her and, if so, to contract formally for the consultancy. She agrees.

At our first meeting, Alison wants to go straight to talking about Brian and the trouble he is causing. I request that we begin by her describing her organization to me, so that I have some sense of context.

> *This also helps to shift the focus from 'individuals' to organizational 'roles,' often an essential first step in dis-entangling relational issues in organizations. Until and if I explore further and meet more people, I have no idea of the extent to which the presented problem is an interpersonal issue between two people, a habitual issue for*

Alison (where a 'new' Brian could easily replace a dismissed one!), or an issue embedded in the division itself.

In addition, I need to decide just who my client is—Alison or her employee group. Will this work be in the form of one-on-one consulting to Alison? (This is sometimes called 'off-line managerial supervision' or 'coaching'.) Or will this be a piece of process consultancy, where the division is the client? Basically and crucially in gestalt OSD, where is my professional and ethical responsibility? Directly to Alison, or to Alison as divisional manager? This is often the first choice-point in the work and always needs careful handling and consideration.

Alison presents the following description of her division:

One of the editors—Dorothy—is also Deputy Manager. Each editor is responsible for a number of authors and, where relevant, illustrators. Alison is a former editor and describes warmly the various well-known authors who had been hers, and how she still lunches regularly with some of them, just as she had done as an editor. The editors work closely with their authors and illustrators, including: listening to suggested projects; sometimes making their own suggestions; supporting them through periods of writer's block; establishing and following up on deadlines; and working with them around revisions and additions. Deadlines are particularly important as the specialist publications concerned have well-established peak periods and pre-publication review procedures—and towards all of these, Alison explains, authors are notoriously blasé. 'But then, they are artists,' she says. 'A good book can't be hurried.'

It is now also clear that all the editors, all the administration staff, and the two design staff (in the Production Department) are women. Brian and one semi-retired, part-time, former Production Manager (Charlie), who assists Brian, are the only men.

Could this be a gender issue of some sort? I ask myself.

She now turns to the subject of Brian, the only problem she has in managing the division. She adds that her opinion is shared by all of the editors. He is aggressive at meetings, uncooperative in general, and always causing problems for the smooth running of the division. He can only see problems, not opportunities.

I immediately notice how I bristle slightly at this remark. In the region, it has become a management catchall phrase to label as a problem anyone in an organization who is in any way different to the espoused norm— generally set by the manager. As before, I acknowledge my response to myself, let it give off steam for a second or two, then return to Alison.

I comment that it is not always easy to distinguish between being realistic and being pessimistic, and that what is realistic to one person may sound pessimistic to another. Seeing either as an absolute statement of fact rather than a personal preference can easily lead to misunderstandings between people.

I am here introducing the notion of 'multiple realities,' a favorite concept at GIC and fully consistent with the field theory of Kurt Lewin from whom Fritz Perls may well have borrowed his illustration in Ego, Hunger and Aggression (Perls F., 1947/1992, pp. 35–37). I am indebted to Staemmler (2006, p. 65) for this. Both Lewin and Perls use the example of how differently the same physical location will be experienced by a variety of different observers.

Alison responds to my comment by repeating how everyone else experiences Brian in the same way, and adds to the list of problems he is causing. There is also quite a repetition of earlier complaints about him.

I know from experience that I am particularly sensitive to being deflected, and I now get the usual signals as Alison responds in this mode. When I feel deflected, I look for what it is I have said that the other needs to deflect. What favorite introject have I brought into question? Alison's refocusing on Brian's shortcomings and the apparent consensual validation within the division is a likely candidate on the evidence before me.

This seems to confirm one of my first thoughts—that for Alison I am here to approve and support the removal of Brian from her division. This brings me back to my choice-point of working client—Alison or the division as a whole. This is always complicated by my opinion of the manager as a manager. In this case, I am slowly reaching the conclusion that Alison as a manager is part of the organizational issue, and that my working client is the division itself. As a therapist, I can feel the attraction of working therapeutically with Alison—and that is neither the purpose of her calling me, nor ethically appropriate. I can also feel the attraction of managerial supervision with her, though doubtful of its efficacy in the short term. So I make my choice, and my decision.

As a result, I explain to Alison that such issues as she has presented are, in my experience, not always as clear-cut as they may at first seem. The 'obvious' solution may not always get at any other root causes that may be present, and would likely remain and possibly resurface. I add that I would like and need to meet more people in the division in order to fully clarify what is happening and support her in resolving the matter for the best of the division and her own peace of mind. After a brief attempt to refocus exclusively on Brian, she agrees. I promise to get back to her quickly with an outline of how I will work, and also ask her to let all her staff know that I will be coming in as an organizational consultant to the division and will be requesting various meetings with them in a number of constellations.

From Practice to Theory #1

The following elements are of specific relevance here to gestalt OSD:

- Entry
- Contracting

Every entry is an intervention—and every intervention is an interruption. While it is true that Alison initiated the exchange with me, my every response can be seen as an entry into her world. Actually going to see her at her workplace and in her office is yet another entry. It is probable that some of her staff—her secretary, for example, and any confidantes amongst the editors—would also have known of my visit and its purpose. In this way, I have also entered the division.

One of the impacts of a consultant's entry into any client organization is to be 'the difference that makes a difference,' to paraphrase Gregory Bateson (1972). This is neither always intentional, nor dependent on any explicit action. Simply being there is enough to create potential change. In Lewinian terms, the life-space of the staff and division has a new environmental element—in this case, me. There is a new field, with new forces and needs organizing it. The work has begun.

When teaching, I make the distinction between the 'business contract' and the 'working contract'. For example, it is clear that my 'business contract'—the agreed task, the time frame, the fee and payment conditions, etc.—will be negotiated with Alison. Should the task be to consult to the division on a broader scale, then the 'working contract' will first be in terms of Alison advising all staff members that such is the case, followed by face-to-face contracting with each member or group as I meet them. In this latter case, actual or perceived confluence with Alison will impact on my contact with staff, individually, in whatever formal or informal subgroups I meet and with the division as a whole. Each of these are at all stages of the work my environmental other.

Contracting is not only a piece of the business end of consultancy. It is also an intervention. In this mini-case, I have negotiated a change of focus with Alison by moving from agreeing that Brian is 'the problem' to a position of exploring further on a wider scale. By agreeing, Alison is at least tacitly open to the possibility that there may well be other issues.

Both Entry and Contracting will be recurring features as the work progresses. I will probably be entering again and in new places with new people. With each new person, I will be negotiating a working contract.

The key theoretical areas which may be seen as ground to the figures of the work are:

- use of self
- organism/environment (PHG)
- person/environment (Kurt Lewin—the Life Space)
- figure/ ground
- awareness

- contact
- contact boundary dynamics
- the contacting cycle

These have been succinctly summarized for applications in organizational settings by a GIC colleague (Jonno Hanafin, 1996), an experienced manager, OSD consultant and trainer as follows:

'Being fully present and selectively sharing our awareness.'

This simple statement contains a wealth of material to be understood, experienced in use, processed and integrated. Use of self: me; who I am as a person; as a 64 year-old, white Irishman of the Catholic tradition; as a trained gestalt therapist and gestalt OSD consultant, living abroad as a resident immigrant, plus all of my other defining characteristics and functional roles. I will be fully present as organism to the other as my environment as well as environment to the other as organism. Or in Lewin's terms, which I prefer, as the person of *my* person/environment Life Space, influencing and being influenced, as all the forces of this me/other field are available to my awareness. My awareness of what is becoming figural for me from the ground of the me–client meeting and its 'selective sharing' is a function of the contact boundary dynamics that arise, embedded as they are in the contact cycle (PHG 1951/1994). This is described as fore-contact/contact/full contact/post-contact. In this opening vignette, Alison and I complete this specific cycle. At the same time, Alison as manager/the division (my client) and I are just in a fore-contact phase.

GIC is known for its extrapolation of the original contact cycle into the Cycle of Experience model (Nevis, 1987), initially as a pedagogical tool for teaching awareness and contact, and later as a tool for practice, particularly in OSD applications. This is now usually given in OSD contexts as Scanning–Awareness–Energy–Action–Contact–Meaning-making–Withdrawal. Using this schema, I have been in the Scanning phase, moving into Awareness and using the Energy I had accumulated to move into Action: the proposal of a business and working contract with Alison. Again, as far as the work is concerned, I am still in the Scanning phase with the identified client: the division.

'Contact boundary' is a core gestalt construct, easier to experience than to understand or explain. It is the meeting of self–other, an in-the-moment happening co-created by all parties to the meeting. 'Contact boundary dynamics' is a construct I use in order to capture the unpredictability and fluidity of this process. As an aid to a cognitive grasp of these dynamics, gestalt practitioners and theorists usually describe a number of patterns which seem characteristic of these co-created processes. The following pairing of patterns and oversimplified descriptions is intended to give some guidelines to the reader not trained in gestalt for some of the references that follow in theoretical and methodological comments on the mini-case.

First, here is what I call the basic social stance of the person to the environmental other:

- Egotism (being apart from the other) – Confluence (being a part of me–other)

This basic social stance is operationalized in the remaining constructs:

- Deflecting (keeping the other out) – Introjecting (taking the other in)
- Projecting (the other as object) – Retroflecting (self as object)

In terms of contact boundary dynamics, I have clearly projected onto Alison with regard to her intentions, as well as my reading of the situation. This projecting has—through my awareness—been brought into the ground of my work. Similarly, my experience of being deflected, and my assumptions of how I co-created this deflecting, have also become available to me. As has the obvious corollary—that I have deflected Alison by not instantly introjecting her version of events. Generally speaking, I judge that Alison is seeking to invite me to be confluent with her with regard to Brian, a confluence she may very well have achieved with her closest confidantes among the staff. Clearly, aware retroflecting of my various gut reactions has also been at play.

Retroflecting—with as much awareness as possible, whether in the moment or on later reflection—is a major competence in gestalt

OSD work. It is this skill that is embodied in the phrase 'selectively sharing my awareness'.

The Division, #2

Within a few days, I have prepared a draft contract and e-mailed it to Alison. This includes:

– how I work
– my daily fee
– a provisional proposal for the flow of the consultancy
– some thoughts about the time frame that may be involved
– a request that Alison inform all concerned about the interview

I always provide a new client with a brief description of process consultancy from a gestalt perspective and its difference from expert consultancy: I will not resolve the issues, nor provide a plan for doing so—I will rather support the division to find perspectives which may allow a resolution to emerge. Any resolution that emerges from within will be more acceptable and potentially more easily implemented than one imposed from without.

The proposed flow is as follows: a 60–90 minute interview: each of the editors; with Brian; with each of the design staff; with Charlie; concluding with an interview with Alison. This may be followed by a second, similar round. Depending on the outcomes, the consultancy could result in a final meeting with all of the above as a whole, all together.

I intentionally place the interview with Brian towards the end of the process, certainly neither first nor last. I do not want in any way to signal that I see him as 'the problem'. The client is the division, represented by the staff members directly involved in interactions around the process, including the author, the illustrator, the editor, design, and production—all of the people involved in the monthly meetings at which Brian is perceived to be difficult.

I am aware that at some point in my own process I had decided not to include the administrative staff in the consultancy. If they were privy to what was going on, then it would be mainly through second-hand ac-

counts and workplace gossip. For whatever reason, I had come to another choice-point, and made my decision. There are always moments like this in any piece of work where I trust my intuition (intuition as I see it is the most refined form of projecting). If I have made an unwise decision, I will find out about it soon enough. This can take two forms: 1) I become aware of a missing piece in the jigsaw puzzle; or 2) the 'missing piece' becomes proactive in drawing my attention to its presence.

I suggest two to four interviews per day, giving a rough estimate of four days for a total of 11 interviews—six editors, four production staff, and Alison. A second round would require another four days, including at least a half-day for a larger meeting. So I suggest a contract for four days, with an option after renegotiation for a further four to five days.

Alison agrees to all of the above and requests a phone call to arrange dates and times to start the work. I call her, hear 'the latest' about Brian, and schedule the first day of interviews.

I neither know—nor want to know—exactly what Alison has said to her staff. A reasonable assumption is that the editors may well have heard one version, Brian another, with maybe even a third version for the design staff. From now on, I will be 'fully present and selectively sharing my awareness' as I move through the Division, influencing and being influenced by my very presence there.

From Practice to Theory #2

I am now approaching a whole series of 'entries' and working contracts with 10 individuals I am meeting for the first time. This working contract will include the following:

- the purpose of the consultancy,
- the format of the consultancy,
- the format of the interview,
- the confidentiality of the interview; and
- my accessibility in the event of afterthoughts.

The first point, the purpose, is the most sensitive. It requires a sense of intention that is general enough (see below) to allow the interviewees to speak freely about their own roles and opinions within the context of the consultancy process. At no stage will Brian or any other specific person be identified as a 'problem' by me. Whatever the internal dynamics, they will emerge naturally as figures from the ground of the day-to-day operations of the Division. It is also essential that each interviewee gets exactly the same information so that I do not create confusion and mistrust. This is also the way in which I will be able to establish my agenda, as opposed to Alison's for example, and my presence in my own right. At no point in the working contract will I encourage the thought that I am anyone's messenger. Soon enough, I will have become the messenger of the editor/production subsystem to itself.

I will describe to each interviewee how I work as a process consultant, and segue into how this will also apply to the interview, in that there are no pre-determined questions—the interview will be open-ended and informal. I tell them that in any reporting that I do, nothing will be sourced to any specific person. At the same time, everything I hear will be available to me to process and use as I see fit in the course of the work. I will give them all my phone number and e-mail address.

The Division, # 3

Having decided on a declaration of purpose and format that can be appropriate, I start the first set of three interviews. The opening format is as follows:

> 'As you know, Alison has engaged me as an organizational consultant. My contract with her is to look at the relationship between the roles and functions of the editors and those of Production. I am therefore having interviews with all of the editors and all in Production to establish an understanding of the interconnections between these functions, and how they seem to be working in practice. There will be at least one round of interviews.'

I follow this as described earlier with the interview process. From this point onwards anything can happen—and usually does!

The first interviewee is Dorothy, who is also Deputy Manager and stands in for Alison when she is out of the office. Dorothy listens patiently to my little prepared speech, then comes straight to the point: 'I suppose this is about Brian? I know Alison has difficulties with him, and she told me that this is what you are supposed to be sorting out.'

I ask her if she has difficulties with him or anyone else in Production. She assures me that while she and Brian do have their 'little dust-ups', they are part and parcel of the nature of their roles and never become either inappropriately personal or long-lived. Once resolved, they disappear—until the next one!

She gives me some background in terms of authors who miss deadlines, illustrators who have differences of opinion with authors, delays in getting finished manuscripts and illustrations, schedules constantly changing. Each change affects if and when a book is ready for printing. Editors are always in a state of uncertainty about the books for which they are responsible, with some authors creating more havoc than others. Since Brian is at the end of the line, it all tends to accumulate on his desk. She adds that he can certainly be somewhat rigid, but that his bark is much worse than his bite. She adds that Alison takes him 'too seriously'.

The rest of this interview is taken up with Dorothy filling me in on details of the publishing business: the trade in general, this publishing house in particular, and the specific issues involved in being a specialist division with nationally known authors spanning at least three generations of readers—with some authors internationally known and translated.

Is Dorothy after Alison's job? Is there a history here worth looking at? Were they competitors when Alison actually got the job? So here are two figural issues to bring with me as ground for my continued work: Brian is 'rigid,' 'his bark worse than his bite,' 'Alison takes him too seriously'— though understandable in context, still the Alison/Dorothy dimension—is there something here, past and/or present?

Over a period of two days, I meet all of the editors. Four of the remaining five editors seem like 'variations on a theme by Dorothy'. Brian is 'difficult at times, but so is his job'. Alison is 'too impatient' with him. And yes—most of the editors would be happier if he wasn't around—but then, on the other hand, there would be no books published—and certainly not for the traditional major demand periods. The one voice with a different opinion is an editor on the brink of her pension, who fondly remembers how it 'used to be with Charlie'. He was a gentleman, always willing to compromise. Brian just says how it should be, and pushes ahead without any consideration for others.

I am aware of some of my projecting falling into place—as well as the attraction such confirmation can have! Again, I listen to myself, then put my voice on hold until I have some alternatives to my fast figures. What seems to be emerging is, generally speaking, questions around Alison's competence in managing the whole division and, in particular, in managing the interface between editors and Production, and Brian as the focal person of that tension. The editors, supposedly in agreement with Alison about Brian—as presented by Alison—are, in the reality they present to me, mostly of another opinion.

And so comes my seventh interview—with Brian. I meet a man in his mid-fifties, casually well dressed in the context of the region, and with a tray on his desk with two cups, milk, sugar, freshly made coffee and biscuits. His room is neat and tidy, his desk clear of anything other than an In and an Out tray, and the pot of coffee. I give him my opening phrases, which he listens to, acknowledging he has been told by some colleagues to expect it—and he's been advised to let me 'get it over with'!

Oh! How I love this moment—when the client starts 'talking back' to me as a novel environment to me as 'person', as 'person' to me as environment. Brian has clearly been informed by one or another of the editors of my style and content—so he gives me enough rope, then reins me in! Beautiful! Change is already occurring from Alison's original presentation. There is actually a degree of cooperation between the editors and Brian on an interpersonal level. And it is they who are enacting it . . . so where is Alison?

In response to my questions about how Brian sees the inter-connectedness of the editors and production staff, he talks with focused energy about how the editors and Alison do not pay attention to the reality of production. First, there is the difficulty for his design staff of being 'manipulated' by famous authors and illustrators into recommending better and therefore more expensive qualities of paper than necessary or appropriate. Unfortunately, the editors usually side with the authors/illustrators, thus putting the design staff under greater pressure. They in turn come to Brian with two alternatives—what the authors/illustrators want, and what they would themselves recommend. In this way, it is Brian who has to take on the editors, on behalf both of his design staff and of his own responsibility for the balance between quality and cost.

The next interviews, with the two design staff, are each centered on the demands of their work. It is they who will recommend the size, shape, format of the books, the type of cover—hard or soft—the quality of the paper, the number of colors, even taking into account the expectations of the book-buying public with regard to certain authors. Some authors will always be only in hardback and European A4 format, with matt paper, etc. Some authors and illustrators will want to influence the choices to be made. This is difficult in relation to who they are—the more famous and popular, the more difficult they can be to refuse or argue with.

Worst is when the editors side totally with the authors and illustrators against the design staff, who then have to go to Brian with requests that they know a) are unreasonable/inappropriate, and b) he will oppose on cost grounds or issues around availability. They appreciate that Brian never demands that they go back to the editors to tell them what the final decision actually is—as head of the Production Department, he is always prepared to do this himself at the monthly meetings. They each speak of him as a good manager—'you always know where you stand with him', 'he really supports us', though he can be 'a bit of a stickler for details and order'. They each confirm how much they have learned from him about the book business from a production perspective, and how he is always willing to answer their questions.

Charlie is the last interview in this first round. Charlie is an amiable person, willing to cooperate fully in supporting any change that will resolve what he regards as 'unnecessary' tensions between Alison and Brian. He talks of how management attitudes have changed in his many years in the company and Division X: it used to be that the focus was on production. The publishing house was in the business of producing and selling books, including having its own in-house printing facility. Now, all that has changed. The authors had moved from being happy to be published, to a more democratically pro-active role in the whole process. There were certainly the occasional special cases in the past—eccentrics, alcoholics, prima donnas, too. Now, the Production function was at the end of a more generally unpredictable artistic process. Editor commitment was now more to the author than to the company. Charlie admitted openly to difficulties handling the change in inter-functional relations, and to finding himself in conflict with the editors. So he had taken the opportunity of an early retirement, with his former assistant, Brian, taking over as Production Manager. In the current situation, Charlie was generally supportive of Brian, though often advising him to tread more softly.

My interview with Charlie confirms what I have already felt regarding the need to contract for a second round of interviews. A figure is emerging from the ground of the 'multiple realities' of Alison, the editors and the production staff. Here is clearly another choice-point for me—to move towards an impersonal inter-functional systemic approach, or a field perspective with its forces and vectors of both interpersonal and dynamic inter-functional forces, all at work simultaneously. I need time to reflect on this crossroads, and see what emerges, examine it critically, and reach a decision.

From Practice to Theory #3

There are many theories and perspectives on organization, each with its specific merits and applications. Increasingly, inter-disciplinary approaches are becoming more evident, with 'pure' organization theory merging with organizational behavior, organizational psychology, and social psychology. A current example of this synthesis is the work being done on 'Organizational Identity' (Hatch & Schulz, 2004). A Danish gestalt colleague is currently exploring gestalt theory and practice as an ingredient in organizational identity theory, with a research project in a Danish trade union (Blom, in press). Another Danish gestalt colleague and I have been mining our combined experience and knowledge of gestalt OSD consulting and training, searching for patterns to support our work. We have identified four main perspectives on organizations (Gaffney & Jensen, 2008), each valid in its own right and individually necessary. Our proposal is that they are collectively sufficient to support both an understanding of organizational dynamics and a very useful lens for the gestalt OSD consultant:

- hierarchical (power, rank, authority, inequality);
- systemic (functional, inter-functional, equifinality);
- relational (personalities, interpersonal dynamics, positioning); and
- field (the totality/wholeness of all of the above in their interacting).

Management often prefers the first of these, while accepting the possible hypothetical validity of the second. The third is often regarded as an inevitable and annoying source of gravel in the machine, while the fourth is the domain of the few. The gestalt OSD professional can move among each of the first three, though always aware that it is the field—the whole—that gives meaning to the parts.

This brings us back to 'selectively sharing our awareness.' Any intervention that is too far away from the ability of the client to receive it will, of course, fall on deaf—or deflecting—ears. The goal is not the 'perfect' intervention, embracing all of the knowledge and experience of the consultant. The only goal—as in gestalt therapy—is one with meaning for the client, which the client may choose to act on or not. When the client is a multiplicity of people, each with their own version of reality—as is the case in gestalt OSD—then the choice of figure and its presentation is the art and aesthetics of the work.

Figural for me in the work is that Alison focuses on the Relational as her preferred organizational perspective. When that does not work to her liking, she moves to the Hierarchical—remove Brian, then all will be well. Five of the editors and all of the production staff seem to hold a Systemic perspective, with acknowledgement of the Relational. Charlie seems to have a glimpse of a Field perspective while at the same time removed himself from a position from which he can influence through the Hierarchical or Systemic views. He attempts to coach Brian from a Relational perspective. From a Lewinian Field perspective, he has become a vector with some direction, though with insufficient magnitude to have an impact on the self-organizing of this field. Since my next scheduled meeting is with Alison, partly to report back and partly to contract for a second round of interviews and for a general meeting, I know that I have reached another—and sensitive—choice-point in the work.

A deciding factor here is the view that if I, as consultant, do not represent sufficient difference, then I have become over-confluent with the client organization. I need to think in terms of being the outsider who brings in what may be missing—in my opinion. If I do not bring in that which is novel and influential in its novelty, then I am reneging on my ethical responsibility to my client.

After some reflection, I decide that a Field perspective would be too big a step in the circumstances—I am the one who can hold this perspective as my responsibility and guiding principle. What Alison does not seem to have is a Systemic perspective in her role as manager of inter-functional issues. These she has chosen to respond to as Relational issues. So I go for a Systemic report, with Relational aspects! The Hierarchical will also be present, respecting her role as manager of a complex system.

The Division, # 4

As I go to this meeting with Alison, I am aware that this is the end of the contracted first phase of the consultancy, and the possible start of a contracted second phase. I have decided to await and/or elicit Alison's understanding of what has happened during phase 1, to 'stay fully present and selectively share my awareness'. Alison seems eager to open the meeting, and goes immediately into a review of what she has heard. This includes a recognition that her opinion of Brian was not as shared as she had thought—which leads her to being critical of the editors who, she now realizes, had not been fully truthful with her. She is inclined to suspect that I have influenced them to be against her—yet stays with the thought that maybe they had not been truthful in agreeing with her that Brian was a problem they could all do without.

I note that her previous certainty is now open to change. Something has happened by the very fact of another presence in the organization (me), and an opportunity for 'the organization' to interact with it (me).

I offer her my appreciation of her willingness to take another perspective, and to acknowledge that the editors may have had another opinion—however previously unexpressed—than hers about Brian. This allows me an opening for a brief discourse regarding the Hierarchical element: she is, after all, Divisional Manager. The first choice of any subordinate may well be agreement with the views of a superior—as may very well be her experience relative to company management. She agrees, and gives me examples of how wrong top management could be at times and how she has chosen to go along with them rather than go into opposition.

Alison is curious about Brian's comments. I remind her of the confidentiality aspect of the interviews, and report to her simply that I did not detect any personal animosity towards her. Brian has a job to do, and wants to do it well. This sometimes means fighting for his corner of a complex, interacting set of functions. She and the editors sometimes fight for another corner. Both are 'right' from their own functional perspectives and 'wrong' from the other. Alison remembers our first conversation about realistic and pessimistic points of view…

I am aware of how impressed I am and moved by Alison's ability to take in other views and reflect honestly about them. At the same time, I can see the delay that occurs in her need for time, feedback and reflection. From a contact perspective, she tends to move directly to Full Contact, bypassing Fore-contact and Contact and/or Sensation–Figure–Energy. My sense now is of a very insecure manager in a role beyond her personal and professional competence…yet again, I can feel the attraction of a therapeutic relationship, while aware of its inappropriateness in the current contractual context. Once again, I as a gestalt therapist meet the dilemma of the gestalt OSD consultant: who is my client? And in what setting? Having made my choice earlier, and contracted on the basis of that choice, I feel a need to be true to my 'use of self' in relation to the people I have chosen as my working focus.

Alison is generous in her openness to now talking about the next steps in the consultancy. I state that there already seems to have been some change, and that a second round of interviews with a general meeting as a closing intervention would seem to be appropriate. She immediately agrees, and we finalize dates for phase 2 of the work. The meeting moves into very general chit-chat about things in general … often a prelude to a more focused topic. However, such a topic does not emerge, so we end our meeting, amicably.

From Practice to Theory #4

– The field
– Self-organizing, self-regulating

The field as Lewin sees it (Marrow, 1969), is a dynamic field of forces or vectors, with origin, direction and magnitude. The need organizes the field—where need is of the field rather than a willed or planned outcome. The need can be seen as the best equilibrium possible in the situation. The situation embraces the particular people, the particular functional roles, the particular context involved. From a field perspective, each equilibrium is a unique realization of what is possible. There are no generic, universal resolutions. This field organizes as this field can. The art of the gestalt OSD practitioner is to recognize this and the skill is to act on it. On entering an organization, I become one of the forces/vectors of the field of me–the organization. I can follow, not lead or direct. My work is to be aware of shifts and changes as they occur—in me, in the other, in the contact boundary dynamics of our interactions.

This field perspective is a responsibility and a competence and an art. It is where the work moves from the practical to the aesthetic (Bloom, 2003). It is where the work 'does' me as much as I 'do' the work. This approach is enshrined in such phrases as 'go with the flow' and 'follow the process' and thus gives them meaning beyond what may sound like clichés. The river will flow where the conditions support its flowing; the process will go where the process can go. The work of gestalt OSD practitioners is to be fully present as part of the flow and process of the consultant–organization field, and fully aware of what is happening to them as this happens—in the moment and over time. Over time, patterns may emerge as figures which can be shared selectively. Receptiveness is of the field. The self-organizing energies may 'accept' or 'reject' or 'adjust' any intervention as an energy, a vector, of the field. The self-regulating energies may do likewise. Our task is to hold our awareness open to these field vectors, and meet them both where they are—and also to appropriately challenge them. By appropriately, I mean with reasonable receptivity, in both the short and the long term, at least with honesty and good intentions, and respect for our understanding of where the client seems to be, as we see it. Of course we can be way off, as most of us can recognize from experience. This is where going with the flow and following the process is part of our willingness to experiment … and re-appraise as we receive the response.

The Division, #5

In my experience, a second phase of this nature can either allow people to consolidate the changes that may have occurred and/or provide an opportunity for the previously unspoken to be aired—and anything and everything in between! In a sense, the organization will be moving between integrating and fragmenting.

Dorothy expresses her appreciation of the changes that have occurred; namely, that Alison has delegated the running of the Monday meetings to Dorothy; Brian is reporting how good it was for him to talk with an interested and impartial outsider, and is behaving more calmly while still holding his ground on scheduling demands; the other editors are happy with the 'change of atmosphere'. Dorothy is concerned about Alison, who seems to be withdrawing from any issues of potential tension. Of particular concern is Alison's relations with David, the Director of Marketing.

Ah! David! A new piece of the puzzle emerges...

Normally, David would liaise directly with the Divisional Managers, both collectively and individually, around production schedules. This inter-functional connection had gradually been eroded during Alison's time as Divisional Manager, and she had generally managed to reduce her contact with David to a minimum. David had taken to direct contact with Brian, and very recently Brian had told Dorothy how this was yet another pressure on him.

So—Dorothy and Brian are connecting! 'Now isn't that interesting!' as Edwin Nevis likes to say when change emerges...

The other editors confirm Dorothy's assessment of changes for the better—including the different relations with Brian—all expressing their appreciation of 'whatever' it was that I had done! None of them mention David. Something similar occurs with the design staff.

Brian is in a good mood, and thanks me for 'whatever' it was that I had done! He reports on somewhat better relations with the editors and smoother processes for and with his design staff. He is particularly appreciative of Dorothy and her competence at running the scheduling meetings. He adds that she is 'easy to talk to' and understands his difficulties with David. I ask him to describe this situation more fully, from his perspective. As Marketing Director, David needs to plan marketing campaigns and liaise with the Director of Sales and Distribution around publication dates. Both of these activities have long lead times and are directly linked to production schedules. Normally, this work 'should' be coordinated by the two Directors with the Managers of the various divisions of the publishing house. Ensuring that the production schedules of each division are in line with marketing, sales and distribution planning is the job of the Divisional Manager. The exception here is Alison, and this Division is getting a reputation for 'sloppy' production standards, as Brian puts it. Another consequence is that David now chooses to go to Brian directly, making demands that Brian has to translate into action. He feels that his hands are tied by inefficiencies in the editorial work, and this causes him to feel frustrated and to dread calls from David. He has now been able to share his situation with Dorothy and notes that she is attempting to support him in practical ways.

I am aware of a clear figure forming of a possible systemic intervention that will have field consequences as the organization responds dynamically. I can feel the consultancy drawing to a close…

And so on to Charlie, who is relaxed and expresses his satisfaction at 'the way things are moving'. He turns our meeting into a discussion of the theory and methods of my work…

… which becomes an intervention as I describe to him the importance of hearing what has to be said by each interviewee, and trusting that they will probably talk about it now that it has been spoken. In this way, information is shared and spread throughout the organization. I also trust that the organization will move towards whatever it needs and is capable of achieving.

Charlie agrees, and we end our meeting.

I am aware of my need to gather my thoughts, examine my figures, reflect enough to allow new figures to emerge before my Phase 2 meeting with Alison. She is clearly under pressure from many sides. The support she had elicited from the editors has been shown to be weaker than she imagined. Her problems with Brian seem minor in the context of the de facto problem David is having with her, of which she is probably aware though maybe deflecting. In a sense, David's actions are undermining Alison's managerial base—a base she herself seems ready to abdicate. How can I support her as a person at the same time as I have doubts about her competence as a manager? She clearly has difficulties managing up to the Directors, and down to her Division. Dorothy and Brian are forming an alliance, and therefore bypassing Alison and dealing with David. Alison seems 'caught between a rock and a hard place' and is soft enough to be squeezed flat. My heart goes out to her.

And then I meet with her. She is open and welcoming, speaking quickly about how much better everything is, how happy she is to have initiated this consultancy. She is grateful to Dorothy for taking on some of her responsibility, and mentions how she maybe could have delegated this earlier. And maybe that she is the only one to find Brian's behavior objectionable, but then says how she has always been sensitive to aggressive behavior.

I notice how my own vulnerability resonates with her presence, a feeling I usually get as a therapist in the presence of psychologically fragile clients … and I also notice how I am balancing two figures: complete the consultancy contract on the one hand, and support Alison on the other. The first can be achieved at the open meeting (yet to be scheduled), and the second is energized enough to act on in the moment…

I ask her what kind of support she has in her life—family, friends, a place to relax and look after herself. She tears up slightly, mumbles a little, and talks of how lonely she feels. She had no idea until recently of how important 'her' authors were to her, their lunches and book launches, their occasional celebrations of a prize or a new sales record for a book. She then suddenly asks me if I think she needs therapy, and if I can recommend someone to her. I give her two names and phone numbers. She thanks me, then asks about 'what next' in the consultancy. I arrange some possible dates for a meeting with the editors, the production department and, if the interest exists, the administration. She assures me that the administrative staff want to be involved as they have commented on how things seem to have changed and are curious.

I am moved by this meeting, as my vulnerability met Alison's, and also moved by her proactive stance in sensing that her difficulties may have had more to do with herself in relation to others rather than any solely external cause. The work is coming to an end and Alison will not be a victim of circumstances.

The Division, Part 6

We have booked a whole day—9 a.m. to 4 p.m.—together. I have asked a female colleague to act as my shadow consultant throughout the day. She and I are agreed that I may turn to her for feedback at any time, and also that she may intervene, either with me, or with the assembled group, should she feel the urge.

Everybody turns up—this session is considered a training day for the staff. I open by presenting Erika, my shadow consultant, and her role. I then ask if anyone has any comments they would like to make. Alison expresses her thanks, and adds that everybody appreciates the impact of my work.

My decision was to focus on the systemic and also the hierarchical dimensions of my understanding of the Division, to see the relational dimension in these contexts, and to allow the field of the whole take care of itself. I first drew a chart of the Division as I had understood it (FIGURE 11.1), and asked them to discuss this in groups of three to five people with a mix of departmental roles—Administration, Editorial and Production. I suggested that Alison could sit this one out since, as manager, she was not a staff member of any of the departments mentioned. She agreed, and we went for a coffee together.

THE DIVISION

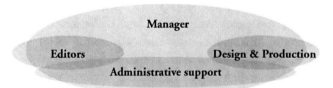

FIGURE 11.1

The reporting-back session that followed was lively and warm, and no major issues were raised. Brian asked that the position of Production be discussed in a more contextual light. I agreed, and added the next visual: FIGURE 11.2.

I explained that I was here attempting to place the division in its organizational context. The Division is not in a vacuum, however

The System

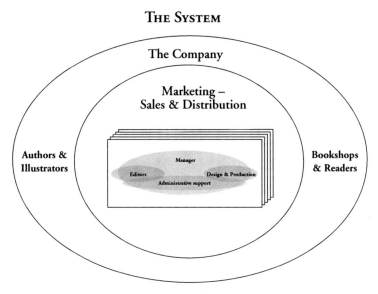

The Company

Marketing –
Sales & Distribution

Authors &
Illustrators

Bookshops
& Readers

Manager

Editors

Design & Production

Administrative support

FIGURE 11.2

much it may seem so in its day-to-day operations. It is one of five specialist book divisions in a major publishing house. It is an integral part of a larger system. From the 'in a vacuum' perspective, the flow of responsibility is editors (plus authors and illustrators) to production, with administration dealing with the back-office needs. From a larger system perspective, production was an integral part of a complex flow from printing to marketing to sales and distribution. The needs and demands of marketing, sales, and distribution were, internally to the organization, focused on production, and through production on into the editorial functions of each division, including, of course, this Division.

As a publishing house, the company would always be juggling with artistic integrity from the creative side—authors, illustrators, editors and design—and production efficiency from the commercial side. These are not incompatible—probably every author/illustrator wants to be published!

Again, I asked them to form small groups and discuss this chart. I mentioned that Alison could take part if she chose, as her role and function as manager was now included. She did.

The discussion that followed was again lively and fully participative. An administrative staff member was pleased to find herself in a large and complex system of interlocking parts—she spoke of how the Finance Director could sometimes involve himself in their invoicing procedures and credit-card use within the Division.

Erika intervened also to ask the group if the gender imbalance was an issue for them. There was some shared laughter, followed by 'Men are men. They can't help it!'

The day progressed with small-group work as themes emerged, whole-group discussions and, finally, an open session on 'What have we learned, and how will this impact on us?'

The day ended in an atmosphere of shared enthusiasm as I closed my contract with the Division.

Epilogue

Some three months later, Dorothy contacted me and requested an individual consultancy. I arranged to meet her for a morning. The company had moved, and I found my way to her floor. As I passed through an open-space office en route to Dorothy's room, I was greeted warmly by administrative and editorial staff. She was now in a temporary position as manager of the Division, having decided not to take the position on a permanent basis. 'I like being an editor too much,' she said. 'I would miss the contact with my authors and illustrators, the creative and social side of the work.' She then added that she had seen what had happened with Alison, and knew that the same would probably happen with her. So she would stay as an editor, and let someone else manage the issues and complexities involved!

Alison had gone into therapy, taken sick leave, and returned to announce that she wanted to change jobs. She had since found an editorial position in a division dealing with books on her major pastime interest, and was feeling well and happy with her work. Dorothy simply wanted to talk through her experience of the period before, during, and after the consultancy, and her role in what had happened. We had a good discussion, I made some minor interventions in her support, and we parted amicably. The work was well and truly done!

Final Reflections on Practice and Theory

This work involved me in engaging with various levels of system (see Kepner, 2008). The interviews were at the level of the individual at the same time as each small collective—editors, production staff—became a subgroup whenever they discussed and/or shared their experience of and discussed the interviews and their context. My general meeting was at the level of the group as a whole with reference to the division, though this in turn became a subgroup, as one part of a larger system. This larger system, the publishing house itself, was not ever part of my contract. Tempting as it can be to expand the work into the higher echelons of the hierarchy, it is a particular skill and competence of the gestalt OSD practitioner to be a respecter of boundaries and contracts. This also covers truly trusting the process of the self-organizing field, and having faith that changes in the Division as an energy of the whole will be part of that self-organizing. Our work is not to intentionally direct or manipulate the environments in which we work. We certainly do influence it—our very presence is often more than enough. Everything else is added value for the client organization.

Some sense of this latter point can, perhaps, be seen in a number of the concrete consequences of the work, and the levels of system at which they occurred. Individually, three of the major players were impacted—Alison, Dorothy, and Brian—and two of them (to my knowledge) made significant personal and professional choices. Also, I feel that Charlie emerged relaxed and satisfied as his gently supportive energy was heard and responded to.

Intergroup relations between the editors and production were improved. Inter-functional operations between the Division and the rest of the organization were at least clarified. In both cases, contact boundary issues, both relationally and functionally, were brought to awareness and the nature of contact impacted.

None of the above was ever a goal of mine, in the sense of being something I wished at the outset to achieve and worked at accomplishing. They were all part of the field at the time, and emerged as energized figures from the ground of the contact boundary dynamics of the work and its impact.

Use of self, awareness, contact, a field perspective and a humanistic trust in people doing the best they can in their circumstances: these are the strong and always flexible foundations of gestalt OSD.

Closing Remarks

Gestalt therapy is a theoretical and methodological discipline that can equally embrace therapeutic, group, organizational, and also social applications (Gaffney, in press, 2010). This chapter has explored a typical organizational application and shown how a gestalt therapy OSD approach allows the consultant to move fluidly between various levels of organization, dealing with the complexity of individual-in-organization as well as subgroup, group as a whole and organization as a whole.

There are many more such stories in our ranks. We all need to hear more of them, as well as to spread our work more widely. Who knows—we may even eventually contribute to fewer people 'growing up absurd'.

References *

Bateson, G. (1972). *Steps to an Ecology of Mind*. New York: Ballantine Books.

Blom, S. (in press). *Organizational Identity: A Gestalt Perspective*. Derby, England: University of Derby Ph. D. Thesis.

Bloom, D. (2003). 'Tiger! Tiger! Burning Bright!': Aesthetic Values as Clinical Values in Gestalt Therapy. In M. Spagnuolo Lobb, & N. Amendt-Lyon, (Eds.), *Creative License: The Art of Gestalt Therapy*. Vienna: Springer Verlag.

Feder, B. & Ronall, R. (1980/2000).* *Beyond the Hot Seat: Gestalt Approaches to Group*. New Orleans, LA: Gestalt Institute Press.

Gaffney, S. (2006). On Being Absurd: Kierkegaard and Gestalt. *British Gestalt Journal*, 15(1), 7-15.

Gaffney, S. (in press 2010). Using the Gestalt Approach in Developing Social Change Interveners in the North of Ireland. In J. Melnick, & E. Nevis (Eds.), *Mending the World: Worldwide Social Healing Interventions by Gestalt Practitioners*. Cape Cod, MA: GISC.

Gaffney, S. & Jensen, I. (2008). Trifocal Lenses: A Practical Field Perspective on Organisations for Managers and Consultants. *Gestalt Review 12*(2), 44-160.

Goodman, P. (1956). *Growing Up Absurd*. NY: Vintage Books.

Hanafin, J. (1996). Teaching materials, GIC International OSD Program. OSD Training Materials. Cleveland, OH: Gestalt Institute of Cleveland.

Hatch, M.J. & Schulz, M., Eds. (2004). *Organizational Identity: A Reader*. Oxford: Oxford University Press.

Hentoff, N. (1966/2004)*. *Our Children Are Dying*. Highland, NY: Gestalt Journal Press.

Kepner, E. (2008). Gestalt Group Process. In B. Feder and J. Frew (Eds.), *Beyond the Hot Seat Revisted*. New Orleans, USA: Gestalt Institute Press.

Kitzler, R. (2006). The Ontology of Action: A Place on Which to Stand for Modern Gestalt Therapy Theory. *International Gestalt Journal, 29*(1), 43–100.

Marrow, A. (1969). *The Practical Theorist: The Life and Work of Kurt Lewin*. NY: Basic Books.

Melnick J. & Nevis, E. (Eds.) (in press 2009). *Mending the World: Worldwide Social Healing Interventions by Gestalt Practitioners*. Cape Cod, MA: GISC.

Nevis, E. (1987). *Organizational Consulting: A Gestalt Approach*. Cleveland, OH: GIC Press.

Perls, F. (1947/69).* *Ego Hunger and Aggression*. NY: Random House.

Perls, F, Hefferline, R. & Goodman, P. (1951/94).* *Gestalt Therapy: Excitement and Growth in the Human Personality*. Highland, NY: Gestalt Journal Press.

Staemmler, F. (2006). A Babylonian Confusion?: The Term "Field". *British Gestalt Journal, 15*(2), 64–83.

Stoehr, T. (1997). *Here, Now, Next: Paul Goodman and the Origins of Gestalt Therapy*. Cleveland, OH: GIC Press.

Smuts, J. (1926/96)*. *Holism and Evolution*. Highland, NY: Gestalt Journal Press.

Wysong, J & Rosenfeld, E. (1982). *An Oral History of Gestalt Therapy*. Highland, NY: Gestalt Journal Press.

* In cases where there is a later edition dated, this later date has been used for publisher data.

༈

This chapter was published in *Beyond the Hot Seat Revisted* (2008), chapter 18, pp. 371-403, published by the Gestalt Institute Press of New Orleans, USA, and is reproduced here by kind permission of the editors, Bud Feder and Jon Frew.

12.

From Theory to Practice:

A LEWINIAN APPROACH

Kurt Lewin (1890–1947) pioneered the application of field thinking in physics to both his early work in experimental psychology as well as in his highly influential theoretical and practical contributions to the development of social psychology in general, and group dynamics in particular (Marrow 1969). His delineation of Field Theory eventually became a methodology embedded in a meta-theory (Gold, 1990).

His thinking supports the notion that 'field' is both ontologically real and present at the same time as it can be phenomenologically experienced. He distinguishes this latter as the 'life space', though uses the terms 'field' and 'life space' synonymously (Staemmler 2006).

Lewin is the author of the formula B = f (P, E). In plain English: behaviour is a function of the person in an environment. He gives the example of how the same, ontological environment will be perceived in distinctly unique ways by a variety of persons, depending upon their roles, circumstances and needs. An example is as follows: A farmer might see a clump of rocks and thick bushes in the middle of a piece of fertile land as an obstruction to be removed in the interests of increased acreage and easier harvesting; a soldier might see it as a place of ambush or hiding; two rambling lovers might see it as an opportunity for some private moments. As such, each life space carries its own distinct set of characteristics as a sub-set of whatever totality may exist.

Should any of the persons in the example change roles and circumstances, then their experience of the clump will change. If the soldier becomes a farmer, then that in which he once hid and found safety will now be either an obstruction to be removed, or a reminder to be cherished. To paraphrase Lewin's thinking, the need organizes the life space. What we see as our environment, how we see it thus and how we then respond is related to our needs. Naturally, when the environment is not a clump of rocks and bushes, but rather other people, then needs meet needs, responses evoke responses and all the unpredictability of being in and of the world comes into dynamic play.

This is also where life space and field can become difficult to separate —and yet, we argue here for the value, both theoretically and practically, for a Gestalt therapist in making that separation. We will therefore now explicate the theoretical intricacies involved in order to establish the parameters for practice from a Lewinian field perspective and present a mini-case to exemplify a life space approach to Gestalt therapy. In addition, this explication will also set the ground for considerations of how this approach may be amenable to outcome research.

For the sake of as much clarity as may be possible with such complexities, what follows is a highly simplified and minimalist description of Lewinian Field Theory. The practical extrapolations from and fleshing-out of this simplification will follow in the mini-case.

An introductory comment here: the person *has* a life space at the same time as the person is *of* the person/environment field. This will become clearer and its relevance more obvious as we proceed. The person will have a sense of being able to observe and describe the environment of her life space. Since we cannot observe that of which we are ourselves a part, the person is unable to describe the field of which she is a part. She can however describe her experience of being influenced—and as soon as she distinguishes what or who is influencing her, she is taking a life space perspective.

The life space is the environment as perceived by a person relating to it, usually depicted as a Jordan curve. Some of Lewin's doctoral candidates liked to call these 'bathtubs' (Patnoe, 1988) (See Figure 12.1).

Whilst the environmental other/others constitute the life space of the person, the wholeness of the person and her environment is the person/environment field, where each element is dynamically contributing to the self-organising in the moment and thus also over time. In this way, a person may experience quite a different sense of agency in respect to her life space than in respect to the field of which she is a contributing force.

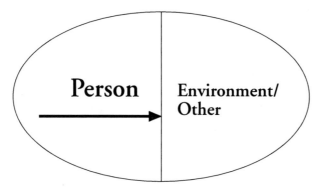

FIGURE 12.1

This point becomes clearer when the environment of the life space is another person and viewed from that other's perspective also and simultaneously:

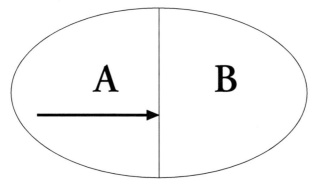

FIGURE 12.2

Here, the life space of A is A in relation to B (**FIGURE 12.2**). Simultaneously, the life space of B is B in relation to A (**FIGURE 12.3**). Merged and inextricably linked, they constitute the field of AB (**FIGURE 12.4**), to which may be added other environmental factors which each brings with them in the 'totality of coexisting facts which are conceived of as mutually interdependent' (Lewin, 1951), and of which only one of them may have been in awareness prior to their interaction. Concretely, each brings with them their past experience as they express it in the present, and their future aspirations as they choose behaviours.

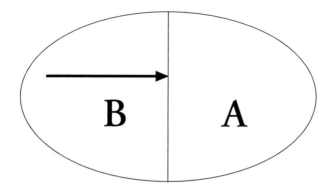

FIGURE 12.3

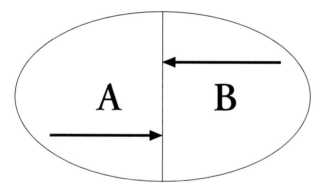

FIGURE 12.4

Assuming that A is the client, the presence of the therapist (T) now adds both a new life space for A as well as a life space for T (**FIGURE 12.5**).

At the same time, A is bringing her life space to therapy, so that it is possible to extrapolate that the life space of T is both A and the life space of A, including B as representing the environmental other/others that A is dealing with in her life and which may well be the theme of the therapy (**FIGURE 12.6**).

The therapist is meeting a client and the world of that client as she experiences it. Together, the combined life spaces dynamically constitute the therapist/client field, where each is both influencing and being influenced by all the other forces of that field. It is precisely this

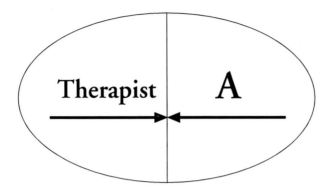

FIGURE 12.5

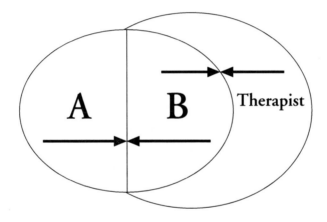

FIGURE 12.6

aspect of the therapeutic work that allows new and often surprising themes to emerge at the therapist/client contact boundary.

This is a good place to add an essential aspect of the perspective being presented here: the slash (/) or even hyphen (-) in the construct organism/environment, usually taken to denote the contact boundary in Gestalt therapy theory, is functionally identical to the line in the Jordan curve which is used to distinguish the person from the environment in Lewin's original work. So the Jordan curve highlights the person-contact boundary-environment dynamics of organism/-environment, though more explicitly from a psychological perspective. We are indebted here to Frank M. Staemmler for his exciting distinctions between biological and psychological models in his ground-breaking article on Field Theory/Theories in Gestalt (Staemmler 2006).

As a Gestalt therapist, there is no investment in changing the client's behaviour per se, and more an interest in exploring her perception of her life space, fully trusting that any change in her perception will emerge as changes to her life space and, therefore, allow her to make choices about her behaviour which she may not have felt were previously possible. The agency is the client's, as are the choices and the actions. The therapeutic process is the possible catalyst for change.

An Illustrative Mini-Case

The original client in this case has given permission for it to be used, has read the draft and approved the version presented here. Some of that client's comments have been incorporated into the final draft. All names and any other particulars which would identify the client have been replaced.

Anne is a new client, who comes to me on the recommendation of a close friend and Gestalt trainee who knows of me through the training institute. Anne is a successful professional in her forties, and moves quickly to her issue, the reason for coming to therapy. She has great difficulties in finding a long-term relationship, though no shortage of possible candidates: currently these are Bernard, Charlie and David. Bernard is her former husband. Charlie is her current lover. David is a former lover, now back in her social sphere after a short absence immediately following their mutually agreed parting.

It soon transpires that Anne is currently meeting all three of them, though only having regular sexual relations with Charlie. She has had a night or so for old time's sake with David, and still feels attracted to Bernard. She feels that she really needs to make 'a final choice' between them and settle down in a good relationship with a long-term commitment.

I become aware as I listen to Anne that there is a disparity which attracts my attention. As she talks of any one of the three, he becomes figural for me as the other two recede into the background. For Anne, mention of any one of them instantly raises the other two as equally energized figures. In life space terms, her environment is not Bernard and/or Charlie and/or David. It seems to me more like BernardCharlie David, a trio as a unit.

This becomes explicit any time I attempt to raise her awareness around her feelings for each of the three—the other two come instantaneously into the work. So I take this as it is, see the trio as her environmental other, and begin working more consistently with Anne's experience of all three as a unit. So I ask her to describe the synthesis of characteristics—both attractive to her and unattractive—which they, taken together, embody. It is in this work that Anne herself begins differentiating between them. For example, she will name what is for her an attractive characteristic embodied in the trio, and then begin reflecting aloud on which of them has 'most' of it, and 'less' and 'least.'

At the same time, whenever one of the three seems to be emerging most clearly, she will immediately correct herself for having omitted each of the other two, and bring them into a newly energized three-in-one or even one-in-three.

As Anne and I move further into this work, I become increasingly aware of another figure forming between us. As the son of an alcoholic father who was often angry and occasionally violent, I have a built-in early warning system for the presence of anger or ill intent towards me. I see this as a form of mild paranoia, generally useful and occasionally more projective than I am aware of in the moment. Anne had a way of glancing sideways at me which set off the alarm bells of my early warning system. Having reflected between sessions in an attempt to raise my awareness around how much of this was more mine than hers, I decided to raise it with her the next time it happened. So she glanced sideways at me, I reacted as before—and I shared my experience with her and asked if she was in any way angry with me. Anne reassured me that she was not in any way the slightest bit angry with me—until I had suggested that she might have been! I asked her if she could accept that I drew her attention to any occasion when I felt myself resonating to possible anger, and she agreed. This now became part of our interactions as the therapy continued.

There were now two major themes present in our work, one of which Anne had brought with her as her existing life space—her felt need to decide between three men and her difficulty in doing so. The other—my bodily response to a particular glance of hers—was clearly of my life space. At the same time, since it did not belong to a relationship with her prior to the therapy, it was clearly of the field of Me-Anne-Anne's life space. My reflections here were exploring my possible anger towards Anne, or even towards any or all of the three men in her life. While I certainly liked her, I did not trace any feelings of emotional or physical attraction strong enough to evoke my jealousy and resentment. And so the work continued.

Session 12 marked a turning-point in our work and probably in Anne's life. She was yet again extolling the virtues of all three men, and becoming self-critical at her inability to decide between them, when I had a sudden image of a pair of gloves. I bracketed this apparently inappropriate image and turned my full attention back to Anne. The image returned, and as I hesitated to deal with it, came at me in a highly energized form, visually and verbally. When Anne came to a pause in her narrative, I asked her if I could share a curious experience I was having as I sat there with her. She agreed. So I told her of how I had had a clear visual image of gloves as well as the thought 'gloves' as I listened to her. She looked me straight in my eyes, sat back in her chair and I saw her eyes water. She sighed, and started crying. Talking through her tears, she told how, as a child, her parents had insisted on her wearing woolen mittens as soon as the weather turned cold. They were itchy and made her feel clumsy as she could not fully use her fingers. When it rained, they became sodden and cold. Sometimes they would be covered in ice and feel heavy and uncomfortable. She had tried 'losing' them, only to be given a new pair almost immediately. After she had left home and started traveling, she found herself beginning to collect fine gloves, usually of soft leather, and always a perfect fit. She now had a special drawer at home for her collection, and would occasionally sort through them—though never wear any of them outdoors.

As she continued to muse on this theme, she began reflecting on her life and how she generally disliked doing anything she felt that she was 'supposed' to do. She could see that she sometimes stayed in an uncomfortable situation longer than she needed, and had difficulties making her own choices and acting on them.

The session drew to a close as the image which had emerged was now transformed—and was still transforming—into a metaphor which had meaning for Anne in her life. This now became the theme for the following sessions, and BernardCharlieDavid receded into the background, with very few references to them other than in the context of this new theme. Anne's life space had changed as an energized figure had emerged from the field of possibilities.

Within three months, Anne had unexpectedly met a teenage love—Eric—reconnected with him and they had become lovers. Within a further three months, they had set up house together and married. Anne continued in therapy with me for a short while after their marriage and we eventually agreed to close our work together.

During this period, I had occasionally reflected on the other theme—that of anger, and the possible connections between Anne, her parents and me. The sideways glance still made occasional appearances. I decided that this was now of the field, and that if it had any figural energy for Anne, then she could choose to raise it with me. She never did.

From Practice to Theory—Some Reflections

We mentioned earlier that the work is not focused on changing a client's behaviour. It is focused on exploring the client's life space from different perspectives and allowing a new behaviour to emerge from any changed perception which may occur. It is clear to me that the therapist did not influence Anne in reaching a new perspective. For her, the environment consisted of BernardCharlieDavid, and attempts at distinguishing between them invariably led us back to her original theme.

The therapist's introduction of anger as a theme, emerging as it did from the past he brought with him as part of the ground of his life space and resonating in the here-and-now with Anne was an energized figure for him, and not for Anne.

The image of the gloves and its transformation into a metaphor is clearly of the Therapist/Anne field. This image emerged in the therapist and connected directly to a significant event in Anne's childhood. Lewin's thinking includes the notion of vectors—energies or forces that have an origin, a magnitude and a direction. The gloves image has its origin in Anne's childhood experience and her strong memories of that experience and its factual—the glove collection—and now metaphorical meaning for her as she sees her life through the lens of the metaphor. And at the same time, the image has its origin in the therapist with sufficient magnitude to remain figural for him and with a clear direction—Anne. The process whereby an event of Anne's past emerges as an image in me and returns to Anne is the magic and the mystery of a field approach. We—therapist and client—are of a field of our life history, our present both separately and together, and are being influenced by the self-organising dynamics of which we are also influential parts.

There is no doubt that the process of the gloves image can be or soon will be open to a generally acceptable 'scientific' explanation. Our interest is not in such an explanation as we are more concerned here with the experience of this process and its validity in a therapeutic setting. By working from a Lewinian Field Theoretical approach we can move from the pragmatics of a life space perspective to being the recipient or channel of an energy of the field of which the therapist is a co-creating part, and back to the life spaces involved.

References

Gold, M. (1990). Two 'Field Theories.' In Wheelan, Pepitone and Abt (eds.) *Advances in Field Theory*. London: Sage Publications.

Lewin, K. (1951). Field Theory in the Social Sciences. New York: Harper and Brothers.

Marrow, A.J. (1969). *The Practical Theorist—The Life and Work of Kurt Lewin*. Basic Books, USA.

Patnoe, S. (1988). *A Narrative History of Experiential Social Psychology*. Berlin, Springer Verlag.

Staemmler, Frank M. (2006). A Babylonian Confusion—The Term 'Field'. *British Gestalt Journal, 15*(2).

ॐ

This case study was written by Seán Gaffney for inclusion in a co-authored article with Brian O' Neill and has been extracted from their chapter entitled Field Theoretical Strategy which was published in Handbook for Theory, Research and Practice in Gestalt Therapy, 2008, chapter 11. pp. 238-256, Newcastle, England, Cambridge Scholars Publishing. It is reproduced here by kind permission of the editor, Phillip Brownell.

13.

Steps Towards a Practice of Gestalt with Groups:

A Mini-manual for Beginners

Introduction

This is a highly subjective and personal description of how I practice 'Gestalt with Groups', written in the first person and offered in the hope that it may support trainees and new Gestalt practitioners —and even other group facilitators—in finding something that may be useful enough to taste, chew, selectively swallow and assimilate—or spit out. My proposals here are for a generic group, facilitated with a Gestalt approach. The particular requirements of a therapy, personal and/or professional development, training or supervision focus is a specific figure to this generic group process as ground. I ask the readers to extrapolate, focus and distinguish freely here from their own knowledge, experience and purpose. Please note also that sub-headings which address specific aspects of the work will be indicated in *italics*.

For many years, I much preferred working with groups from a Gestalt perspective rather than *writing* about it. My foray into publication was an exciting challenge and a rewarding experience. I discovered that I 'knew' more than I thought (though not always exactly where it came from!) and also had a contribution to make to theoretical thinking on the subject. I also found how much my practice was being influenced by my writing. New perspectives and insights occurred regularly and became embodied in my practice. I had moved from *doing* it to writing *about* it, back to *doing* it—and here-and-now to writing *about doing* it! As such, the statements, opinions and perspectives I offer here are simply confident expressions of where I am in my current practice.

Summary of my Basic Premises about Groups from a Gestalt perspective

Since these assumptions inform my practice, I want to be explicit about them. Should any or all of them differ from yours, then you will now already know which aspects of my practice may be of little usefulness to your knowledge and practice; or more of a challenge to your current understanding, to which you will be responding; or an encouragement to your thinking and practice; or even a complete mystery.

- What I call the 'Actual Group' is that particular collection of members who have registered to join and who attend regularly.
- Such a collection, taken as a whole, is greater than and different to the sum of its members as a collective. I call this the 'gestalt of the group', or 'Group Gestalt'.
- What I call the 'Imagined Group' is the wholeness of the collection of implicit and explicit images of what 'a group' is or should be. These images/expectations are brought into the room by group members, whether based on personal experience or hearsay.
- Awareness of my own Imagined Group is essential here, and how it connects with, and disconnects from that of the group members' Imagined Group.
- The process of the Group Gestalt—continuously becoming precisely that—is done by and through the members who are present at any given time (the Actual Group), and will include the interplay between it and the Imagined Group.
- Group members are thus involved in both the in-the-moment dynamics of the Actual Group and the developmental process over time of the Group Gestalt.
- In other words, the here-and-now dynamics of the parts are embedded in a then-now-next process of the whole.
- I have no desired or required outcome nor normative model for the developmental process, which I see as self-organising and self-regulating. My focus is on following the dynamics and process of *this* group, and no other.

- As the formal therapist and/or facilitator, I am not a member of the group.
- At the same time, the group members and I are of the field which we, together, are continuously creating simply by being together.
- Individual members very quickly become subsumed into subgroups, explicitly or implicitly. Explicitly through voiced agreement/disagreement with others and implicitly through the same behaviours.
- Simply participating in a group, its dynamics and process, is in itself therapeutic and developmental for all concerned.
- Part of this therapeutic/personal development process is participating in, influencing and being influenced by, whatever movement may occur between the Actual Group and the Imagined Group in the developmental process of the Group Gestalt.
- Being fully present and contactful and selectively sharing my awareness are fundamental to my practice.

This list will, I hope, suffice as background to my practice as I continue. Let me now start to put these together both as context, and also within additional contextual aspects, to provide some of the essentials of my practice of Gestalt with groups. I suggest that readers get a grasp of the full gestalt of this article before exploring the parts. After all, it is the whole that gives meaning to the parts.

Starting a Group

It is clear that different therapists and/or group facilitators will want to present their core message and their function differently as they market their competence and their group work. When I advertise an upcoming group, the central message is that the group members themselves and their interactions are the core therapeutic/developmental agents. As facilitator, I present my two main functions as I see them: the *first* is to support the group with appropriate experiments and interventions intended to follow and raise awareness around the group's own process and the contributions of its members to its in-the-moment dynamics. The *second* is to use interactive teaching sessions based on actual and current events in the group as an aid to the members' understanding of individual, interpersonal, sub-group and collective aspects of group life, thus supporting an experiential/cognitive whole for each group member. I like to be general enough to leave myself room to manoeuvre when I sit there with the group for the first time and begin the co-created contracting process—for the first (though probably not the last) time. I like to keep my written course descriptions as simple, clean and clear as possible, and leave the complexities to the opening session when the working contract is negotiated for the first time.

Giving a maximum number of members is as important as a minimum number to start the group, since it provides potential members with a sense of social context. The starting time/day and ending time/day for each module are clearly and unambiguously stated, as are costs and what they include. Also, information on how to register and pay, and a confirmation that every registration will be quickly acknowledged.

I generally prefer to give my e-mail address for any questions that may arise, rather than my phone-number, as e-mail gives me time for a considered response. There is also the fact that I have had my fill of calls at 7.30 a.m. or on a Friday evening as I settle down for the weekend…. When individuals specifically request that I phone them, I will do so.

Numbers

I regard five to eight members as a small group; from eight to fifteen would be a medium-sized group. In my own opinion, above fifteen we are definitely looking more at a small organisation than a group. My own take on this issue is to do with the probability that, at some stage in the question of numbers, sub-groups will become more indicative of group dynamics and process than individual members (see below). I believe this begins to be the dominant dynamic already with a group of three. For example, this number allows the emergence of three distinct pairs, each with its corresponding single. Add two members—a group of five—and no fewer than ten pairs and ten trios can emerge, or five quartets, each of the latter with its corresponding single. These examples can be easily understood using small squares of differently coloured paper, moving them around in all possible combinations. Each additional member adds layers of complexity exponentially, a complexity of which my presence in addition is a contributing factor to the dynamic self-organising of us as a field.

As a therapist and/or group facilitator, I find ten to twelve is about my limit for even considering individual therapy in a group setting. Above that number moves us all into a level of complexity which some members will find overpowering and therefore disempowering. I regularly work with training groups of twenty where I accept that individual members will become so inextricably a part of the facilitator-group field, and thus part of our shared inter-connectedness that I choose therefore to work more specifically at the level of the group-as-a-whole, including sub-group dynamics.

The size of the group is one of the factors I will consider when introducing the nature and focus of my interventions when negotiating the working contract.

Contracting

Arising from my work in organisational consulting, I like to distinguish between the *business contract* and the *working contract*. The business contract covers all aspects between me as supplier and the client as paying customer, the client here being the group members. In a training institute or organisational setting, the business contract is between me and the relevant representative, and covers such items as details of the particular service being purchased, its timing and duration, its costs and payment procedures etc., all the commercial and legal formalities of a seller/purchaser relationship.

For a group on the open market, each member is purchasing a service from me, as described in any advertising or presentation of the proposed group and its work. The same principles apply here as in the preceding paragraph.

The working contract is between me and the specific people in whatever group with whom I will be working. This is to do with what we will be doing and how we will be doing it. It is our negotiated contract with each other, and is treated more fully below in 'A Sample First Module/Session'.

Some Terminology

Some terms I use in my group work, both for my own orientation and for that of group members are:

- PROCEDURES—formalised, recurring events.
- PROCESS—the flow of change over time.
- DYNAMICS—the in-the-moment interactions as the process unfolds.
- INTERVENTIONS—my behaviours in the above contexts.

'Procedures' are any formalized and recurring events which are likely to occur, and which carry enough predictability of occurrence to be included as part of the practical planning. For example, 'Today's/Tomorrow's Logistics', 'Open House Sessions', 'Reflections and Applications', 'End of Module Feedback', 'Checking In' and such items.

'Logistics' are questions around starting and ending the formally scheduled group-work time each day, length and frequency of breaks, length of lunch and dinner breaks, variations due to special circumstances which are all put out as a shared responsibility to be treated with great flexibility.

It is quite usual in my experience for issues around time to become more and more an aspect of the group's dynamics and thus its process, than any logistical or procedural point. For example, the always on time and always late sub-groups can have this apparently formal aspect of group life as a tension between them. Often, a whole group will seem to reach a silent agreement about always starting late, whether in the morning or after every break, or extending every small-group work session beyond the mutually agreed time. However, no matter what happens, I will bring them up at the beginning of a course and of each module; also at the end of a module in respect to the following module.

I use 'Open House' sessions at the beginning of every session or module (except for the first one—see below), usually each morning, and sometimes also after a lunch break. It is a fully open session where members can say whatever they choose, need, wish to say; they are free to respond to each other, ask questions, and add perspectives.

'Reflections and Applications'—I always include formal and scheduled sessions for reflections and thoughts around application, both personally and professionally. These are briefly reported in plenum in order to share learning in the group as a whole.

'End of Module Feedback' is just that—a 30 minute or so session (depending on numbers and the dynamics of the module) before we close the module, devoted to comments on anything and everything pertaining to the experience of the module, each other, and me.

'Checking In' is the opening of each module/weekly meeting etc. from the second one on. It is like an extension of the original presentation, and includes any new or relevant information in addition to what group members have already shared. This is a space for such items as a new job, a divorce, a new relationship, or any other significant event in the life of that member.

'Process' means the flow of change over time: how a collection of people (the Actual Group) somehow takes on something at least analogous to a recognisable collective personality (the Group Gestalt). As such, group process can be seen over the period of a session, a day, a module (say, three to five days) and also from module to module. It is how the Actual Group is 'coming along.' The process of the group is best seen in periods of relative constancy, so process, in a sense, moves from constancy to constancy, through the dynamics of change. I deal somewhat more fully with this point under 'Change over Time'.

'Dynamics' are embedded in the process, and are the emergent in-the-moment events that influence it and are influenced by it, the figures to the process as ground. The dynamics of the group express the changes in, and consequences for its process. Specifically, while they occur in the Actual Group, they contribute to the process of the Group Gestalt.

'Interventions' are any action on my part related to the work of the group members.

A Sample Module 1 / First Session Opening

I still tussle with the timing of my presentation of myself—first or last? Clearly, if it is a group that has gathered as a result of advertising then I will need to be welcoming, and more so if it is taking place in my house. Increasingly, I have tended to welcome the members, and say that I will wait to say a few words about myself and then the work we may be doing after they have each presented themselves to the rest of us. This is a matter of context and preferred style, and I encourage new facilitators to experiment freely, respectful both of their own style, the context and the group members.

Presenting last allows me to match my content to that of the members and make connections with them where appropriate, such as having had the same trainers, or shared interests, or any connection which was figural for me as the members presented. One of my favourites was a professional academic, socially un-practiced, totally new to the thought of doing personal work in a group, who switched from speaking of his nervousness to speaking enthusiastically about the Steve Earle (American singer-songwriter) concert he had attended earlier that week —as had I. His face visibly lit up when I mentioned this as I presented myself. A therapist who also likes Steve Earle! Generally speaking, when I present myself last, I will rarely initiate any verbal acknowledgement of individual presentations—the group members are not presenting to me, we are each presenting to each other. I will always present first to a pre-existing group, a training group for example.

I will then move towards logistical matters, such as the availability or otherwise of tea/coffee making facilities, the whereabouts of toilets, smoking areas and so on. If on a residential, then logistics will include some choices around timing and length of lunch-breaks, whether to have evening sessions (much loved by some) after dinner, or a later dinner and thus a longer afternoon session, starting times in the morning etc. Such issues allow people with special requirements, such as diabetics for example, or people on a strict diet, to have an opportunity to legitimately give voice to their needs. Talking logistics is also a content-based topic which allows the members an opportunity for their first exchanges around shared issues, an opportunity to take each other's measure, to get a first feel for this group, these people. This is also where the Actual and Imagined groups can start to make their presence felt. The work has truly started!

I will then turn to the program, course or whatever commitment they have registered and paid for. Clearly, if it is a training group with an institute, then there is probably a module description which I have certainly seen, maybe even written, and will need to have as figure in the context of the training. The same will roughly apply to a group on a specific and advertised theme. For therapy or personal/professional development groups, the work is more open-ended, the content less predictable.

Whatever the focus, I find that I can support all the variations within the framework of Procedures, Process and Dynamics—and now I add 'Interventions'. I will present my take on the possible work we will be doing in some version or other of the following: the work of this group is primarily experiential and thus centres around its process over time—from hour to hour, morning to afternoon, day to day, week to week, module to module—and the specific dynamics which occur in the moment, however apparently or un-apparently related to the process they may seem. My interventions as therapist and/or facilitator may be focused on one or more of the following:

1. one-on-one work with individuals,
2. and/or supporting interpersonal issues between members as they arise,
3. and/or intervening primarily if not exclusively with the group members-as-a-whole, which will include sub-groups rather than an indiviual or one-to-one interpersonal focus,
4. all of the above.

In some groups, my role is covered by Point 4. In others, I will declare a focus on Point 3, and suggest that they themselves take care of the individual and the interpersonal work as natural aspects of group life and dynamics. My focus on Point 3 is particularly relevant where Gestalt group-work training groups are concerned, as well as with management training groups.

The other aspects of my interventions will include interactive teaching sessions, as much as possible figural to actual events in the group as ground. The content here will clearly include generic material, and I find that timing is of the essence here. Introducing a didactic history of group dynamics session in the middle of charged, dynamic events is probably not the best timing in the world. Or it may be just that! Nothing is 'a given' with groups, apart from the fact that nothing is 'a given'.

I will also present to participants the procedures of our sessions and modules, as described above. A summary on a flip-chart of this kind of opening would look something like this:

- An experiential focus on the group's own process and dynamics.
- Facilitator interventions at the level/levels agreed.
- Facilitator theory input sessions, based on and/or exemplified by both of the above.
- Recurring procedures as described above, as a support structure.

Thus, having taken my responsibility as convenor and/or assigned facilitator, I throw this framework open to the group for questions, discussion, change or confirmation. I am now negotiating the *working contract*. The business contract of registration and payment etc is either behind us or in good progress towards completion. It is very important with the working contract that I stay with and hold myself at the aspect of content and not dynamics. During this contracting session, I am not their contracted therapist, and they are not my clients. This in fact, is one of the issues we are negotiating. Any behaviour on my part which disrespects this, disrespects the group members and invalidates our contracting.

While it is clear that the working contract is being negotiated with the Actual Group, it is also here that the issues of the Imagined Group begin to emerge as lively figures. It is not unusual for such items as 'individual work' and 'confidentiality', for example, to be brought up here. Depending on the context and the agreed theme, I will or will not agree immediately to work individually with individuals. I may even end up agreeing to do it with some specified people, and not with others, or work individually on request.

As for confidentiality I explain that I am ethically and legally bound by my profession as therapist to maintain confidentiality. Where such exceptions are applicable, I will explain that I am legally bound to report child abuse, and danger to self and others through a threat of suicide, violence or murder. Clearly, I will certainly bring my work with the group to my supervision and not in any way identify or make possible the identification of any particular person. Should any episodes of our journey together find its way into one of my articles—which is always likely—then the people concerned may even have difficulty recognising themselves. Otherwise, the issue of confidentiality is up to them to resolve as they need to, following an open discussion. This is another content issue which gives a taste of future dynamics and process as the group members work their way through their individual needs, doubts, indifferences, demands, requests, and all the 'oughts' and 'shoulds' of the Imagined Group in this discussion.

I also like to leave the door open here for any other issue any member wishes to raise that can be addressed at this point. This can include such items as 'rules' about attendance, absence, late arrivals, early departures etc. In such cases, I am willing to state my own preferences, invite others to do likewise, and let the exchanges continue until some form of consensus has been reached—or not! In this way, group members get a sense of their own responsibility, both individually and collectively, and also of their influence on me and each other. I also like to see this period as the first engagement between what is imagined and what is actual in this particular group.

My focus throughout this phase is to establish a working contract which will inform our work together. All contracting specifically to do with my role is open to re-negotiation at the opening of any session or module, when I remind group members of our previously agreed working framework. I also reserve the right to explore the possibility of this re-negotiation as an expression of group process and/or dynamics.

My work with this group starts from the moment I send out advertising and shifts qualitatively the moment I arrive at the location of the group. The opening session, including the logistical and contracting aspects, is very much intrinsic to the wholeness of the work. It is not unusual for some group members to regard these scene-setting sessions as time-wasting and wonder when the 'real work' will begin. Indeed, I regularly meet participants who don't bother coming to opening sessions, even of modules after the first one. They usually define the 'real work' as the formal session, led by me, including exercises and/or therapy and/or teaching. This is my opportunity to clarify that, from the moment we committed to this group, we had started working together. Our every interaction, from then and now on, is part of our work, including scheduled sessions with a fixed starting and stopping time, coffee breaks, lunches, strolls in the grounds whether alone or with others, evening gatherings in whatever constellations, contact between sessions and so on. All of the latter points may now become more material for our discussion in the here-and-now of the opening session.

And Then What? #1

At some stage, the initial contracting comes to a close, however provisionally. This may be at the end of the first of a series of weekly meetings, or the opening sessions of a residential.

After the punctuation provided by a break of some sort—coffee, end of weekly session, whatever—I move to the next step. Until the initial contracting is completed, my role has been that of convenor or chairperson.

Now, I am in my formal and contracted role as facilitator. I like to then move to introducing the 'Open House'. This means inviting group members to give us their voices, their silences—to give us who and where they are in the moment, and to respond to each other as they feel appropriate. This is now where our contracting goes from words to actions; where individual figures become shared ground, out of which figural themes for the group can emerge. I remain fully present throughout, my active participation is being in my awareness of what is happening for me, and what patterns of behaviour or themes may come to my awareness as the session develops. This is also where group members find how they can/cannot and want/don't want to relate to each other, and to me.

Please note that an Open House session is anything but a 'round' in the sense of every voice being heard—including that most enforced paradox of them all: saying that you have nothing to say! An Open House is just that: everybody welcome in their own time, at their own pace, and an excellent opportunity for group members to begin their experience of how a group not only self-organises but also self-regulates, as each person responds to the experience of their membership.

From this moment on, I am in the wondrously unpredictable any-man's land of group process and dynamics. Whatever happens is of the field of us, here in the room, embedded as we are in our environment. We bring who we have been, who we believe we are, and who we are co-creating—our potential future selves in their becoming—and our attitudes to each of these expressions of who we are. We bring those aspects of our environment which impact on us, for example, a training institute, a war, a dramatic news-item, a sudden family issue. We bring ourselves into the room, influencing and being influenced, and always in a process of change.

People speak and are met with silence, affirmation or an invitation to dialogue. This is how sub-groups emerge, in group members' reactions to each other—'she's right; he's stupid; I hadn't thought of that so she's worth listening to; he seems to know what he's talking about; I knew the moment I saw her that I wouldn't like her and I was right', and so on.

Sub-Groups

A sub-group is any constellation which implicitly or explicitly shares a characteristic, an attitude or an opinion which becomes expressed through behaviour in the group. Sub-groups may be formal or informal, they can also be stable or dynamic (and everything in between).

Formal sub-groups are generally explicit: male, female, gay, straight, lesbian, bisexual, trans, older, younger, married, single, parents, non-parents, black, white, of one nationality or another, employees, self-employed, etc. Some of these are immediately obvious, others may have become apparent during the presentations, some evolve as people get to know each other.

Informal sub-groups are those which form in the moment and which may or may not last beyond that moment. Members who agree or disagree—vocally or in silence—with a statement by another member have joined a sub-group in relation to that opinion, and the person expressing it, whether they know or intended it. Many of these initially silent and invisible sub-groups form more concretely during breaks, walks, evening gatherings and other non-scheduled group time. They bring their energy into the room as a force of our field, one of the many self-organising and self-regulating forces of the group process and dynamics.

Amongst these will be my fan-club sub-group, as well as that of my critics, and that of the un-influenced either way. Each of these is a huge magnet, an attractor, as support, as challenge, as question-mark. Every teacher knows the temptation to 'preach to the converted' and keep the fan-club happy—or deal with the critics, whether through confrontation or appeasement or whatever. I work hard at bracketing the various attractions of these particular sub-groups, seeing them as expressions of the whole group's dynamics and process. After all, I may very well be the most figural environmental other for the group, individually and collectively, and the dynamics involved in relating to me are part of our work together. The interpersonal has now moved from the traditional level of individual/other individual, to the more complex level of sub-group/other sub-group, each representing a force of the field of our togetherness in our setting.

In this way, sub-groups can represent such forces as sameness or change, process or structure, being or doing, closeness or distance and so on—as well as every nuanced distinction along the continuum of any apparent polarities. The work of the Group Gestalt is now being done by the sub-groups of the Actual Group, in the moment and therefore also over time.

Sub-groups and Informal Leaders

I am the formal leader, either as initiator or through being assigned as such by senior management. My status includes particular responsibilities, authority of some nature (whether as perceived by members or as delegated by management), an assumed competence, and more. While much of my status has strong cultural connotations, there is (anyway and always) a hierarchical relationship of some nature between the formal leader and group members. Whatever else applies, removing a formal leader is a major event and effort for a group.

Informal leaders are of two types: the self-appointed and the group-appointed. The self-appointed informal leader does not necessarily have any followers in the group, though this can change according to circumstances. The group-appointed informal leaders (plural!) are created by sub-group followers, and may not themselves be aware of their position. They are people whose comments, actions and participation evoke support amongst others inasmuch as they (the informal leaders) in some way represent the others, however temporarily. This is a crucial distinction: an informal leader can be 'deposed' effortlessly, simply by their vocal or silent followers switching allegiances.

It is seldom crystal-clear for me when a member's work is to be responded to as 'individual.' Apart from always being field-emergent, I will tend to explore to what extent the presented issue is at least just as much a sub-group issue as anything else. The implications for my practice are covered below.

And Then What? #2

With the first 'Open House' up and running, the dynamics of the group emerge in terms of work. Some patterns and themes from the opening session may well make a re-appearance. Variations and new themes will also emerge.

My work here is to raise awareness of these dynamics as they emerge for me as figures and bring them to the attention of all, in support of whatever change processes may be at work. For example, some members may be expressing a preference for more facilitator-led exercises (even giving examples from other groups); others may be expressing their appreciation of open, more process-oriented sessions. This is where sub-grouping and informal leadership can become apparent, as the theme becomes figural. I will share my awareness of the theme as I experience it. I might use the theme of structure/process, giving the data of my phenomenological observations as ground for the figure of the theme; the comments I heard, the nods I saw, the silence of others —all the data I have gathered and now selectively shared, which group members can now use to inform their responses. Whatever happens, sub-groups will become somewhat more defined.

I invite them to participate in what may be something of a para-dox: an experiment with overtones of an exercise, fully process ori-ented! Should there be agreement, I ask the people whose comments introduced the theme, to repeat them. I ask anyone who more or less agrees to join the speakers. I add that anyone is free to move to another grouping at any time. Each grouping is invited to share their perspectives with each other within that grouping. This is followed by an invitation to each grouping to explain their perspective to the others. Depending on the atmosphere in the room—serious, playful, confused, or withdrawn—I may suggest to each grouping that they do their best to 'sell' their perspective to the others and thus allow the forces of influencing and being influenced to self-organise the membership of the sub-groups as well as the dynamics and process of the group-as-a-whole. In this way, the group has an opportunity to explore a common theme which emerged as figures from the group as ground, voiced by some members and now gestalted in the here-and-now by all. As the movements settle, accelerate, settle again and the group arrives at a sense of where it is collectively, work is occurring spontaneously both individually and interpersonally. Awareness becomes insight and potential change. The experiment closes as I invite group members to re-configure in self-selected groups of minimum three, maximum five, to share their experience and their learning—and their questions, confusions, curiosities. I then offer the opportunity to share these in plenum—in effect, a theme-focused 'Open House', which then becomes the ground for further figures.

I have become attached to 'minimum three, maximum five' for self-selected small group work. This format offers everyone a choice where 'being in the limelight' is concerned—somewhat more possible in three than five. It also gives everyone an opportunity to have their voices heard, to the extent they choose. In addition, this is a natural part of the sub-group and informal leader dynamics and process. Finally, time-management is easier—a twenty to thirty minute frame covers most eventualities. It is never my purpose that everyone will have said everything they want to say. Whatever is spoken or left unspoken is still ground for the continued work in and of the ground. This methodology—sharing my awareness of emerging figures which, if meaningful to the group, are worked with experientially and experimentally—then becomes a general feature of the group work as we continue on our way into the specific world of *this* group as it unfolds over time.

I want to distinguish here between an experiment which emerges in the moment as a 'tailor-made' event for a specific group, and an 'off the shelf' exercise, used before and which often has a pre-determined, or at least intended outcome. Both have their place, and we facilitators have our preferences. Certainly the methodology I propose may seem more like a repeatable exercise. This is true—in format only. The thematic content is the secret to its experimental nature, since the theme emerges as figure from the ground of the group. The reality that some themes seem to be applicable to just about any group, simply points to the developmental processes of groups and their generic character. Nevertheless, I will only introduce such an experiment (or many others) in response to an emerging figure. Doing 'Process/Structure' as an exercise 'in order to' do something to the group is not my style, nor is it consistent with a Gestalt approach.

Teaching

Adding a cognitive element to an experiential group, while often decided by the setting—formal Gestalt training, management training etc.—is also a natural ingredient in a holistic approach like Gestalt. The choice is often between 'before or after'. In other words, how much knowledge input will support a group in advance of experiential work, or is such work the necessary foundation for cognitive learning? In some cases, where the process work seems to be temporarily at rest, I may punctuate the work with a general input which is neither building on that which has gone before, nor preparing intentionally for what may follow (though it will, of course, be influential anyway).

I always find it most exciting to be able to use some current or recent dynamics or process issues as a stepping-stone to some theoretical input. An example here might be a piece about phenomenology when members comment on the differences between their experience 'of the group' and mine, when I have suggested an emerging figure. This is a good example of making a cognitive connection to our experience.

Change Over Time

As mentioned earlier, some themes—however group-specific they may be in the details involved—can be recognised as, in some way, typical of other groups also. This is the basis for the many group models which exist, and the exercises which often accompany them. These models are often generally linear and sequential, often normative in consequence—if not intention. Most of us have a particular favourite and tend to apply it. From a Gestalt perspective, my basic stance is staying with where the group is in the moment and trusting that the group will make whatever movement is appropriate to its current needs and potential. It is precisely in this process and its relevant dynamics that learning can take place. All learning brings change, just as all change brings learning.

In other words, my skill as a Gestalt practitioner lies in my willingness and ability to track and follow the group's process, rather than prescribe and direct it in any direction. The group really *does* know best about its own potential as it emerges, and will become what it may best become. I have no desired outcome for any group. My pride will sometimes push at me to show how good I am by 'giving' them a great group experience – whatever that is. I'm still learning to recognise the signals of this push, and attending closely to how much of it is recognisably my projecting, and how much is me-with-the-group. Is this a group desire resonating in me? How cleanly can I share my sense of what is figural for me as material for the group to work on? This is where competence and experience transform into co-created art as we explore such a core issue with as much mutual transparency as we can manage.

At the same time I need to deal with my sense and experience that a collection of individuals somehow becomes a group, easily distinguishable from any other group. This is what, above, I have called the Group Gestalt; that distinctive 'something' which is greater than and different to the sum of its individual members. Co-creating this is what I have called the process of the group over time, from one apparent state of relative stability/constancy to another. This moving is through the in-the-moment dynamics of the members as they both co-create and grapple with the disequilibrium involved in the shift.

From the perspective of practice, I find that I am becoming faster and even more accurate at using my awareness of the co-created me/group contact-boundary where process and dynamics are concerned. When I am feeling relaxed and confident in the presence of the group, with a sense of 'where they are', then it is probable that the process has slowed into a period of relative stability/constancy. I will usually draw the group's attention to this, and ask for any comments. When I am feeling lost, confused, isolated, pulled in different directions—then it is likely that the dynamics of change are in the room. While I have no guarantees that I am 'right', I am prepared to trust my feelings and experience as the only reality I have. One of the dilemmas here is that group members are likely to be so into what's going on, that any sharing of my feelings can often be met with blank faces. I also attend more closely to the contact-boundary dynamics that seem to be thematic amongst the members.

An example here might be: 'I notice that some of you are making comments and suggestions within the group and I hear no responses. Sometimes, I have heard a change of topic and context which I found difficult to follow. Does this make any sense to any of you?' If my observation has any value to the members, at least one of those whose inputs have had no explicit impact is likely to reply in the affirmative —or not. Whatever happens, the group now has an observation to relate to about their possible interpersonal and sub-group dynamics. Awareness may have been raised for some and may well become a topic of conversation during the next break. The theme of taking in/ keeping out the influence of others (introjecting/deflecting) is now at least of the field, ground from which a figure may soon emerge. I see the contact-boundary dynamics of introjecting and deflecting as one of the many ways in which sub-groups can form and informal leaders emerge. In other words, I work with attending to both process and dynamics, with the dynamics always being in-the-moment, and the process emerging as change over time.

'What is'

Gestalt's phenomenological stance brings with it a focus on our experience as embodied selves. I see, hear, smell, taste, touch, have proprioceptive sensations—and, of course, interpretations of and opinions on my experience. Describing what I have seen or heard, or physically sensed, is a description of my experience and not necessarily anyone else's. At the same time, it is my reality in the moment of the contact boundary dynamics of me-group, individually and collectively (whole or sub-group).

Any distinctions between 'what was' and 'what is' are difficult to capture in flight; swallows which swing and flit and swoop in one instant of startling agility. Over time—say one module/weekly session to another—I may have a sense of what was then and what is now.

'What was' is the context for 'what is' as it emerges in the moment. Change is what I work with, in me and in others. Awareness of such change and selectively sharing my awareness of it, is part of my work with groups.

This brings me to bracketing, that exceptionally difficult phenomenological effort to see what is, in and of itself. From the perspective of Gestalt psychology, the wholeness of what is includes not only what most recently was, but also what will become of it—the completing of the gestalt in the future. This is for me a core methodological issue— staying with what is, in the context of what was, and bracketing the future.

What I mean here specifically is this: I will bracket any opinion I may have about group movement in a particular direction towards a predictable state (as in linear phases of group development models), or any model which prescribes specific facilitator interventions in order to achieve specific, model-bound movements and change. This means also bracketing my considerable experience and competence with groups, my sense of where the group may well be headed ... I know all too well (and with some embarrassment) how easily I will be tempted to fulfil my own prophesy. This includes how easily a particular sense of possible group direction will influence which figures emerge for me.

I find this to be a complex challenge, filled with contradictions and dilemmas; I am of the field of me/group members/our environment and thus a force and influence of that field—as well as being influenced by other forces. In this latter case, I am just as much a voice of the self-organising of the field as anyone else. I am also the designated facilitator and therefore the environmental 'other' of the group members, individually and collectively. I see clearly that it is my professional responsibility to hold my awareness of this continuum—me as part of the field and me as apart from the group—and selectively share my awareness in support of my client, the group. This can sometimes mean an intense period of silent juggling with my awarenesses from each perspective. I will also sometimes choose to openly and explicitly juggle with them in full view, and see what happens ... either way, this is one of many major choice-points in my work, and probably the most difficult intervention for me to predict. Usually, I go with the flow of my awareness in the moment and the self-energised contact boundary dynamics which emerge. So I may choose to hold back (retroflecting with awareness), put out my figures (projecting with awareness), or await an energy shift to another theme (deflecting with awareness).

I identify two overarching qualities of silence, each with any number of variations: restful silence and restless silence. In each case, I need to rely on my awareness of what is happening to me in relation to the group as my environmental other, that is, my sense of our contact-boundary dynamics. Am I feeling a pull towards action, though unsure of what action? In punctuation terms, is this silence a semi-colon, with the remainder of the sentence still to come? Or am I feeling at peace with myself and with the group, and clearly capable of sitting calmly and silently until something happens. Are we slowly turning the page to the next chapter?

Amongst my choices here, I usually join and wait out the silence, and see what happens. Occasionally, when I feel strongly that this is a 'new chapter' silence, I may formalise it by tentatively suggesting we take a 15-minute break—and see what happens.

So I stay, (with as much presence as I can muster), with *what is*! Whatever will be, will be—and then a new 'what is'. This is the art of seeing any group event as a 'stopping point', while acknowledging that it is simultaneously a 'starting point' for what is emerging.

Closing the Door and Locking-Up

With the exception of on-going and open-ended groups, most groups have a scheduled first and last meeting. In other words, a defined beginning, middle and end. Part of my responsibility as facilitator is to orchestrate the beginning and the end, by providing sufficient structure to support each of these formal elements. The first of these is easier (see above), since we are all concerned with similar issues at more or less the same place and time, entering something new together. The second is more delicate and more complex. As we approach the transition from the middle to the beginning of the end, group members can literally be 'all over the place', though in the same room at the same time. Some members and sub-groups can't wait for the end to finally come; some become aware of missed opportunities which they may want to revive; some project their own unfinished issues onto others, encouraging them to take their last chance and so on.

At some stage—the third-last session of a weekly group, the opening session of the final module of a formal programme, or other appropriate point in another setting—I will present the structure of how we will be ending. This will typically include a clear indication of the final 'Open House' session which will end with a punctuated long coffee break, or lunch on a residential. This is followed by an extended 'Reflection and Applications' session, covering the whole programme, with a plenary session where the combined learning of the group emerges in all of its disparate glories.

'Finished and Unfinished Business'—this is where each member has an opportunity to address each of the others with whom they feel that they have had issues of one sort or another, and either finished to their satisfaction or still feel are alive and well and will not be finished in this group. Then, a final 'Feedback Session', this time for the whole programme, followed by the first and only traditional round, including me, to formally close and end our work, and say goodbye to each other.

And then the hugging starts...

✌

This article was previously published by the *Gestalt Journal of Australia and New Zealand*, (2008), Vol. 5(1), pp.32-51, and is reproduced here by kind permission of the editors, Richie Robertson and Nickei Falconer.

A Thematic Presentation of the Contents

Apart from Personal & People (Chapters 1 – 4), the following themes can be followed in their development over time:

INDIVIDUAL THERAPY

Chapter 12: A mini case-study of Lewinian field theory applied to a therapist-client interaction.

GROUPS

1) Theory, Methodology and Practice in general.
   Chapters 7, 8, 9, 13.

2) Training and Educational Settings
   Chapter 9.

ORGANISATIONS

Chapter 5, 6, 11.

SOCIETY AS CONTEXT

Chapters 5, 10.

THE CROSS-CULTURAL CONTEXT

Chapters 2, 4, 5, 6, 7, 9.

THE INFLUENCE OF KURT LEWIN

Chapters 5, 7, 8, 11, 12.

Commentators, Conversation and Co-authors

<small>(AS ORIGINALLY PUBLISHED)</small>

TALIA LEVINE BAR-JOSEPH, PhD, is former director of Gestalt Ms.C program at Metanoia Institute London and co-founder of the Jerusalem Gestalt Institute. She is a registered clinical psychologist with experience in PTSD, cross cultural work, and group work; a business consultant in Israel, Europe, and the USA; and author of *The Bridge—Dialogues Across Cultures.*

CLAIRE ASHERON BARTRAM, PhD, has been working as a Gestalt psychotherapist since 1991 and is a therapist, group leader and supervisor living and working in London. She is also a mother, stepmother and grandmother. Her own doctoral study has arisen from her own circumstances and is an exploration of the narratives of mothers in stepfamilies. Among her outcomes are the finding that stepfamilies can be a useful metaphor for certain therapy group situations and the founding of an organisation StepIn ASAP Advancing Stepfamily Awareness through Psychotherapy.

PHILIP BROWNELL, PhD, is a licensed clinical psychologist, organizational consultant, and coach. He is the Director of the Gestalt Training Institute of Bermuda, Editor of the *Handbook for Theory, Research, and Practice in Gestalt Therapy*, and author of *Gestalt Therapy: Guidebook for Mental Health Practitioners.*

MARK FAIRFIELD, LCSW, BCD, is on faculty at the Pacific Gestalt Institute in Los Angeles. He is the Clinical Director at Common Ground—The Westside HIV Community Center in Santa Monica and he has a private practice in West Los Angeles.

BUD FEDER, PhD, is a psychologist with a long-standing interest in groups. He has just published *Gestalt Group Therapy: A Practical Guide* (Gestalt Institute Press).

IsABEL FREDERICSON, PhD, lives in semi-retirement in Santa Barbara, CA with her husband, Joseph Handlon. She is still active in AAGT.

JON FREW is a Professor in the School of Professional Psychology at Pacific University in Portland, Oregon. He is also in private practice and works with individuals, couples and as an organizational consultant. He is an Associate Editor of the Gestalt Review and has published widely on a variety of topics related to Gestalt therapy. He is one of the directors of the Gestalt Therapy Training Center Northwest and has been active as a Gestalt trainer since 1982. Recent publications include *Contemporary Psychotherapies for a Diverse World* (2008) and *Beyond the Hot Seat Revisited: Gestalt Approaches to Groups* (2008).

JOSEPH HANDLON has his doctorate from UC Berkeley. He is a graduate of the Gestalt Institute of Cleveland and the co-founder of the Santa Barbara Gestalt Training Center.

CARL HODGES, MSW, is past President of the New York Institute for Gestalt Therapy and of AAGT. He teaches periodically at the Gestalt Centre London and Instituto di Gestalt, Italy.

MARY ANN HUCKABAY, PhD, has been a lecturer in Organizational Behavior at Stanford University's Graduate School of Business since 1990, where she directs a small group facilitation program. She is a professional member of Institute of Cleveland.

ANNE MACLEAN co-founded the Gestalt Institute of New Zealand and was on the faculty. She co-edited two collections of New Zealand and Australian articles and in 2002 wrote *The Heart of Supervision*. She established the *Gestalt Journal of Australia and New Zealand*, and was a co-editor. She is in private practice and on the faculty of the Healing Energies Foundation of New Zealand.

BIRGIT NIEBUHR is a medical doctor with a diploma in Sociology, with 15 years of experience in development cooperation. She is a recent graduate of the OSD course of the Gestalt Institute of Cleveland.

EDWIN C NEVIS, PHD, co-founded the Gestalt International Study Center (GISC) together with Sonia M. Nevis, Ph.D., in 1979. He is the author of several books and numerous articles on Gestalt therapy and its application, and he has been teaching therapists, consultants, and executives since 1960.

BRIAN O'NEILL, BA(HONS), MAPS, Brian is co-director of the Illawarra Gestalt Centre, and visiting faculty member of Gestalt training programs in Australia, the USA and Europe. He is past President of the Association for Advancement of Gestalt Therapy (AAGT), founding editor of the *Gestalt Therapy Forum* (New York), and on the editorial boards of the *Gestalt Review* and *Studies in Gestalt*. In 1996 the Australian Governor General awarded him the Mental Health Gold Medal for achievement in research, education and practice. He is currently the regional manager for Relationships Australia in the Illawarra.

PETER PHILLIPSON, MSC (GESTALT PSYCHOTHERAPY), is a UKCP Registered Gestalt psychotherapist and trainer, a teaching and supervising member of the Gestalt Psychotherapy & Training Institute UK, a founder member of Manchester Gestalt Centre, full member of the New York Institute for Gestalt Therapy, senior trainer for GITA (Slovenia) and a guest trainer for many training programmes internationally. He is the author of several books, and many papers on Gestalt therapy.

CHANTELLE WYLEY lives in Cape Town, South Africa; she is a partner in Baobab Consulting and Training which specialzes in development managements in Anglophone developing countries. Besides her training in Gestalt OSD, she brings to her work experience as an historian, librarian, anti-apartheild activist, yoga practitioner, homeopath and mother.

Publishing Websites

EDITOR'S NOTE:

I find pleasure in thanking all the editors who kindly gave permission for articles to be published in this collection.

This list of websites shows the breadth of publishing for people interested in writing about Gestalt and its many aspects; and in this case is only possible through the generosity of Anne Teachworth and the Gestalt Institute Press of New Orleans.

My warmest thanks to all of you.

— Anne Maclean

British Gestalt Journal
www.britishgestaltjournal.com

Cambridge Scholars Publishing
www.c-s-p.org

Gestalt Institute Press of New Orleans
www.gestaltinstitutepress.com

Gestalt International Study Centre
www.gisc.org

Gestalt Journal Australia and New Zealand
www.gjanz.com

Gestalt Review
www.gestaltreview.com/

Gower Publishing Ltd
www.gowerpub.com

InnerSense Journal
www.illawarragestalt.com/innersense.htm

International Gestalt Journal
www.gestalt.org

NTL Handbook
www.pfeiffer.com/wileyCDA

Ravenwood Press
www.illawarragestalt.com/Index_files/Page619.htm

Routledge
www.routledge.com/

Studies in Gestalt
www.studies-in-gestalt.org/home.htm

Eccentric Genius

An Anthology of the Writings of
Master Gestalt Therapist
Richard Kitzler

ECCENTRIC
GENIUS

An Anthology of
the Writings of
Richard Kitzler,
Master Gestalt Therapist

Foreword by Dan Bloom

The new Second Edition, published in memoriam, contains 100
more pages of photos, articles and essays than the first edition.
Eighteen gestalt therapists have contributed essays in addition to
Richard's many previously unpublished articles, combining philosophy,
gestalt and the development of process groups. Also included are photos
of Richard's life and friends. A valuable addition to any gestalt library.

THE GESTALT INSTITUTE PRESS
433 Metairie Road, #113, Metairie,
LA 70005, USA

<small>VOLUME 2 OF</small>

Gestalt at *Work*

<small>INTEGRATING LIFE, THEORY & PRACTICE</small>

Seán Gaffney

"The culmination of years of work in integrating Gestalt theory and practice. Gaffney's fertile and agile mind ranges across all levels of human development intervention."

<small>EDWIN C. NEVIS</small>

THE GESTALT INSTITUTE PRESS
433 Metairie Road, #113, Metairie,
LA 70005, USA

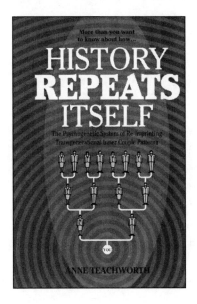

Books from
Gestalt Institute Press

**Eccentric Genius:
An Anthology of the
Writings of Master
Gestalt Therapist,
Richard Kitzler**

$40

**Beyond the Hot Seat
Revisited: Gestalt
Approaches to Group**

Editors: Bud Feder & Jon Frew

$30

**Why We Pick the Mates
We Do**

Anne Teachworth

$20

History Repeats Itself

Anne Teachworth

$20
(available 2010)

Gestalt Group Therapy

Bud Feder

$20

**A Funny Thing Happened
on the Way to
Enlightenment**

Lenny Ravich

$20

Those Who Come After

Renate Perls with Eileen Ain

$20

**The Bridge: Dialogues
Across Cultures**

Editor: Talia Levine Bar-Yoseph

$40

**Suffering In Silence:
The Legacy of Unresolved
Sexual Abuse**

Anne Schutzenberger &
Ghislain Devroede

$20

Gestalt at Work (Vol 2)

Seán Gaffney
(available 2010)